The Saliscape Project

A TIME FOR
PURPOSE

A SURVIVOR'S PATH TO TRIAL, TRUTH & JUSTICE

STEPHEN J. O'CONNOR

For information about permissions to reproduce selections from this book, translation rights, media inquiries, or to order bulk purchases, please contact us through our website: atimeforpurpose.com.

Cover by Lindsay Gatz at vonRocko Design
Author photo by Olan Mills
Cover photo by Gail O'Connor
Publishing mgmt by The Publishing World

O'Connor, Stephen J.
A Time for Purpose: A Survivor's Path to Trial, Truth & Justice
ISBN 978-0-9981080-0-1

1. Biography & Autobiography — Personal Memoirs. 2. Family & Relationships — Child Abuse. 3. Religion — Christianity/Catholic. 4. Law — Personal Injury.

Printed in the United States of America
Distributed by Ingram

A TIME FOR
PURPOSE
A SURVIVOR'S PATH TO TRIAL, TRUTH & JUSTICE

A TIME FOR PURPOSE

FOREWORD BY MICHAEL T. PFAU

PART ONE

FOREWORD

Although statistics vary, if you ask any trial attorney, they will likely tell you that approximately 95 percent of civil lawsuits settle before trial. There are myriad reasons for this, but in the case of lawsuits involving adults who were sexually abused as children, settlements are often driven by a desire to resolve claims before an abuse survivor has to testify publicly about the most intimate and personal experiences in one's life. Moreover, discussing the abuse can tear the bandage off wounds that are decades old and bring back frightening memories and emotions, along with causing new pain and mental anguish. For the perpetrators of abuse and the institutions that harbor them, a lawsuit brings public scrutiny to its practices and the grave mistakes of its past.

Our law firm has represented hundreds of sex abuse survivors in cases against the Catholic Church, the foster care system, schools, the Boy Scouts of America, and other institutions where children were abused. It has been my experience that it takes a tremendous amount of courage for a sexual abuse survivor to even pick up the phone to call a therapist or an attorney, let alone be subjected to the rigorous discovery process of a civil lawsuit and the publicity associated with a high-profile trial where one's story is public. When Steve O'Connor walked into my law office in October 2009, neither one of us could have anticipated the journey that would lead to Steve's trial and verdict. Nor did I know, at that time, of Steve's own heroism in Vietnam and as a police officer.

My clients often comment when going through the civil litigation process at *how different this is than TV,* where actors seemingly perform vigorous examinations of adverse witnesses and give passionate closing arguments, effortlessly. Plaintiffs in a civil lawsuit end up realizing the extraordinary cost, tireless work, and meticulous attention to detail that goes into preparing for and eventually trying a case in court. In sexual abuse litigation, there will be depositions of family members, friends, acquaintances, employers, previous relationships, and the subpoenaing and scrutinizing of an abuse survivor's employment, military, medical, and psychiatric records. In essence, a sex abuse survivor who has the courage to try his or her lawsuit in a court of law lays their life story bare for all to see.

While Steve O'Connor and I are a generation apart in age and grew up 2,000 miles away from each other, there were similarities that drew us together as lawyer and client. We were both raised Catholic, the parishes and schools we attended were similar, and the demographics of our neighborhoods were comparable. In the world of a youth, the important role of the Catholic priest to Catholic families and Catholic communities in the 1960s and 1970s was very different than it is now and hard for non-Catholics to understand. At that time, no one could have imagined the dark secrets the church harbored and the grave danger Catholic school students faced due to the perpetuation and cover-up of child sexual abuse in Catholic churches and schools.

While this is a story of those dark secrets and the church's cover-up of sexual abuse in the 1960s and the present, it is also a story of Seattle in 1962. It was a time before Amazon and Microsoft, when the World's Fair and the Space Needle were a very big deal in this far parochial corner of America. It is the story of a boy whose life was not different than most boys growing up in Seattle in 1962, but how the course of his life was forever altered when he was sexually abused by a Catholic teacher and that abuse was covered up by the parish priest. It is also a story of that boy's journey into manhood and how adversity can be addressed and eventually conquered. Nietzsche writes, "That which does not kill us, makes us stronger." Sadly, while this is not true for all abuse survivors, one can argue that this is the story of Steve's life. Finally, this is a theme about how to live one's life the right way, through service to others and one's country, and how to overcome life's adversities with courage. It has been an honor to represent Steve O'Connor in his quest for justice.

Michael T. Pfau
Seattle, Washington 2018

DEDICATION

To say that the endeavor of writing this book was one of the most difficult challenges of all that has happened in my life would be an understatement. From the moment the jury returned their verdict, I pondered, *what the hell do I do now—that's as far as I can hit the ball.* The answer was clear: Tell the story.

I knew right then: the events of the last nine years would once more take possession of my soul. Haunting me yet again from the confines of St. Benedict grade school, to the jungles of Vietnam, to the last radio transmission for "Stanwood unit 1433." To the testimony heard in the courtroom.

But I did have complete solace in knowing that one small part of the book would be quite simple: the Dedication. For this tribute must go to the true heroes of this tragedy.

For I have known real heroes. I have walked in the path of real heroes. Many are chiseled into vertical granite panels in Washington D.C., their names appearing in the order in which they were taken from us. Many others are visible on the Law Enforcement Memorial in Olympia, Washington.

One hero in particular can regularly be found in his office on the fifth floor of the Columbia Tower, enjoying his third, fourth, or fifth cup of coffee, preparing to "slay dragons" before most of us have awakened from sleep. Some have affectionately referred to him, as *The mighty Michael Pfau,* though not in his presence.

But the dedication of this book must go to two special heroes. Two men who had nothing to gain, who mustered the courage to do the right thing. To step forward and testify at my trial. To have to relive their trauma, for someone whom they did not know and had never met before.

They are the true heroes of this story.

And so, I wish to dedicate this book to Robb Kingsbury and Richard Fish, with my heartfelt thanks and admiration. And to all of those who survived—and those who did not—the horrors of child sexual abuse at the hands of the Catholic Church.

Stephen J. O'Connor
Seattle, Washington 2018

PART ONE

Show me a hero and I'll write you a tragedy.

—F. Scott Fitzgerald

PART ONE

CHAPTER 1

THE 100TH ANNIVERSARY

November 2008

They arrive at the well-lit school on a typical rainy November evening in Seattle. It's the celebration of the one hundredth anniversary of St. Benedict Catholic School and Parish, established in 1908. The school is an imposing three-story brick building on the corner of 48th and Wallingford Avenue. The entrance is framed with white arches contrasting the red-brown bricks. A statue of the Sacred Heart of Jesus is at the top of the building in a small white alcove. It's slight compared to the size of the building, as if the act of placing it there was an afterthought. Under the statue, carved in stone is, *St. Benedict School AD 1924*, the year the permanent school was built. Above the front door is a stained glass circular window with the initials *OMI*, which stands for Oblates of Mary Immaculate.

A steep staircase leads to the main entrance. Straight ahead, large double doors open into the school auditorium. At the center is a stage framed by dark burgundy velvet drapes. It's been close to twenty-five years since Steve has been inside this school. The last time was when he drove his teenage daughters to a Catholic Youth Organization event. He's kept his distance from St. Benedict's.

Steve is now sixty years old. His face is etched with equal parts frown and laugh lines. Despite this, no one who saw him this evening would have any trouble recognizing him from the twelve-year-old boy they knew in 1961. Beneath the weathered face is a youthful, fit frame, quick in its pace, light on his feet after all these years.

1

He enters the school building and immediately looks over to the boy's patrol closet just to the right; it's a small room in which the patrol team, who would help students safely cross the neighboring streets, stored their sashes and flags. Another few feet into the school, he glances to the left of the auditorium, down the hall to the principal's office. This is where the large bronze bust of a former teacher and principal stood the last time he was inside the school. Steve remembers that the bust was an eerie likeness of the teacher: a flat-top haircut, a sports jacket with patches at the elbows, and a bow tie. Below the statue was a large brown plaque from his waist to the floor and it read, *Daniel T. Adamson Memorial Scholarship Fund.* It's gone, and Steve wonders, *where the hell is it?*

He's ready to deliver an academy award performance tonight. He is adamant that he will protect the twelve-year-old self he's carried inside since the events at St. Benedict's so many years ago. He will rely on his *blockers.* His blockers, carefully developed over the years, repressing and putting terrible memories and trauma into a box, nailed shut. He can never let his wife or children ever know about, or be exposed to, this tragedy. He can't drift back to what happened to him, or it would all come flooding out on a night like tonight. As a veteran Marine in combat, or as a police officer who had to respond to reports of child abuse, kidnapping, or child molestation, he knows how to guard the twelve-year-old from exposure.

When Steve first heard about the St. Benedict's anniversary celebration, he encouraged his wife Gail to attend with a grade school friend, Ginny. Ginny was Gail's bridesmaid at their wedding, and they had gone to several high school reunions together. Steve, however, made it clear to Gail that he was definitely not going.

Then Gail got a call from the anniversary committee, asking if she and Steve could share memories of their school days in a video interview the night of the celebration. They are a rare couple who met at St. Benedict School, married at St. Benedict Church, and were still together after nearly forty years of marriage. As the week of the anniversary drew near, there were several feet of snow on the ground where they lived in Spokane, and a storm was predicted in the mountain pass leading to the west side of the state. Because of safety concerns, Steve reluctantly agreed to drive Gail to Seattle, a three hundred-mile trip, and attend the anniversary.

Early in the evening, Steve and Gail are whisked away for an interview to a classroom located in the basement of the school. They sit on folding chairs side by side in front of a video camera. People come and go into the classroom during the interview. The first question for the couple:

"When did you meet?"

The performance begins. Grinning, Steve holds up two school pictures—one of himself and the other of Gail in the second grade.

"This is when we met."

"When did you get married?"

He pulls out another picture, their wedding day in 1969 at St. Benedict Church. Sergeant O'Connor, at twenty years of age, is in his Marine Corps dress blue uniform. Two years of almost constant combat, a near fatal bout of malaria, and multiple gunshot wounds have left him a shadow of himself, old before his time. Gail is petite, with long, golden-blonde hair, wearing a white empire-waisted bridal gown, and holding a bouquet of white stephanotis flowers.

"We were baptized here, received first communion, first confession, and confirmation. We were married here, and buried our parents here. Most of my life skills I've learned right here in these halls."

"Who was your favorite teacher while you were a student here?"

The actor pauses, looking around the room. He must improvise immediately.

"Who was the most influential person here at St. Benedict's?"

"One of the most influential people in my life was our seventh-grade teacher, Mr. Adamson."

In recent years, when Gail asked Steve about Adamson and the rumors of his reputation as "strange," or a "pervert," Steve's answer was always, "Greatest guy on earth." Once again, with his wife sitting next to him, the actor carefully responds:

"Well, it was quite a support system."

Steve waves to a classmate walking by.

"Hey, there's Joe Barton*, a blast from the past."

Some of his grade school buddies Steve has not seen since eighth grade, or high school.

Gail talks excitedly about Sister Mary Thomas, her favorite teacher, who taught piano, and how originally piano lessons were in

3

the auditorium, but later moved across the street to the new nun's convent.

Gail nudges Steve, laughs, and says, "Oh, and remember all the reel-to-reel films we saw with Mr. Adamson, and how he chose you to learn how to run the projector for all the films?"

Silence. Steve slowly removes his arm from around Gail's shoulder, his head and upper torso drooping toward his hands clasped together in his lap. Gail keeps chatting away about her grade school experiences. After a few minutes, Steve's head snaps up and he cuts her off mid-sentence; his arm slices through the air in front of him, signaling that the interview is over.

"That's about it. It's been a wonderful life."

After the interview, Steve and Gail roam the halls and go from room to room. They come to the second-grade classroom where they first met. Steve remembers only one event from second grade. As they enter the room, he looks at the rows of desks and thinks of the teacher, Mrs. Malone*, and her anger at two young girls for talking in class. The teacher yelled at the girls as she tied them to the seats of their small desks with thick rope. Steve was never sure why she would have rope on hand, but maybe it was a kid's jump rope. She wrapped the rope around the two desks, back-to-back, and pushed them into the dark, narrow cloak room, the desks tipping over with the two girls still tied to them. She slammed the overhead door shut and the rest of the class listened to the girls' whimpering cries. Mrs. Malone walked calmly back to the front of the class and resumed her lesson plan. Steve thinks of his own children, when they were in second grade, so small and frail. He recalls other faculty at the school and their treatment of children: Sister Roberta, who frequently singled out students and railed at them for being "spineless and stupid"; or the pastor of St. Benedict's, who in front of the class on report card day withheld some of the kids report cards, telling students that their parents needed to pay tuition.

The classrooms look exactly as they were, as if frozen in time. They meet up with a few old buddies and head to the third floor to check out 7A, Adamson's room. It is the exception. It's been converted to a library. They remember Adamson's desk next to the door, facing the students, and behind them the tall windows facing

Wallingford Avenue. They imagine how the desks were arranged. Missing is the cloak room with the guillotine-style doors that held their coats and lunches—and served as an isolation closet reserved for those students foolish enough to merit the wrath of Adamson. They linger in the classroom, talking about the good old days in 7A. Steve separates himself, slowly walking away from the crowd, backing out of the classroom into the hallway. He bumps into Ginny, who is standing in the hall. He stares at the doorway to the room.

Steve turns to her, but there is no eye contact. He looks past her, focusing on something else down the hallway.

"Oh yeah, scene of the crime."

He thinks, *this is the crime. The moment I stepped into this classroom, I was doomed.*

Ginny notices his mood has turned somber. Not sure what he means, she lets out a nervous laugh and says, "Right, we were always getting into trouble in Adamson's class."

He turns and walks across the third floor hallway, glancing in the direction of the open projector room. What was blocked from his memory is right in front of him now; he must protect his twelve-year-old self who is crying out to be heard, his voice silenced for so many years. He begins to remember: the fear, his broken belt, and running home after the 'trouble' in the projector room. His blockers begin to fail. He descends the three flights of stairs to the basement, wanting to escape.

There is a large lunchroom with folding tables and chairs lined up against the wall, then classrooms *2A* and *2B*, the boiler room, the janitor's closet, and the boys' bathroom. Alone now, Steve slowly walks toward the bathroom, his left hand next to his belt as he would do as a police officer, ready, as if to pull his duty weapon, anticipating the unexpected. As he pushes the door open with his right hand, he is not prepared for what's next. He looks inside and then slowly enters the bathroom. The plaster is still cracked in the same places, there is the same ivory tile above the sinks, the iron radiator, and the metal-framed windows that open outward. He runs his thumb along the glazing around the window, gouging the pliable putty as he did as a twelve-year-old.

Steve walks past the bathroom stalls, one by one. He stops before the end stall, his body rigid, shoulders erect. He takes another step and stares at the familiar stainless steel door, scratched and dented in the same places he remembers. He opens the stall door. He feels the cold backdrop of the toilet on his face as he is bashed up against it, large stubby arms locked around his neck, choking him, and pushing his face down to the man's crotch.

He smells the stale cigar smoke and hears the footsteps of those heavy *wing walker* shoes shuffling over to the sink, then the running water, and the door slamming. Steve backs away from the stall, his back facing the bathroom door leading to the hallway. He barely breathes, his hands out to his sides, waist high, palms down, pumping up and down, desperate to block that memory, to control the twelve-year-old. He bumps into the door, steps to the side, still backing up and out into the hall, as slowly and quietly as possible.

He leans against the wall in the hallway, his shoulders slouched and his body limp. Steve feels dizzy, he wants to throw up. He can't call up his blockers. They're gone. He takes a deep breath, hearing footsteps in the distance on the linoleum stairs, coming closer.

"Hey, you're Steve O'Connor, aren't you? You had Adamson for seventh grade, right?" He introduces himself.

"Yeah," Steve says, recognizing the man as a student a grade behind him in school.

"Everything looks so much the same. Have you noticed there aren't any pictures of Adamson?"

"Yes, I saw that."

He turns his head from side to side, looking for an escape.

"You were kind of like one of Adamson's boys—did you ever go down to his basement and see his train set? Did he ever show you those girlie calendars from Rex's Texaco gas station?"

Steve holds his hand up abruptly.

"Stop…stop…just stop!"

He turns and walks away.

A few minutes later, the main presentation for the night is about to get underway in the auditorium. Gail, Steve, Ginny, and a few grade school buddies are heading to claim a table. A stocky older woman with a neck brace walks over to Steve, looking squarely at him.

"I bet you don't know who I am."

"No, I don't."

"I know who you are. You're Steve O'Connor."

Smiling, he says, "You caught me."

He does not recognize her until she tells him that she is Sister Nathan, a former teacher and principal at St. Benedict's. She is without her black and white Dominican nun habit. She now goes by her lay name, Joann Unger. She is one of those who recommended Dan Adamson's promotion to principal in 1969.

Steve is hoping that on this occasion someone will speak about the facts of St. Benedict's and come to grips with its past. How it was a great mission parish and school for sixty years, until the 1960s, when it was overtaken by a criminal element. How the parish and church has since implemented changes so that no child will ever be harmed in the future. Instead, as the presentation begins, he hears nothing.

The formal program is underway and the master of ceremonies, a graduate of St. Benedict's and the current archdiocesan education director, is speaking about the unique beginnings of the school and how it shaped so many students throughout the years. He praises the Oblates of Mary Immaculate, the religious order of priests who controlled the parish for one hundred years, and the Dominican Sisters for their dedication to the parish and school. A short video clip about the centennial history of St Benedict's is played. Next, an eighty-year-old mother of twelve children, all alumni of St. Benedict's, is honored for her support and dedication to the school. At the podium, she praises the school as a wonderful place to raise children.

Steve looks around the room at everyone clapping and laughing, and he feels detached from it all. His face is white, his jaw clenched, and he crosses his legs. Leaning back in the chair, he's hoping the next speaker will talk about the dark period at St. Benedict's. As the program ends, Steve realizes he might be naïve thinking that St. Benedict's, let alone the Archdiocese of Seattle, would ever admit that something terrible had happened at the school.

As the celebration draws to a close, Steve observes again that every mention and picture of Adamson is wiped clean. His name and picture are missing from the roster of former teachers and principals, even though he worked at the school from the mid-'50s to the mid-'70s. It's obvious that somebody knows about Adamson and what he did. This tragedy must have been revealed. *Maybe they know about me too and remember me as one of Adamson's boys.*

At an after-party at a friend's home, a block from Dick's Drive-In on 45th, Steve is not in the mood to party. He grows quieter and paces around the house. He walks outside and heads to Dick's.

Thoughts intrude. Not just me, there were other victims. What about that guy in the basement tonight, was he my replacement? What if I had stepped up and done more, instead of running away? I could have prevented other crimes from happening. I replaced someone, and then I was replaced, and the creep gets away with it, emboldened. He is never caught. When I confronted Adamson in high school, threatening to tell my coach, Adamson was never nervous: "I'm untouchable. No one will do anything. I own people."

All I did was create more victims by running away to Vietnam. I'd like to run away again, never look back at St. Benedict's, and forget what happened there. Be an unknown, anonymous victim. But I can't run away again. I've lost my blockers and can no longer suppress the twelve-year-old's voice. What am I going to do now?

I am not the guy who runs away from things—not in the Marines, not as a cop. I will stop this. I don't have any idea how, but the truth must come out.

CHAPTER 2

WALLINGFORD (CIRCA 1961)

October 2009

I knew the dark, wet days of winter would soon be upon us as my eyes drifted to the vibrant vine maples lining the mountain pass. The repeated road trips from Spokane to Seattle had become a ritual since attending the 100th year anniversary last November at St. Benedict School. Soon, the trips would become less frequent due to winter's grip on the mountains. The need for the truth to be told burned hotter than ever, yet nearly one year had passed since the anniversary and I had not made much progress.

I had hoped that returning to Wallingford would help somehow. As a police officer, I had learned to revisit the crime scene, several times if need be. Putting myself there physically helped me to visualize what happened more clearly. I could focus better on the details of the crimes, and even identify the criminal's motive. I had in fact accomplished this one thing: I recognized that what had happened to me was a crime. This was not a scandal, not isolated incidents, not negligence on the part of those who were supposed to protect children, but premeditated, selective acts of criminals that involved an unimaginable cunning and grooming of innocent children. Every time I returned home to Spokane, I would ask myself once again why I hadn't solved anything after yet another trip to the crime scenes.

In Spokane, the daily news was filled with the bankruptcy proceedings surrounding the child sexual abuse scandal in the Catholic diocese there. I overheard conversations filled with wild rumors that a group of attorneys from San Francisco, led by someone named "Foo," was on a nationwide campaign to bring down the Catholic Church. These rumors claimed that all parishes would be affected and that the resulting bankruptcy would cause the loss of Catholic schools and require that other church property be sold.

My eldest daughter, Stephanie, whose children attended Catholic schools had taken it upon herself to research the "Foo" law firm that was involved in the Spokane negotiations. She revealed that it was not "Mr. Foo," but rather Mr. Michael Pfau (rhymes with *wow*). His firm was located in downtown Seattle, not San Francisco, on the forty-sixth floor of the Columbia Tower. When she read me his curriculum vitae, I learned that Mr. Pfau had graduated from Boston College and had received his law degree from the University of Michigan. I was impressed. Further, Stephanie had seen his picture, which she described as a refined version of Bruce Springsteen, rather than an Asian man.

Today, as I cleared the Lake Washington bridge and made the turn northward on Interstate 5, I glanced to my left at the imposing structure. I wondered: *Is the Columbia Tower even open on weekends? Do you just walk in and ask Mr. Pfau's secretary if you can see him?* I doubted that. I could just camp in front of the entrance door on Monday morning and look for somebody who resembled "the Boss," only dressed in a suit and carrying a briefcase. One way or another, I knew I had to talk to this guy.

Today was a stellar day. How I loved autumn in Seattle, with its clear, crisp blue-sky days. The leaves on the trees were in a golden state, the change of seasons bringing out their finest hues just before they fell to the ground, creating a majestic blanket covering the landscape. I remembered in particular the gorgeous fall days at Woodland Park spent in high school with Coach Morgan, the "Zen Master," during cross-country season. Images of the fifteen-year-old gliding effortlessly over the fallen leaves crackling beneath his resilient stride.

Part of my Seattle ritual had to include a stop at Dick's Drive-In, where in 1964 a cheeseburger was 24 cents, fries were 11 cents, and they made hand-dipped cones and old-fashioned milkshakes. This was a favorite stop for me back then. It was a place to eat, see friends, and watch the souped-up cars come and go. Watching the crowd as I waited in line, an all too familiar scene develops with the customer to my left. Any native Seattleite would know when you order a cheeseburger at Dick's, there are two givens, and no exceptions: first, the burgers only come Dick's way, not your way; second, it's cash only. This guy was asking for no pickle, no onion, and requesting extra cheese. Following this exchange, I could feel what was coming next: *What, you don't take debit?*[†]

Yes, indeed, you would be hard pressed to find a single soul who had grown up here. Oh, how Seattle had changed. In my childhood, there was no Starbucks, not one freeway, no Microsoft, and no Amazon. The Space Needle was brand new. But if you looked hard enough now, you could unearth old Seattle. The school, church, and apartment where I grew up were all still in place.

I drove by these familiar haunts and headed for Green Lake with my cheeseburgers in hand. I drove past the baseball fields, tennis courts, and track. I pulled into an unusual find—a parking spot at the edge of the lake where I could enjoy the fall foliage. As I devoured my cheeseburgers, I reminisced about the innocent days at Green Lake.

July 1961

When I was twelve, the summer before seventh grade, I couldn't ask for more than a quiet spring Saturday morning. After throwing my bed together and tossing out the kitchen garbage, the day was all mine. Just be home in time for dinner at five o'clock.

It is a typical Seattle spring morning; having rained for days, the sun is finally breaking through the heavy gray clouds and glistening on the rain-drenched sidewalks. I am headed out on my Columbia Roadmaster, which my mother (an aspiring writer) won in an essay contest sponsored by Quaker Oats: *Why I feed my children Quaker Oats.* I feel so free to be out riding on my new balloon tire bike. I have access to any activity imaginable for someone my age with this special machine.

---

† In 2013, Dick's began taking debit cards.

This is a true luxury, living in the Wallingford district. My usual routine is to first ride up and down 45th to see what's up in the neighborhood. I hope to run into my Protestant friends; my dad thinks they are all going to hell because they aren't Catholics, and that I will probably go there too because I am hanging out with them. They are all good friends to me. We do things at the Wallingford Boys Club together, and we play summer baseball on the same team.

Wallingford is just north of the Aurora Bridge, just west of the University of Washington, and at its center is Green Lake. This neighborhood has everything a family needs. There is a butcher shop, grocery store, bakery, hardware store, appliance store, pharmacy, library, post office, police and fire stations, beauty and barber shops, and to top it off, Fuji's five and dime store—where you can buy just about anything. Fuji's is a perfect stop on the way home from the library on a Saturday morning to pick up penny candy to be consumed while reading your books. At the other end of 45th, there is a tavern or two and the local Chinese restaurant, The Moon Temple. We even have our own theater, and on special occasions they put on matinees for us kids for just 25 cents admission.

As I ride by, the businesses are just opening. Saturdays are busy days for them because all stores are closed on Sundays. Some of the owners give me a wave as I whisk on down the street to my destination of Interlake Elementary School; this public elementary school has an enormous paved playground, perfect for bike riding. I spend endless hours here. This is always my first stop for locating my Protestant friends, who attend school here. Today it seems they have slept in, so I will pedal by the Food Giant store. I might find my friends at Seven Sweets Bakery, a family-run bakery where you can buy great maple bars and Bismarcks if you are lucky enough to have change in your pocket. The yeasty smell of fresh baked goods is enough to draw anyone inside, especially on a dreary damp morning. Still no sight of my friends, so I pedal down Wallingford Avenue a couple blocks past St. Benedict School and glide down the hill to Green Lake and Woodland Park. On the way, I say *Hi* to the milkman, who is leaving dairy goods on the porches of the homes.

I pass the rows of houses that surround the lake on Green Lake Way. I make the turn past lower Woodland Park to *Pitch and Putt*, where one can learn to play golf on a mini nine-hole golf course that borders the dirt pathway winding around the lake. I will have to carefully make my way over the tree roots protruding from the ground and attempt to avoid the mud puddles left from the deluge. I wonder if the path around Lake Michigan in Chicago is dirt, or paved? I will have to ask my dad, since he grew up there. I also wondered if he ever rode his bike around Lake Michigan. How long did it take to complete the trip all around the lake? When we go on vacation, we don't visit cities. My parents love the mountains. We visit my mother's relatives and do a lot of fishing in Montana.

I pedal by Evans Pool, which is an indoor swimming pool, one of only two public pools in Seattle. As I pass the lake, I'm eager for when summer will be upon us and the lake area comes alive with all sorts of activities. The choices are incredible, and most of them are free. And they don't require a parent to accompany you. There is swimming at the public beach, which is supervised by lifeguards. There is free tennis at the upper and lower courts at Woodland Park. There is unlimited grass for Frisbees, several open baseball diamonds for working on your game, and a hike up the hill leads you through the old growth maples, chestnut, and evergreen trees to the concrete bridge leading to the zoo.

There is no gate and no admission fee for the zoo. We can just wander through the park to find the caged animals in their cement structures. I feel sorry for the leopard that paces in its glass-enclosed observation area; it is small to start with, and the cat strides incessantly back and forth, looking for a way to escape. There are bears in outdoor cement caves. On a rainy day, you might find me in the bird house, a building which has cubicles of exotic birds that you can observe through the glass. There is an outdoor monkey island. There are pony rides and even elephant rides. These huge creatures lower to their knees and you are hoisted by their trainer into a fancily painted box which sits atop their strong backs. They take you across the grassy hills of the park.

Then there is Seafair, a city-wide festival that seems to last all summer. Every neighborhood hosts a parade, there are hydroplane races, lots of pirates, and more. All the Seattle neighborhoods elect a princess to represent them and they compete against girls all over the city for the coveted position of Seafair Queen; she rides on the biggest float in the main Torchlight parade in downtown Seattle.

The competition is intense, and the queen crowning takes place right here at the Green Lake Aqua Theater, which houses the Aqua Follies. The swimmers perform like Esther Williams, joined by her synchronized swim team dressed in beautiful aquatic costumes. They swim and dive at the Aqua Theater prior to the crowning of the Seafair Queen. It is no small audience; this outdoor theater holds two hundred people.

The finale for Seafair is the unlimited hydroplane races on Lake Washington. On the last Sunday of Seafair, people in boats line the area and tie up together around the course to watch the hydroplanes and soak up the sun. It is fun to watch the rooster tails of the boats as they skim at high speed around the corners of the course.

Finishing my ride around the lake, my eyes are drawn to the dock that hosts one of the best things a twelve-year-old can do in the springtime. This is one of my favorite activities that I share with my friends. All five of us descend upon Green Lake at dawn on opening day of trout season. The hotspot is this T-dock, which extends fifty yards out into the water. It helps my buddies and me get out to the best fishing in the lake, especially since our equipment is nothing but beat up, worn-out baitcasting rods and reels we acquired at St. Vincent's salvage yard. With these old bamboo poles, it is essential that we get out to the farthest point of the dock to maximize our casting. There is an exception in our group, however. Last year, Bill Hawk* had a Garcia Mitchell 303 Spin/Cast Combo with a fiberglass rod and a stainless steel spinning reel with ball bearings. He was able to cast way out into the lake from anywhere on the shore.

This year will be different for me. I have discovered the benefits of doing odd jobs for people. I recently did a job for one of my friend's dad. He was cleaning up roof shingles and stuff from the back of his garage. He paid me one dollar to help, significant wages for someone my age. With opening day of fishing season just around the corner, I decided to look for more odd jobs. There is a blind woman who lives with her small daughter just across from the apartment building where I live with my parents. I had done a couple of lawn jobs in the past. I didn't have a lawnmower, but if someone did, I would mow lawns for one dollar. I went over and talked to the blind woman a couple weeks ago. She has a small front and backyard. After our discussion, she hired me to mow her lawn. I was in business now. It seemed kind of funny to me, however, that when I finished mowing her lawn she would open her wallet in full trust and lay out currency on the table. This consisted of a couple of ones, fives, tens, as well as twenty dollar bills. She suggested I select a one-dollar bill for payment. I never considered taking two bills or anything like that. She said I could continue to mow her lawn through the spring and summer.

Already I had three dollars saved. I knew one of these dollars would have to go toward the bait and tackle needed for opening day of fishing season. This gear is very specific. You need to have a size 12 bait hook, not a *worm* hook, made out of brass. You also need two feet of 4-pound leader, along with three slip weights that go up and down the line, and lastly, a perfect swivel that these weights will bump up against. Speaking of bait, there is only one type of bait that works at Green Lake: Pautzke's Balls of Fire salmon eggs. To my knowledge, the fish will not look at any other type of eggs. You have to carefully position one egg on the hook, gently handling it so as not to squeeze too hard or you will break the skin of the egg, since that warrants starting all over baiting your hook. Once it is in place, you can then gently cast your line out over the water, watching the bright red egg at the end of your line enter the water. If you're doing everything right, the wait shouldn't be long.

When I started my odd job business, I spied a top notch fishing combo set on the wall at Tweedy and Popp Hardware. It was a Garcia Mitchell 303 spinning rod and reel on display, just like Bill Hawk had. The price tag read *$12.00*. I had two dollars in my pocket and decided to get a sales pitch together to present to Mr. Tweedy. I hung around the store to talk with him, but I could see he was very busy. I wandered in and out of the store a couple times that Saturday and about thirty minutes before closing, I walked in and he was alone. The store was empty of customers. I decided it was a good time to approach him and greeted him with a big *Hello*. He knows me quite well, because I am a regular visitor to the store. I had practiced my sales pitch and knew exactly what I was going to propose.

"I mow lawns for the blind woman," I said.

He said, "Yes, I know Mrs. Reed*. She is a regular customer and we try to help her out where we can."

I continued with the fact that I mowed her lawn on a regular basis, and that she paid me one dollar each time.

"I have a solid income of at least one dollar per month and some months it is two dollars."

"Why are you telling me this?" Mr. Tweedy asked.

I could tell now he was trying to finish up a long day.

"I am telling you this because I feel you should sell me that Garcia Mitchell rod and reel spinning combination."

He turned to the wall, took down the set, and put it before me on the counter.

"Great. That will be twelve dollars."

I immediately went into my sales pitch.

"I think you should sell this to me with two dollars down and I will pay you one dollar per month for the next ten months." It never occurred to me that there should be interest on top of this.

I think Mr. Tweedy was quite amused, and seemed to be laughing. When he realized I was serious however, he stopped laughing and asked that I go with him to the back of the store to his office. We walked through the aisles of chain, pipes, and other gadgets to the door that led to the tiny closet he called his office. He asked me to have a seat next to his desk. He pulled a 3x5 card out from his filing cabinet. He had me complete the card by putting down my full name, date of birth, address, and phone number. He also asked me to include the school I attended, my year in school, and what kind of grades I was getting. I thought this was odd for an application, but there was no questioning from me. He asked me to include how much I would be paying per month and to include my parents' names. I was then asked to sign the bottom of the card.

Then he had me follow him to the front counter of the store and he handed me the rod and reel. I burst out with *Thanks!* and a big smile then streaked out the door of the store, running home to show my mother and father.

I explained how Mr. Tweedy had let me buy my fishing gear on credit with my odd job money as future payment. They both burst into laughter.

My dad commented, "Gee, I can't even get credit at the hardware store! Just how did you do that?"

I need to get back home for dinner now, so I turn the Roadmaster toward 45th Street. I pass by the Wallingford Police station. I have to wonder how many bad things happen in Wallingford? It sure doesn't seem like much. The police cars are all parked at the station and I never hear sirens or see red lights flashing on top of the police cars. Crimes seem to be few and far between.

October 2009

I finish my cheeseburgers and exit the car heading to my favorite bench by the lake where I spent many hours as a young boy. The bench where I made awkward advances, actual or imagined, toward my girlfriend. It is the bench where in the wee hours of April 1969, while back from Vietnam, and on a weekend pass as a patient at Bremerton Naval Hospital, I sat with my childhood friend, Gail. She had written letters to me for the past two years: letters written on a daily basis, taking weeks to arrive in Vietnam. We decided we would place all our belongings in my car, get married, and head off to wherever the Marines would send me after I recuperated.

Sitting here today, I realize that the twelve-year-old is not going to be suppressed any longer. He is tugging at my soul to let him be heard. He has suffered too long. I have suffered too long. And so I must relive it with him. Through our pain, we will be released, and find the justice the Catholic Church has never offered.

CHAPTER 3

THE SELECTOR

It's the spring of 1961, before the end of sixth grade. Our class has just returned from the end-of-school-year picnic at Lake Wilderness, and Sister Roberta announces that Mr. Adamson, one of the seventh-grade teachers, is coming for a visit. As he enters our classroom, I think how he resembles a balloon character from the Macy's Thanksgiving Day Parade. His body looks swollen; his checkered shirt and tweed jacket are so tight it looks like he might pop. He has a reputation for being tough on boys, losing his temper, and shoving kids around.

It seems like he's on a mission today as he walks around the classroom. I catch a distinct whiff of stale cigar smoke. Looking down, I notice his unusual shoes, which I learn later are *wing walkers*, once worn by aircraft mechanics in World War II. His argyle socks are exposed below his too-short, baggy pants. Overall, he is a peculiar looking man: a military-style flattop, bright red hair slathered with the hair cream, Brylcreem; a wide ruddy, freckled face and thick neck; black horn-rimmed glasses, ill-fitting with ear pieces that barely wrap around his ears.

I hear the *clop, clop, clop* of his heavy shoes as he threads his way around each student's desk, occasionally tapping on someone's desk with his large, stubby fingers. He pauses at my desk: *tap, tap*. I'm not sure what the tapping on our desk means, but I've heard from older classmates that this is how Adamson selects kids for his seventh-grade class. I sense my fate is sealed, but will have to wait until the first day of school.

In the sixth grade, I worked hard to get good grades. I was also in the boys' choir and on the school crossing patrol team. I had never been in trouble or sent to the principal's office. My older brothers, Jerry and Frank (nicknamed *Heckle* and *Jeckle* by my parents), were always in trouble at school: fighting, breaking windows, climbing flagpoles, smoking, starting fires, and cutting class. They were kicked out of St. Benedict's, transferred to Blessed Sacrament grade school, and ended up in public school; eventually, one dropped out and the other was expelled from high school. This is what Father Conrad and the teachers at St. Benedict's knew about the O'Connor boys. I didn't want teachers to think that I was anything like my brothers. Besides my brothers' reputation, my parents had trouble paying the tuition. That could be another black mark against me, or the fact that my mother never volunteered at the school, always waking at noon each day to her coffee and cigarettes.

The only time Father Conrad got on my case was in third grade, when he handed out report cards; he noticed my last name, *O'Connor*, and that I was absent from school for eleven straight days. He wasn't happy about it, especially having dealt with my brothers' history of cutting class. I tried to tell my story about how I jumped off a porch and cut my foot on a ragged, sharp edge of a coffee can that I used to store my marbles in. I could barely walk, and my parents kept me home from school. That didn't matter to Father Conrad. He railed at me and said, *I don't want to hear your excuses and stories, boy.*

The hierarchy and chain of command at St. Benedict's begins with the pastor, Father Conrad, a stern, authoritarian figure who knows all that goes on under his watch. We dread report card day at school when he stands at the front of the classroom and calls out individual students to come forward and receive their report card. Reviewing our grades out loud, he scolds kids who have failing grades or bad deportment. I feel bad for those kids. The primary mission for the Dominican sisters is teaching at the school, and they live across the street in a convent. Along with teaching piano and directing choral groups, they attend to the priests' laundry and meals. During the 1960s, the principal of the school was normally a Dominican nun; she and the other sisters were under the authority of, and obedient to, the pastor, Father Conrad, a member of the order of Oblates of Mary Immaculate (OMI).

Adamson is a powerful figure at St. Benedict's, right up there with the priests. It's hard to place him in the hierarchy. In addition to being a seventh-grade teacher, he directs the CYO teen club and men's choir. He is the church organist, and manages all the audiovisual equipment at the school. Adamson is omnipresent. He has his own parking spot at school, and when his car is there during non-school hours or weekends, no one else ever seems to enter the building. A single man in his forties, he lives at home with his mother. No one ever sees him in the community: at Food Giant, Tweedy and Popp Hardware Store, Woodland Park Zoo, Green Lake, or just walking down 45th Street. Occasionally, he is spotted getting gas at Rex Jordan's Texaco, or visiting the local train hobby shop. Except for time spent on his elaborate model train set in his basement, he has a side business tuning pipe organs. Most of the time, he is at St. Benedict School and Church. The working class neighborhood parish and school is run on a tight budget, unlike some of the city's more affluent parishes; Adamson is saving them countless dollars through his volunteer time. He's a phone call away for anything that needs fixing at the school or parish: electrical, lighting, sound equipment, organ tuning, and general maintenance. The Oblate priests, Dominican sisters, parents, and parishioners come to depend on him at St. Benedict's. *What would they do without Adamson?*

It is rumored that he knows some of the dark, secret scandals in the parish, in particular about Father Conrad (and his favorite altar boys). This seals Adamson's unique position of authority and power that he amassed at St. Benedict's. He had something on everyone. He "owns people," is how he puts it.

He avoids interfacing with the women of the parish, or the school's Dominican sisters. Adamson's mother makes his lunch every day for school and places it in a brown paper bag marked *Danny*, neatly printed on the outside. Most days he eats his lunch alone in the seventh-grade classroom and shuns the faculty lounge. He is known for his face, neck, and arms turning brilliant, reddish-pink when he is angry. Adamson is large in stature, nearly six-foot tall and over two hundred pounds, but with no athletic capabilities.

One day as he walked on the playground at recess, a baseball was hit into foul territory and bounced against his shins. Startled, he picked up the ball and threw an overhand, effeminate lob back to the boys. He turned reddish-pink all over and stormed off the playground, quickly disappearing into the school building. We boys burst out laughing. The nickname *Pinky* stuck, only uttered behind his back.

Pinky may remember me. I know that when I was in the first grade he visited my house to talk to my eldest brother, Jim, about a hiking trip for the teen club. At the time, he was attending the University of Washington and volunteering for the St. Benedict's teen club. He visited again, five or six times that summer, talking with my dad about St. Vincent de Paul, a charitable organization where they had both volunteered. My dad painted each of the trucks with the words, *St. Vincent de Paul All Over the World* in distinctive, Old-English-style lettering. I remember my dad talking to Pinky about the seminary. He often tried to recruit young men to the priesthood. By the time I was in the fourth grade, Pinky was hired as a teacher by Father Conrad after years of volunteering for the school.

CHAPTER 4

YOU BOYS WANT SOME LEMONADE?

September 1961

On the first day of seventh grade, I see Mr. Adamson as I walk up the stairs. He's getting out of his cream-colored 1958 Borgward Station Wagon. I continue inside and walk upstairs to the top floor; this floor is exclusively for upperclassmen, seventh and eighth graders. Excited to find out who my teacher will be, I spot the list of assignments on the door of each classroom. I check out the list for Sister Nathan's class, *7B*. No, I'm not on that one. Maybe I'm not on either list; it could be that the latest tuition promises from my parents fell through.

I go to the list across the hall, *7A*. There's my name, halfway down. It's real now, I'm in the feared Mr. Adamson's class. The nuns could be mean, but he is a completely different animal.

In the fall of seventh grade I was twelve years old. I had heard about last year's popular student who worked for Pinky, taking trips tuning organs around the state and working weekends running lights and audio visual equipment in the school auditorium for CYO functions. *And* he was paid for all of these jobs! That would be the ticket: the prestige of being Adamson's boy and paying jobs. So for the first two weeks of seventh grade, I was driven, eager to prove myself worthy of being selected.

I approached Mr. Adamson one day after school and asked if I could stay and wash down the blackboards. In the back of my mind, I was thinking what a *brown nose* I was. He said OK and I turned a fifteen-minute job into an hour, getting the job done to perfection. I cleaned the blackboards with a rag and then dried them until they were spotless. I carefully dusted the chalk trays with a small whisk broom and then broke the chalk into equal lengths and set the pieces in rows at the three blackboards so they were uniform and set dead center. Then I took all of the erasers and pounded them outside against the brick school building until they were meticulously clean; inside, I aligned them on the tray, and set them an equal distance apart. Pinky didn't have much to say, but I thought he was impressed. Finally, he said *Good job*.

"Well, thank you, Mr. Adamson, for giving me the opportunity to do this job."

I felt good and my hopes were high that I might be 'selected'. A few days later he asks me to stay after school.

"Oh, sure Mr. Adamson. You want me to start working on the blackboards?"

"No, we're going down the hall and I'm going to show you a few things in the projection room."

My thoughts and heart race. *My gosh, maybe this is my chance to be the projectionist.* The projectionist was a kid who Adamson trained to run the projector for Friday afternoon movies on big reel-to-reel spools, usually sixteen-millimeter film running through the gigantic projector in a maze of sprockets, clicking loudly if the film got stuck. If you didn't know how to clear this kind of jam, the intensity of the projector lamp could cause a fire. The rest of the job was about keeping the lamp clean, splicing tapes, and managing the organization of the film canisters. This is all very big to me—a huge responsibility—and if I can get this down, it's a dream job.

School has been out for twenty minutes. The kids are headed home and the nuns are back across the street in their modern, brick convent building. It's just Adamson and me on the top floor, walking to the projector room. I walk dutifully behind him, hearing the shallow echo of his crepe-soled shoes squeaking in the empty hallway. I watch as he pulls his large key ring with a dozen or more assorted keys out of his pocket and unlocks the door to the projection room. I've never seen anyone else with a key to this room. Adamson was the only one who ever entered the projection room.

His large body squeezes into the narrow entrance to the room. I am small enough to walk straight in. The room is long and narrow, about seven or eight feet long and three feet wide. To the right there is a cutting and splicing table, a small bottle marked *Isopropyl Alcohol,* and Q-tips. There is only one light bulb, which is red, with a small pull chain attached. A flashlight with a red lens is on the table. Everything is meticulously clean to keep any dust away from the film.

He begins to explain the parts of the projector with the huge reels.

"If the sprocket doesn't have enough slack in it, it will stick in front of the projector lamp and burn the film."

His fingers touch the reel as he spins it to adjust the slack.

I could only imagine what would happen if that mistake was made, what he'd do to me. So I listen carefully and do everything he tells me, and I take mental notes to make sure I remember every detail.

After three trips to the projection room, I have a working knowledge of how to splice film and change the projector lens and bulb, all while wearing white cotton gloves so that no prints get on the lens or the bulb.

Nobody messes with Pinky's boy, and there are several perks of the job: going to the bathroom whenever; wandering the halls freely; taking messages and notes from the classroom to the principal's office, and never being questioned by a teacher or nun in the hallway. And, Pinky won't throw erasers at you in class, or beat you with a wooden pointer, or yell at you.

As the boy in training, I get home from school about four o'clock every day; my mother knows that I stay after school for a good reason, working under the tutelage of Pinky, and she and Dad are proud of me. She no longer has to worry about going to the principal's office after school to pick up one of her errant sons. I am proud of myself, and my self-esteem is through the roof; I was going to make it through St. Benedict's.

It's four weeks into school and I've arrived—I'm Pinky's boy. After school one day, he asks me to stay and clean up the projector room and get films ready for mailing, placing labels on the canisters and delivering them to the principal's office. One of the things Adamson talked about was to always close the door to the projector room once you are in to avoid the florescent light shining into the room. He explained that a person needs to adjust their night vision under the red light in the room, so they can see their work. I am impressed and imagine that maybe he was a captain of a submarine or something in World War II.

As I work at the splicing table that afternoon, I hear the shuffling and *clop, clop, clop* of his wing walker shoes coming down the hall. Maybe he's bringing me a cookie or piece of cake left over from his lunch, as he had done last week. This was one of the perks of the job. At my house, there was no baking of cakes or brownies, and no cookies in my lunch or after-school snack. My lunch consisted of a piece of Velveeta cheese with mustard slapped on a piece of stale bread.

I keep my attention to the task at hand. Whenever he approached me, I never looked at him directly or made eye contact. Now, with my head down, I see him out of the corner of my eye as he slides sideways through the door of the projection room. Without a word, he shuts the door behind him and reaches up to the ceiling, pulling the chain to the light bulb. Suddenly, we're in complete darkness. I keep my hands on the cutting board and freeze, quiet and still as possible. I hear him shuffling up behind me and he starts to breathe hard, huffing and puffing. I don't understand what he's doing, then he puts his hands on me, grabbing my sweater, thrashing me around, pushing me down the little stairs that are against the projector. He grabs me in a headlock and I think, *this is Adamson just doing what Adamson does.* But as the attack worsens, I'm screaming, internally, *what did I do wrong? Why is he beating me up?* My breathing is shallow as he cuts off my circulation with the headlock, but he's breathing real hard and using his other hand to grab me in the front.

After a few more minutes, he pushes me back down to the floor, releasing me, and backs out of the room. I hear him adjust his pants, hear the belt buckle, the zipper, and the wing walkers fade away down the hallway, then the classroom door slams shut.

I wait a minute or two, and then I turn on the red light, open the door, and tiptoe over to the window to see if his car is still parked in front. It's there. *I've got to get out of here.* I stand still, not wanting to move. I can sneak out of here, but he might catch me. He could be waiting at the bottom of the stairs to beat me up again. I walk quietly to the other end of the hall and run down the stairs, picking up my pace when I get outside. I'm pulling my pants up because my belt is broken. It's just a second-hand St. Vincent de Paul leather belt, but the force of how he grabbed and pulled my pants from behind must have broken it. I'm running all the way home, thinking I've done something terrible to upset him. Once home, I run straight to my bedroom and look in the mirror. I have a large bump on my forehead and there are scratches on my neck. I'm not so much afraid as despondent. I'm surely going to be fired as Pinky's boy.

My bedroom is damp, the heat turned off again. Probably due to an overdue bill at the oil company. I lie on my bed staring at the ceiling, hoping some answer will come to me. *What did I do wrong in the projection room?* If I can figure out what I did wrong, then I can approach Mr. Adamson and tell him it will never happen again. It's an extra-long weekend, as we have a Holy Day of Obligation and school is out on Friday. For three days, I keep wracking my brain: Did I break a projection bulb? Put the wrong film in the canister? No, it couldn't be any of that; I paid attention to every detail.

Monday is coming soon and I'm distraught, worried. Maybe it didn't have anything to do with the projection room. Maybe something more powerful is going on. *I've done something sinister. Did I lie to my parents? What about my fleeting thought of shoplifting at Food Giant grocery store? What about impure thoughts?* Maybe some supreme being knew about something, and I was being punished for it. I sift through any possible reason outside of the projection room. At home Sunday night, sitting in my room, catching up on arithmetic homework, I stare down at the numbers in the book. Normally, arithmetic is a cinch for me, but the numbers are blurring together and I've lost concentration.

Then it comes to me.

Do not walk with a girl in Woodland Park woods alone. My sixth-grade teacher, Sister Roberta, warned me to never do this. Not because of any outside danger, but because it could cause impure thoughts about girls. The teachers and nuns had endless list of dos and don'ts. If you failed, punishment would come in some form, from some greater being. We learned early on that God is all-knowing and all-present. *That's it, I walked my friend Gail to the upper tennis courts, through the woods. I was alone with a girl. The higher power knows this. God was watching me, and he told Father Conrad, and Conrad went to the "enforcer," and the enforcer beat the crap out of me—my punishment for this sin.* By the end of the weekend, this seemed logical to me; there could be no other reason for the attack in the projection room.

Monday dawns and I am uneasy as I trudge my way back to school, to the seventh-grade classroom. I expect to be grabbed by the throat, thrown against the wall, admonished in front of everyone in class, fired from my job as projectionist, and ridiculed in front of all my classmates. Instead, nothing happens. No dirty looks from him, and later in the afternoon, he calls me to his desk and gives me a note to take to Sister Marie in the principal's office. There is no harshness in his voice, nor anger on his face.

On my way to the office, relieved, I try to make sense of it; I had sinned and Adamson was assigned by Father Conrad to punish me—he was just doing God's work. Over the next few days, things are back to normal and Adamson gives me several tasks and errands to run, all of which I take great care in doing.

I am anxious about my job and tread lightly, staying under the radar, avoiding any of his wrath. After school one day, he talks to me about future plans to have me work more in the projection room. I'm thinking, *Well, the upside is, I'm still Pinky's boy, but the downside is that I might be exposed to more thrashing as the projectionist. Maybe it just happens randomly?*

The next week I ask if there is anything he wants me to do after school.

"Yes, there is. I want you to go downstairs, outside, and sit in the front seat of my car and wait for me. We're going down to my house."

I am ecstatic. I had heard from other students that if you were invited down to his house, you were on your way to being hired... hired to be the pipe organ tuner. The boys who were invited to his basement told fantastic stories about this elaborate set-up that held a large pipe organ set into a chiseled-out stone foundation, ham radio equipment, and a model train set—all of this under magnificent bright lights.

For me, as a young boy, I can hardly wait to see all of this, which I've heard about and imagined. As I wait in the passenger seat of his car, I fixate on the dashboard right in front of me, the word *Borgward* prominent on the metal dashboard. He opens the door, sliding onto the driver's seat that is encased in a plastic cover. I keep my head down, never looking his way, mute and starring at the *Borgward* logo on the glove box.

This first time going to his house, I am afraid I might not find my way home. As a seventh grader, if you were to plop me ten blocks away from my house, I'd be lost. I only know St. Benedict School and the Wallingford and Burke Avenue Apartments. If you were to leave me on the other side of Lake Union, or Capitol Hill, just a mile or two away, I would not find my way home. As it turns out, we drive only a few blocks to his Wallingford bungalow, stopping at a gravel alleyway with a small garage in back of his house. The car fits only part way into the garage, with the back end sticking out in the driveway. There is a garden staked off in the backyard, and a fish pond nearby. Adamson gets out of the car and motions me to follow him to the back of the house. There is a screen door in the back and three steps up is the kitchen to the right as you enter. He says something to a person as we walk in and I see an elderly woman wearing a flower-print housedress washing dishes. It's probably his mother. He walks down the stairs to the basement as she speaks.

"How are you boys doing?"

I hesitate, unsure if she is talking to me or if I should respond.

"Yes, Ma'am," is all I manage.

There is a sweet, inviting smell of cookies, or a cake, baking that fills the house. I stand rigid at the top of the steps to the basement and see bright florescent lights and a set of wooden stairs; the stairs are without a railing of any kind and they open up to a concrete floor. The lights are a contrast to anything I've ever seen in Wallingford, especially my dark rental apartment building. Even the Food Giant is dark and dingy. The brightest lights I'd seen were in the hospital. On 45th Street, where everything closes at five o'clock, nothing is this bright in the neighborhood. To see this kind of light is astounding…

special. As I walk down the stairs and look up at the low ceiling, I see florescent light after florescent light after florescent light all butted up close to each other. It's ten times brighter than the sun shining.

I see the bench with all of his radio equipment, ham radio gear as I learn later, with a set of headphones and aerials. He could talk to people from all over the world on that radio—Australia, Hawaii, the South Pacific. He built the ham radio from a *Heath kit*, he said. And not only do I notice the light in this basement, but it's warm, a heater going against the wall. The usual basements in the Wallingford district were dark, cold, and damp with single, low-watt bulbs hanging from the rafters.

In the corner of the basement, up against the chiseled out rock, and wedged between the stone, is a large pipe organ with pipes and bellows and keyboards. I'm not sure how he was able to get that monstrous organ down to his basement. It's bizarre looking, the way the organ is positioned within that rock, like in a grotto, or cave. The organ was on a riser and he sat up on the stool to play. It was so loud—an amazing sound in this small space—different than the pipe organ at St. Benedict Church, which stood out in the open in the choir loft at the back of the church.

"Come over here, I want to ask you some questions about the projection room and running the projector."

It sort of feels like a test and he appears fine with my answers.

"I want you to run the projector for a history film next Friday."

I am astonished. He just announced to me that I was going to run the projector by myself for an auditorium full of sixth, seventh, and eighth graders, teachers, nuns, and the principal.

As we sit in front of the bench with the radio equipment, he asks me if I know how radios work.

"Do you know anything about wiring, soldering, and metals?

"No, Mr. Adamson, no I don't know anything." Even if I had, I would never speak up to an adult and say what I might be knowledgeable about. Our St. Benedict's upbringing instilled in us a sense of low self-esteem; we were way beneath anyone in authority.

"Well, we're going to be installing a speaker system for the school next summer and I think I'm going to hire you to help with that. First though, you need to know what a wire is, which one is hot, which one is ground, and how speaker wire is different than house wire. Then you need to learn how to solder connections with the soldering iron. You'll need to pay attention to all this. I don't want you messing up or I'll find someone else and I won't pay you."

I'm excited and overwhelmed with the stimuli of things in the basement and all the information he throws at me that I've never heard before.

He excuses himself and goes upstairs. I hear him talking to his mother in the kitchen.

I look around the walls of the basement and for the first time I notice that he has calendars everywhere—the same year, 1961, but not with pictures of lakes, mountain scenes, or a seascape; these are all of women and the advertisement at the top is for a gas station, Rex Jordan Texaco, in the Wallingford district. In the pictures, the women are doing things like sitting on a swing or holding an umbrella in a raincoat. The pictures are on a Mylar acetate, a type of clear plastic.

Adamson comes back downstairs and starts explaining about wiring speakers. He turns on the speaker on his wall, which makes a loud radio static and I hear *whoooie, whoooie,* as if tuning into a channel, then voices of people talking to each other.

"What do you think of my calendars? Go on over to one and take a look."

I walk over to a calendar nearest to me and Pinky follows. He takes it off the wall and has me sit on the stool. Then he lays the calendar in my lap.

"What do you think of this one?"

I look down and see it's turned to the month of October; there is a woman with an umbrella in a raincoat standing next to a park bench. I really don't know what to say.

"It's OK."

He has a pin holding up the picture and he takes the pin out and lifts up the first piece of Mylar. It's the same woman standing there, but now the raincoat is gone and she is wearing a one-piece bathing suit. I think, *That's odd.* He lifts up the next piece of Mylar down and she still has an umbrella, but her bathing suit is off her shoulders, down to her waist, exposing her top. For the first time in my life, I not only see a woman partially clothed, but a woman with

30

no clothes on top at all. I'm not exactly sure what I'm seeing as a twelve-year-old and start to feel weird sensations.

He closes it up and hangs it back on the wall and then in a loud, abrupt voice says, "OK, I'll see you tomorrow."

I quickly walk up the stairs, with Adamson in front of me. His mother is still in the kitchen.

"You boys want some lemonade?"

I keep my head down and without a word walk out the door and all the way to my house.

When I get home, my mother is sitting at the kitchen table, smoking.

She asks, "You been working for Mr. Adamson today?"

"Yes, I went down to his house today."

She seems excited. "Oh yeah, did he drive you down to his house?"

"Yeah, and I saw his basement. He's got all these florescent lights, and a big pipe organ."

"I heard he has some neat stuff he plays with down there, and that he's quite the hobbyist."

"He has some type of radio equipment."

"A ham radio, probably." She seemed familiar with them, maybe because they used them in World War II.

I definitely leave out the part about the calendars.

As we eat our dinner, I am quiet, the images of the woman and the umbrella flashing in and out of my brain.

That Friday, I am quite nervous during my trial of running the projector on my own. The auditorium is packed with students, teachers, nuns, and the principal. Pinky is outside the projection room, but it all goes off without a hitch; the sprockets don't stick, the bulb doesn't go out. Nothing goes wrong and I am really happy with myself.

A few weeks later, around Halloween, Mr. Adamson asks me to go down to his car again and wait for him after school. I sit there, like always, staring at the *Borgward* logo on the dashboard. After a while, he slides into the driver's seat and we drive to his house. I am less anxious this time, as I know where his house is. We walk into the back entrance of the house, into the kitchen.

"Hi boys, how are you doing?" His mother is in the kitchen again.

We walk down the stairs to the basement. I stand in the basement, looking at the calendars on the wall. They all seemed normal: the woman with the umbrella has her raincoat on and the woman in the swing is in a white sundress with wide shoulder straps. Sitting at the desk, I learn more about the radio equipment, and then he motions for me to follow him to another area in the basement, to a big wall and large door.

"I'd like to show you something."

There are about eight light switches to the right of the doorway and a box with fuses that supplies the additional electricity to whatever is behind that door. The wall is plastered and painted and there is a nice frame around the door. This is all located past the pipe organ, the radio equipment, and a giant fish tank, four feet wide and three feet high. I thought the basement couldn't possibly have any more lights, but then he turns on the switches and opens the door. It's as if he just opened the door to Mars and there were flying saucers, Martians, and all that was foreign to me. And the lights are even brighter than the rest of the basement! Just inside the door, there is a wooden two-by-six board set waist high, and connected to that is a large plywood hatch, which Adamson unbolts and opens. Then he crouches down, crawls in, and disappears.

My eyes slowly comprehend the space that I'm standing in. There are multiple miniature train sets circling around the room. I marvel at the little mountains, lakes, and green hills. Tracks are running everywhere. There is a replica of a train station with miniature people walking their tiny plastic dogs. One of the electric trains has an elaborate engine with *Great Northern* painted on the side and pulling five cars, all painted the orange and green color of the Great Northern Empire Builder. There was a tiny bubble vista dome on top of one of the cars with miniature people seated near the windows, an exact model of the train that I once rode to Montana. The whole room seemed like an elaborate movie set. I thought maybe this is how they filmed movies like *Godzilla* or *Invaders from Mars*, it looked so unbelievably real. It wasn't just one train on the tracks, there were other trains higher up, coming down little hills around mountains. For now, they were all motionless.

I don't know where Adamson has gone. Then a hinged green mound opens up in the corner of the room, about five feet away, like the top on a flying saucer. Adamson pops out like a jack-in-the-box, standing in the middle of a field where a mountain had been. I flinch at his sudden appearance. Later I realize that he has four or five access spots, so if a train derails he can go to the area, pop up, and put the train back on the tracks. It also allows him to create the landscape around the tracks. He uses cinnamon for roads and pathways, he explains to me, and glues on a variety of spices—red, yellow, and orange—that make the hills alive with color. He uses substances such as bits of dried parsley to make the trees and shrubs. All of these carefully ground up and set in containers.

At the place where he disappeared, I notice a large rectangular plate with lots of switches, big and little, and two main ones that are primitive pieces of metal rods, thicker than a coat hanger, like a big fat nail, and with a rubber base. He tells me to back up as he comes up from underneath, then makes his way to the control panel. He points to the panel of switches to the right and says, *Watch this*. He turns up a large black dial (later he explains it's called a rheostat switch) and as he rotates it to the right, the train accelerates, going faster and faster. Then he hits another switch and a second train starts moving down the hill, around the mountain, and as they pass each other at high speed, maybe an inch apart, I imagine them crashing.

Adamson leaves the room for a minute as these trains are running. I don't dare touch anything. He comes back with a stool, tells me to sit in front of the switches, and then starts explaining which lights went with which trains and what dials ran the trains and which ones ran the whistle and then a separate switch for the roundhouse—a disk that turned the train around so that it ran in a different direction. All of these trains require a huge assortment of control switches!

Never have I witnessed such elaborate toys in my life. I look at the room now, and how the path from the train set leads up into forests, mountains, and blue sky, all murals painted on the wall, like a scene from *The Wizard of Oz*. My senses are overwhelmed with the lights and color of the whole set: the sound of the train wheels turning on the track, the bells ringing and whistles blowing, and the smell of cinnamon and other spices.

There's no sign of the calendars in this room.

I sit on the stool as he instructs me on how to use the toggle switches to run the trains. My hands are busy, my mind fascinated with this train set. He reaches around and grabs me, pulling at my pants again, "goosing me," like he does on the playground, and then I hear him breathing hard again and he's grabbing at my sweater, rocking me back and forth, butting up against me. His hands move around on himself and then he suddenly leaves the room. I sit and watch the trains running on the tracks and hope they don't derail, as I'll get blamed for that. I'm sure these trains cost as much as a brand new car. In a few minutes, he returns and I sit motionless. He reaches around and snaps two large switches to the off position and *poof*, everything stops.

"You can go now."

He walks back out the door. Turns out all the lights. Closes the door.

I run up the stairs, taking them two at a time, and out the back door, passing the garden and little fish pond. I look at the fish pond and remember how Adamson came out with an old red Prince Albert tobacco can that now contained fish food and threw a tiny scoop out to these giant fish—they'd make rattling noises, like piranhas jumping up from the pond, stirring up the water and making it turbulent.

When I round the corner of the house, I encounter an old shriveled up man in a pair of black and white striped railroad overalls. I nearly jump a foot. The guy is dressed exactly like the children's TV character, Brakeman Bill. He's even got the engineer's hat and red handkerchief around his neck. We make eye contact, I say *Hello*, but he doesn't say anything, just goes back to his gardening. I feel like I'm looking straight at a ghost and wonder if this is Adamson's grandfather. Later, I learn that he is Adamson's *dad*. A lot of people in the neighborhood described him as *a weird duck*.

As a twelve-year-old, I'm wondering what would be next for me. I've been to his basement where these weird things happen, yet when he asks me to go sit in his car another time, I dutifully wait for him after school at three o'clock and go to his basement again, leaving for home at five o'clock. This happens again and again in the fall of 1961, always between three and five o'clock.

I'm hoping that maybe sometime soon Adamson's going to ask me if I want a job tuning pipe organs with him, and I'd say, *Heck yeah*. I'll do everything to do that, because that's the next step. All the while, I am doing better at all the jobs he gives me, impressing Adamson and getting more perks. Lemonade from his mother, cookies, and money for some of the jobs after school.

Down in the basement again by the ham radio equipment, he brings over more calendars and goes through the same routine of de-clothing the women through the magic of Mylar. The woman in the bathing suit is on the swing now, then the bathing suit is coming off, and next she has nothing on except her big white headband with her hair in a ponytail. These pictures are more and more revealing and I'm starting to think about them a lot. In a matter of minutes, he's hanging the calendars back on the wall. As if choreographed, he quickly changes the subject.

"You know; I think you've got what it takes to follow instructions. Now, you need to learn soldering and know something about musical notes. You don't need to know how to play the piano or organ, just know the notes."

"Well, I'm in piano lessons right now, so I can read notes."

"While you're on the job, tuning organs, I'm going to ask you to put your finger on a note, like a C, or C sharp or B, B flat, or D, and I'm going to be in the organ loft area opening and shutting these pipes, or vacuuming out the pipes where they meet the bellows, so I'll be calling down to you. So you think that's something you can do?"

"Yes."

"You'll get an opportunity to travel all over the state."

I'm thinking, *Wow, this is it.*

"You'll have to talk to my parents."

"No problem."

A few days later, on a Saturday, he stops by the apartment. My mother answers the door. He quickly looks past her and says he needs to talk with my dad. My dad calls him *Dan*, and Adamson explains to him that he'd like to give me a try at this job. My dad seems thrilled. Standing by the door next to my dad, I listen to them talk about me. My dad seems anxious for me to get this job.

"Oh, yeah, Steve's really good at paying attention to things. We'll make sure he gets any of his studies or book reading done and be there on time."

Tugging at the too-short sleeves of his sports jacket, Adamson says, "Good, I can pick Steve up on Saturday morning and bring him back Sunday afternoon."

At first, my thoughts are, *I hope he's paying me and that I'll have a chance to make a lot of money.* But now, I'm confused about this arrangement. Did I hear this right—overnights with Adamson? Before, at least I could get away at five o'clock. When he first mentioned trips around the state, I thought he would be picking me up on Saturday, work all day, and then head home Saturday night; on Sunday after Mass he'd pick me up again early and deliver me home that night. An overnight with Adamson feels weird to me— not only driving across the state, but staying in some strange town with my seventh-grade teacher. It wasn't what I envisioned for after school or weekend jobs.

My parents understand that I'll be gone overnight for this work. They agree to the arrangement no questions asked, with a lack of curiosity about the overnights that shocks me. What about where we'll stay: in the cathedral, in the rectory with the priest, a hotel? No, instead my parents are totally accepting, they completely entrust me into the hands of Adamson. They are proud, happy, beaming.

My dad sits me down in the living room after this visit from Adamson and lights his cigarette.

"You're seeing the consequences in your life—cause and effect— the positive consequences that are coming to you now."

Making sure he can't see me, I roll my eyes. Here we go again. He's always into *consequences*, explaining elaborate Jesuit theories and philosophy from Aristotle that I don't understand.

"If you work hard and do what you're supposed to do, positive consequences will come. When he says jump, you say, *yes sir, no sir, Mr. Adamson*, just like with the nuns, and that's what you do. He says *Jump*, you say *How high*."

This is how the next progression begins. I am traveling all over the state with Pinky and at the end of the day, he'd buy me food: a cheap cheeseburger, or hot dog, and lemonade, always lemonade. We'd stay in some cheap, fleabag hotel with a single bed. When I come back from these trips, I am more ingratiated, more special to him. He pays me three dollars a day. I keep my money in the top dresser drawer and by Christmas season, I save about fifteen dollars. I feel good about earning my own money, and I buy my mother a candle for Christmas and a gift for my dad, a humidor or package of pipe cleaners for his pipe, or maybe a paint brush from Tweedy and Popp hardware. It's fun. I'm thirteen years old and I'm buying my parents Christmas presents.

The Wallingford Boys Club shows movies on the weekend. They are black and white thrillers about Godzilla, or man-eating giant ants. I was removed as I watched the giant ants devour these desert towns. The ants were in the desert, so it couldn't happen to me, since I lived in a city. That's how I started to get in my own life; I was watching this scenario, what's happening to me, as a horror movie. I'm developing life skills—all learned at St. Benedict's. Pinky is not doing these things to this child, not to me. I'm watching this from afar, like a rerun, and I know what's going to happen next. *But that's not me on the hotel bed, that wasn't me being tortured, exploited, having terrible unheard of things happen to a thirteen-year-old, no that wasn't me. I was just watching.* This would be the start of what I would refer to later in life as my *blockers.* If I can do that, I can go back to the basement, back to tune another organ in Yakima, and when I return home, that *wasn't* me, and that *isn't* me. I know how to make money, an accomplished projectionist at school, and I'm learning how to solder, do wiring, fix and make speakers, starting to run the train set on my own and oil the engines and put the rear wheelers on and switch plates, making sure the trains are going slow while turning the electric switch. I'm helping with the grasses and making mountain sculptures and it's all fun. I only hope that I can continue to look at the downside of this boy from afar. It's painful and it's horrendous. I still don't understand it, other than it's a physical thrashing. But Pinky seems to enjoy it and he's not mad when he's done. It's a weird kind of beating up, way different than my brothers taking a pop at me or roughhousing, and apparently Pinky seems to really like beating up on kids.

Bumps, bruises, and scratches are starting to show up all over my body. Things have gotten worse, I'm worried about this and so I think about the Wallingford Boys Club and once again, it's my savior. I learned how to play basketball, pool, and baseball by signing up for teams or classes, so I decide that now is the time to sign up to learn how to box and join the boxing team—that way I can explain away a bruised eye, scratches, or puffy cheeks—blame it on the boxing team. I learn how to separate myself psychologically and physically from what is really happening to me.

All the while, my parents are really happy with me. I'm hanging out with Dan Adamson, and I couldn't possibly be getting into trouble. I certainly am not going to say anything. If I say anything about Adamson, maybe my parents will think I'm a *homo*. In the Wallingford district back in the early sixties, if a guy was ever found out to be a homosexual, they would be banned from stores like Tweedy and Popp's or Food Giant, not to mention the church and school. You would be treated like a leper or outcast, along with your whole family. You could be a juvenile delinquent, a rink, involved in petty theft, breaking windows, getting into fights and people would at least think you were a tough guy, but a homo, you might as well move as far away from Wallingford as possible, to another town or country.

I never consider that Adamson would get into trouble. He has immunity. If I reveal what is going on, I won't be allowed to go to his house to work on the train set anymore, there will be no more jobs tuning organs and making money, and I won't be Adamson's boy. These are things I don't want to give up.

I hate myself at this point in time.

CHAPTER 5

TAKING ONE FOR THE TEAM

The first incident was in the fall of seventh grade. We were at recess and Father Dillon, who periodically came out on the playground, called us boys over to the baseball diamond. He seemed quite angry with us.

In his fresh Irish brogue, he shouted, "You're acting like a bunch of dogs!"

He was talking about the *goose fights* out on the playground. Goose fights started in sixth grade. At recess, we would hide from one another and when somebody ran by us, we'd jump out, surprising them, and quickly grab them by the crotch and try to *goose* them.

Dillon's tirade went on.

"I want these goose fights to stop. Do you know what I'm talking about?"

At this point, I blurted out that we had learned it from Mr. Adamson and that he was the one who showed us how to goose each other. It was then that Father Dillon marched us into school and Sister Marie, the principal, disciplined us, threatening to call our parents or suspend us if we continued playing this *vile game*.

Around this time is when the boys at St. Benedict's would start being asked about *impure thoughts* at confession, which happened once a month. Within the church there were three or four confessional boxes with each priest's name over the confessional door. Not long after the goose fights incident, I selected Father Dillon for confession, hoping to steer clear of Father Conrad. I entered the small dark room and a light went on as I knelt down next to the priest's box. I pulled open the small door above the kneeler. There was a grate covering the window so the priest and penitent could both hear each other but remain invisible. I started out with *Bless me father for I have sinned,* and recited my usual venial sins: lying once, being angry three times. When I finished, he asked me if there was anything else I wanted to confess, and if I was having any impure thoughts. That was strange. He had never asked any questions in the confessional before.

I had heard about impure thoughts from an older classmate, however. This student had said that when you're in seventh or eighth grade, Father will start asking you about these thoughts, things like fantasizing about a person in a sexual way, or viewing photographs of naked women, or lustful thoughts of any kind. They may be things you have not acted upon, but imagined doing in real life: impure thoughts. Now I was faced with Father Dillon asking me about these thoughts and I felt compelled to confess that I did have impure thoughts—three, maybe four times.

He asked me, "How are you addressing these impure thoughts, and what are you doing about them? These are grievous sins."

Sins are divided into two categories: mortal sins (grievous) and venial sins (minor). Lust, or impure thoughts, is one of the seven deadly sins or capital vices—also known as grievous sins.

"Father, these impure thoughts are actions," I said, "actions with Mr. Adamson. I had impure thoughts with Mr. Adamson."

I heard nothing as I pressed my ear against the small opening. After a few minutes, Father gave my penance, more than I've ever received before—not the usual three *Our Fathers,* three *Hail Marys* and an act of contrition. This time, it's big—reciting an *entire* rosary. I knelt down right outside the confessional and I was there a long time, saying my penance.

Later that winter, while in confession with Father Conrad, I had the same experience—a question and curiosity about impure thoughts from him, and my confession of impure thoughts, again, telling him about the naked women on the calendars. Nothing seemed to happen though, except for a large penance. I was not struck by lightning, and outside the confessional no one asked me about my impure thoughts with Mr. Adamson. I wondered if I was the only kid who was confessing these grievous sins.

I started playing baseball with my Protestant friends through the local Wallingford Boys Club. I was fortunate to be a member. My dad's work bought memberships to give to company families. The baseball fields were just blocks from the Boys Club. If you didn't have a dime to your name, you could play for any one of a number of local organized little league teams. The Kiwanis would have you if you were really good, but teams were sponsored by the local pharmacy, gas station, grocery store, and hardware store, as well. Here you learned the rules of the game, teamwork, and good sportsmanship (win or lose) at a very young age. These sponsored teams had great uniforms and plenty of equipment. The previous year, in sixth grade, I started playing for our school-sponsored team. It was a CYO city team in Seattle. Each parish sponsored a team.

This year I am playing on the St. Benedict's seventh-grade team. We are playing pretty well. St. Benedict's doesn't have a very big budget to provide fancy uniforms and we have the bare minimum for equipment, but nothing will stop us from playing.

Our sixth-grade uniforms were pretty worn because they had been passed down year after year from the seventh and eighth-grade teams. They seemed oversized: huge, baggy wool baseball pants, and stirrup socks that were all stretched out from wear and would fly out of your shoes. Most of the uniforms resembled hand-knit socks made by someone's grandmother, and they were also adorned with holes from moths and snags from metal cleats. The shirts were without any printing—no player names or even the name of the team or mascot. They had hand-cut pieces of felt that some parent had labored over to complete the letters *ST BENS*; not even an apostrophe was included. Our uniforms were cream colored and the letters were bright blue, as were our caps, which bore the letters *SB*. These woolly garments went through a lot during the wet season in Seattle.

To allow the field to dry out, the coaches would take a five-gallon can of kerosene and pour it into the standing mud puddles. Then they would use a Zippo lighter to light the puddles on fire. After the high burst of flames died down, there were billowing black clouds of smoke permeating the field. This dried out the puddles so we could play. Charred chunks of dirt and grass were left in the puddles, which resembled an old campfire site. This didn't help the wool uniforms any, as it left a greasy residue in the puddles. If you slid into base, you got up looking like an old ball of steel wool.

Then came our equipment. In sixth grade, we had one bat for the whole team. It was cracked and nailed together. This repair was covered by wrapping friction tape (not to be confused with electrical tape) around it. Friction tape consisted of a very sticky fabric that had glue on both sides. I would imagine I was in the big leagues and had just tarred up the bat. You hoped the bat didn't break when you were up to bat, because that meant we had to borrow one from the opposing team. Our sixth grade season had been pretty good, with a 5–3 record.

Our seventh-grade uniforms are much improved. They look pretty sharp, resembling a Yankee uniform—white, with blue pinstripes. They happen to be my favorite team. Donned in these uniforms, we play with a bit of confidence. We are having a great season, winning game after game. This year we have two repaired bats, friction tape and all, but at least the embarrassment of having to borrow from the opposing team is less frequent.

There is a member of our team, Dick Davis*. He isn't a great player; he rides the pine most of the time, but he is a really nice guy. His dad showed up at practice the other day and our coach, Mr. R, who is also a teacher at Ballard High School and father of one of our players, called us over to the edge of the field. Mr. R directed us toward DD's dad's car, a 1959 Plymouth with wing-like fins. He opened the trunk of his car and my eyes shot wide open because laying in the bed of the trunk (which was large enough to hold groceries for six months) were nine brand new Louisville Slugger baseball bats of various weights and lengths. I had no idea how much they must have cost, but they were the real deal…Louisville Sluggers! The surprise didn't end there, though. He also had a dozen brand new Rawlings baseballs.

The season is great and as April turns to May, it looks like we will have a chance to advance to the CYO City Championships. To advance, we will have to win against the team from St. Anne's Parish, however. Considering how we have been playing, especially with all this new equipment, we feel we have a pretty good chance of winning.

Most of the seventh-grade team is in Pinky's class. Bob is our pitcher. He is a tall, dark, and handsome kind of guy. He is very studious. To me he is "Mama's Boy"; his mother comes to every game. I always remember his frequent outbursts of crying in class when we were in the first and second grade. I will give him credit, though—he is a good pitcher, or I guess we wouldn't be winning all these games. Next is our catcher, John. He seems slower than the seven-year itch. When he winds up to throw, however, it looks like the ball will fly halfway around the world; in reality, more often than not it makes it to second base on a couple of hops. He has a head of hair like a mop. He is calm and collected. I am the southpaw first baseman. I am not an exceptional baseball player, but I do play most of the games. They say I am serious and seem old before my time. Because of this, the opposing team feels my presence. I swing at anything. I don't take balls and I strike out more than not. Occasionally, however, I have been known as the lefty who can "rip it." Next comes our second baseman, Dennis. He is an excellent fielder. He has trouble deciding whether to be right or left-handed. He plays baseball right-handed. In class, he writes with both hands and when he eats he switches back and forth. He is never late to practice. He probably learned to be so punctual by doing his paper route every morning at the crack of dawn before he heads off to school. I would describe him as methodical and the best voice in the boys' choir. I never saw an audience he didn't like! He is short, but not shy. Lee is our shortstop. He also has the highest batting average. He always goes deep into the count and can read the ball like a Yankee. He's not a power hitter, but he hits down on the ball. When he connects with the ball it is hard to field it. Our third baseman, Gregg*, is sullen and very serious. He seems like a grown-up at times. In the summer, he is always taking care of his younger brother. When it comes to baseball, he is the most talented on the team. When he has a hit, he parks it. He has the quickest moves and always swings for the fences. He is my best friend. Gregg has leadership qualities; we all follow his lead, for sure. He is in charge of the patrol boys at school and he is also the lead altar boy. Now for another paper route guy, we have Tom. His route is after school, so during baseball he hires a substitute so he can play baseball. He is a serious left fielder. He seems sort of the European-type, maybe Italian from his name. He has a serious

43

demeanor. Our center fielder is Ray. He comes from the Philippines and has an infectious smile. Earlier in the season, he got hit in the head by a baseball and had a concussion with amnesia. Pinky didn't cut him any slack though in class when he seemed confused. Jim is the coach's son and an outfielder. He is a great student and an adequate player. He knows all the rules and talks strategy with us. He is very polite, and always in a good mood. Lloyd plays multiple positions. He's been at St. Benedict's since first grade. Though he's not a candidate for most home runs, he is a good "mitt," short and quick on his feet.

The whole school knows we have a good team. Pinky never stops by to see our games, but he reads the local Catholic paper and our team's results are published there every week. Some of the parents stop by to see a game now and then, especially since we are doing so well this year. Our good attitude as a team and all the new equipment has paid off. We have made it to the playoffs and we'll need to beat St. Anne's.

It is Monday before the big Saturday game. Pinky decides to pull an old trick of his on us. He gives the entire seventh-grade class a pop quiz in history today. It is multiple choice like all his quizzes, but there are only ten questions. We have been studying explorers for the past couple weeks, but today's quiz has nothing to do with this; it is on the War of 1812, which hasn't even been mentioned in class. The rules in his class are very clear and there is no appeal process when it comes to grades and playing sports. If you fail a quiz in his class, you will not be allowed to play in the upcoming game and your coach will be notified, no matter what your sport. If we miss four questions today, we fail and we will not be able to play baseball on Saturday.

I miss six out of ten questions, as do many others on the team. Even the "straight-A" girls in the class failed. There is no question in my mind, because I know him better than anyone, that this is one of Pinky's schemes he dreamed up. He is always planning his next "deal." After school, the team and I go to baseball practice but the coach says nothing. Maybe Pinky is having second thoughts. Not likely; he probably couldn't reach the coach by phone. We are keeping our fingers crossed though.

It is Tuesday's practice when Mr. R calls us aside to talk to us. He asks everyone in Mr. Adamson's class to raise their hand.

"Mr. Adamson contacted me today and said under no circumstances would you boys be playing in the game Saturday. He said that you have all failed a history quiz."

Mr. R is a teacher in a high school, so his attitude about academics and sports is quite serious.

It is no surprise to me; I knew this was coming. The other players seem quite shocked that he would do this to us, knowing it was such an important game. Mr. R will have to play on Saturday without five starters, which doesn't give us much hope for beating St. Anne's.

As my teammates listen to our coach breaking the dismal state of affairs, I see their heads hang dejectedly as we all sit on the bench.

"Steve, can't you go to Pinky and see if you can talk him into letting us play, retake the quiz or something? He will listen to you."

Mr. R responds, "He won't listen to Steve. He won't listen to anyone."

Another player pipes up and says, "But Mr. R, Steve is Mr. Adamson's boy."

"What do you mean he is his *boy*?"

"He gets invited to his house to play with his trains, he goes on trips with him, and he even works for him after school. He is our class monitor and talks to Mr. Adamson all the time. I just thought he could go to his house maybe, so he thinks nobody knows about it, and he could talk him into letting us play after all."

At this point, my heart is racing as the whole team turns and stares at me with pleading eyes; they are joined by our coach. I quickly drop my eyes and stare at the ground.

I hear a voice from the back of the group ask, "Steve, would you please do this for us? Just talk to him, maybe he will listen to you. If anyone can change his mind, you can."

I realize now how important this game really is to my friends and classmates. The possibility of a championship for our team is their dream. Feeling the peer pressure, and being put on the spot by the coach, I remember that I am probably making a visit to Pinky's house on Wednesday, anyway. I go home to dinner, finish my homework, and compose a sales pitch to give to Pinky on behalf of the baseball team.

As I expected, Pinky asks me to come down to his house after dinner on Wednesday. I arrive right on time and enter the house via the back door, which is just past the fish pond. I close the door, feeling a bit nauseated with the anticipation of what might happen during tonight's visit. I notice right away that he is seated on his stool at the bottom of the stairs in the basement where the trains are located. He would sit there if he wanted me to come downstairs from the landing. By this time, I knew very clearly that the basement—even though it was a horror story in itself—wasn't anything compared to what would happen to me if he sent me up the landing to the attic.

I had hoped for the basement direction all day, as this was the only place I could deliver my sales pitch about Saturday's game. As I glance down the stairs, Pinky turns on the stool and motions for me to come down to the basement. He invites me to help with some of his train set-ups, and that goes on for about an hour. My anxiety has calmed somewhat by now and I take advantage of this free time with the trains to ask if I can talk to him about something regarding school. He seems to listen attentively to my entire spiel. I give him all the reasons why I feel it is an unfair decision he has made regarding the baseball players. I don't want to make him mad or anything. I am speaking with maturity and confidence now, presenting a case before him on behalf of my teammates. I try to be very apologetic. I go into detail about how we might have done better on the quiz, but we were concentrating so hard on the explorers last week and this quiz seemed to just come out of the blue. I plead with him to accept our apology, and finally, ask if he would consider letting us play in the game on Saturday. It appears he is listening and he says he will think it over. Nervously, I continue to help him with the trains, soldering the tracks and placing artificial grass on the mounds of his train landscape.

Pinky suddenly turns on his stool and glares over at me.

"Like I said, I will think about it tonight."

He raises his large freckled hand and points directly to the landing of the stairs that lead to the attic. It only takes a second for my stomach to be in my throat. I feel the muscles in my neck give way as my head hangs low, eyes cast downward.

As I pass his mother in the kitchen, she asks, out of the blue, "How are you boys doing? When you finish up, maybe we can have lemonade and cookies before Steve goes home."

I turn and head for the stairs that lead to the attic. Halfway up to the left of a little landing, there is a small, dark water closet with a toilet, sink, and mirror. As I continue all the way up the stairs, I can see a door open to an undersized room with low ceilings, part of the attic that held a bed and dresser, nothing like a formal bedroom. As I freeze on the stairs, he walks past me and motions for me to come into the room. I dutifully follow. I am thinking that these old houses don't have any insulation and you can hear everything from one floor to the next. I figure he's not going to thrash me upstairs right above his mother's kitchen. She's home and I'm shocked that she has not done anything or said anything in the past, but if something really bad happens, she would know about it.

In this attic room, there is a small window to the south and a tiny black and white TV sits on the dresser. An ashtray overflowing with cigar butts is on a side table next to the bed and cigar smoke lingers in the air. It looks as if he was just there, lying on the bed watching TV prior to my arrival. As he had done in motels, he motions for me to go over to the bed and place my hands on the bed. I see a red and white tube of something lying next to the ashtray. It looks like hair cream. I remember the ads on TV about Brylcreem and guys with crew cuts rubbing this oily stuff into their hair and the little jingle playing in the background. I hear the noise of the lid coming off the tube and the sound of his hands rubbing together, in back of me. He recites the jingle: *Brylcreem—A Little Dab'll Do Ya*. Then he laughs, like he's leading a chorus of monsters.

What's happening to me gets worse. This time by the end of the evening, it is too vivid, too painful, and too close and personal. I have not mastered my blocking mechanisms. I'm *unable* to remove myself from what is happening to this thirteen-year-old boy. I cannot remove myself from this reality. Can't his mother hear the thrashing, crying, and screaming? She must hear it all.

When it is over, Adamson goes downstairs. I slowly creep down the rickety wood stairs and halfway down on the landing, I glance at the mirror in the water closet. I do not like what I see. I am no longer looking at these episodes from afar, I am participating. As I rearrange my disheveled clothes and arrive at the bottom of the stairs, his mother turns to me.

"Do you want some lemonade and cookies?"

I am speechless and escape swiftly through the back door, the screen door slamming behind me.

I hear her calling after me. "Good-bye, and have a good time tonight, now."

Yes, we will play that baseball game with St. Anne's on Saturday. To some, it might not seem that important. I just remember the pleading eyes of my teammates when they asked me to talk to Pinky.

Saturday is a dry day for baseball, so no need for the kerosene show today. We are all suited up in our spotless uniforms for the St. Anne's game. We go out onto the field with a true spirit of confidence. The game is close all the way. Just when we think we can pull it out, our third baseman makes an error. The St. Anne's fans are ecstatic and start heckling him about the botched play. Unfortunately, this arouses Gregg's anger and he proceeds to scoop up a handful of pebbles from the field and throw them at the cyclone fence, peppering those in the bleachers. Play is stopped by the umpire and he takes Gregg aside for a pep talk to cool him off.

There are a few sets of parents at the game today. My parents aren't coming. They never go to my games or athletic events. They always say if players have parents rooting in the stands, their son is a sissy, or a "mama's boy."

The game comes to an end and we just don't have enough to pull it out. We played well, and it was intense all the way, but no matter how good the teams, one has to lose. We walk out in a line to congratulate the other team. There is no crying or throwing of mitts; it had just been an honor to make it this far. A couple of the players pick up their gear and walk off the field to head home together. Some of the boys are going home with their parents and I am sure some will stop for an ice cream cone on the way home.

I make it a point to wait until everyone is gone from the dugout. I look around the diamond as the parking lot empties. In the distance, I can see the 1958 Borgward station wagon pull up into the parking lot where I will need to pass on my walk home.

I slowly make my way across from home plate to the rubber of the pitcher's mound, then I cross second base, and finally make my way at a snail's pace across the 220 feet of grass and clover. The outfield is filled with honey bees, just enjoying the sunshine today as most everyone is. I know it's not going to be this way for me, however. I reluctantly walk across the field, desperately wanting to be like the other boys, on their way home, but for me, it's another defeat. Overwhelmed by shame, and aware of the captive victim I have become, I approach his car.

I can smell the hair cream mixed with a strong cloud of cigar smoke. Then the door of the station wagon opens and I see that freckled arm and hand giving a silent mandate addressed to me: *Get in, shut up, and do what I say.*

CHAPTER 6

COMPLIANT VICTIM

After that, the attic episodes continued. Emotionally and physically, I was pushed to the limit as the abuse progressed. The injuries kept getting worse, now that he was more into the physical torture. I developed ways to avoid going to Pinky's house, creating all kinds of excuses. Eventually, I did a pretty good job fending the brutality off, to once every other week. At thirteen, I was developing muscles and athletic abilities. I was getting tougher and could actually push back during Adamson's attacks, preventing them more often than not. Many times I would just leave the house, saying to myself, *why go down there? Adamson's just going to continue to blackmail, extort, and coerce me through his usual methods.*

Deep down, when I was honest with myself, I knew why I kept going back. The money was important to me, coming from a family that was barely making it financially, at times. It gave me a sense of power and security, and I didn't want to give that up. Not only was it the special jobs and money that I didn't want to lose, I also feared that Adamson would tell someone I was a *homo*. He continued to bring up the ever-present threat that my friends and others could hear rumors about me. If I told anyone, or tried to defend myself, it wouldn't matter; they'd believe the seventh-grade teacher before a kid like me.

I was resigned to the fact that I was going to be Adamson's boy all the way through school, however. I was still popular as we started eighth grade so I decided to run for class president, courting the "chick" vote. I won. On the outside, I was successful, getting good grades in school, playing sports, class president, and soon...I'd be graduating from grade school. My parents were ecstatic—that's how low the bar was set at our house. I would achieve what my brothers did not: An O'Connor boy was finally going to graduate from grade school. My parents were probably thanking God for answering their novenas, intercessions, and prayers for me. They also gave a lot of credit to the perfect role model and good influence of Dan Adamson, who led me through it all.

The next time Pinky told me to go sit in his newly purchased 1962 Chevy II station wagon and wait for him, I waited in the car and watched the school boys on patrol team as they passed by, ready to help school kids cross the street, wearing their sashes, holding the red flags. I felt alone, thinking, *oh yeah, look at me all right, 'I'm Adamson's boy' and at what a price.* Then I saw Sister Marie, Sister Nathan, and the other nuns in their habits—white floor-length tunics with black and white veils—standing right across the street, carefully monitoring the children. Occasionally, they would turn and look in my direction as I sat alone in the car waiting for Mr. Adamson. They also knew that I was his favorite boy, going down to his house, to play with the train sets, and going on overnight trips tuning pipe organs.

I wondered why they thought it was OK. Why they approved of me spending time with Adamson. Why did Pinky's mother think it was OK? Didn't she hear the crying and screams? Why did my parents think it was just OK, and what about my older brothers? I guess that's just the way things were at St. Benedict's.

After informing Father Dillon and Father Conrad about Adamson on two separate occasions when in confession, as well as and the principal, Sister Marie, I decide to make another attempt when an opportunity comes up to talk with Father Conrad, alone. One Saturday afternoon in the winter of my eighth grade, I join a group of students for a leadership skills training session with Father Conrad at St. Benedict Church. All the students in the group have important roles at St. Benedict's, Seattle Prep, or Blanchet High School. I am the eighth-grade president, in charge of scheduling the ushers at the nine o'clock Mass; another attendee was awarded the prestigious Ad Altare Dei certificate and is in charge of scheduling the altar boys and the school patrol team. Two other students are from Blanchet—a star athlete and another on the debate team.

As we finish the training, Father Conrad says he wants to talk to me and pulls me into his office in the rectory. I'm not sure what it is about—maybe he wants to talk to me about Adamson. Instead, he tells me that as the head of the nine o'clock Mass ushers, and the person responsible for collecting the offering and taking it to the rectory after Mass, that I should deliver the baskets to the Oblate priests in the rectory right after the second offering, and not to wait until Mass is finished.

"Yes, Father, I understand."

He is standing now, and paces around his desk. Then he sits down and rifles through some paperwork, impatient.

"Father, could I possibly talk with you about something?"

"Go ahead, what is it?"

I sit in one of the St. Benedict's metal folding chairs directly across from him. He seems just like he was at the leadership meeting: he was never friendly, but he isn't mean or mad today. I've seen him when he was mad, and you better stay out of his way.

"Mr. Adamson has been doing things to me. I've almost been choked to death on his bed, and he attacked me in the projection booth and the boy's bathroom."

I tell Father Conrad what has been going on with Adamson over the last two years in detail, and I use explicit terms such as, *pecker*.

He immediately gets agitated, and I can see right away that he is angry.

He leans forward in his chair.

"This is the first time in all these years I've known you that you've ever been in trouble."

He propels himself from his chair, rushes over to me, and points his index finger at my chest real close.

"You are a liar, and you must never speak of this again. You are going to hell, and I can send your parents to hell too."

As I leave the rectory, my hand on the doorknob, he stops me.

"By the way, tell your parents your tuition is not paid. It's overdue, and if I don't get a check by Friday, you're out of this school."

He shames me right out of his office.

I slowly walk the several blocks home. It's my fault. I'm definitely in trouble now and Conrad is condemning me to hell. A priest, the representative of God on earth, had the power to condemn you to hell. Worse, what if he tells Adamson, the enforcer? My life will be over for sure. All the things I've worked so hard for—making money, popularity, good grades, class president, and the baseball team—won't mean anything. My sense was that he believed me, yes, but why was he so angry? I expected that maybe Conrad could help me, make Adamson stop. I was surprised at his response, his anger. Something wasn't right, and I tried to think of what it could be. I wondered about the times that I played basketball with friends on the blacktop at the playground across from the church and witnessed the boy who exited his car on a Sunday night—the favorite altar boy, following behind Conrad for a session in the rectory.

Once home, I think that I should at least tell my parents that Father Conrad was asking about our overdue tuition. I can't tell them anything else about my meeting with Father Conrad; they wouldn't believe me anyway. The next week, I saw my dad enter the rectory in his white overhauls carrying his paint brush, roller, and cans of paint. He must have figured a way to barter with Conrad for the tuition.

That spring and summer, there is an opportunity for me to help Pinky with the wiring and installation of new speakers at the church. The upside is that I'll have an ongoing job, making money, but the downside is the crimes will continue.

Over the last year, the incidents have moved from the projection room to the basement, to the train room, to the attic, back to the school, and as eighth grade progresses—and most unsettling to me—now to the actual church. At fourteen years old, having these things happening to me in the church choir loft brings a whole new level of fear. I'm burdened with guilt and shame taught to me since the day I walked into St. Benedict School by the nuns, teachers, and priests. Now, I'm participating in these grievous sins and crimes in the actual holy of all holies.

The choir loft, which overlooks the congregation and altar on the main floor, has a large circular stained glass window with the initials *OMI* and the words, *To Preach the Gospel to the Poor He Hath*

Sent Me. A mid-sized organ sits in the middle of the choir loft facing the choir. It looks like an electric organ, similar to one found in your living room, except larger. Because the pipes are concealed in the pipe organ room, many people think it is electric, but in fact it is a real pipe organ.

The pipe organ room, designed by Adamson to house the pipes, is on the north side of the choir loft and he has a key to the room. It is a narrow room, almost as narrow as the projection room, and measures about four feet wide and eight feet long. The pipes are lined up along the west side of the room at six inches wide, shrinking the room farther. The room is dark all the time; it doesn't seem to have a light switch. The pipes in the room are made out of tin and lead, and are in the shape of long cylindrical tubes that are tapered at the bottom. They have jagged edges at the opening. There is a key for each pipe that opens them up or moves them back—part of adjusting the organ key note. The key turns like on a sardine can, rolling back and forth. The edges are like a knife, and can cut you or snag your sweater if you brush up against them. On this job, we aren't actually tuning organs, but running wires and preparing to install speakers for a new sound system in the church. We just end up running wire through the pipe organ room, since it's the shortest route through the second story of the church.

I think about the frequent places of being trapped by Adamson in narrow confines with one opening, no way out, unable to move right or left, to escape. Now in the pipe room, he attacks and overwhelms me by wrestling me to the ground, pulling my shirt collar, and all the while I'm trying to stay away from these pipes, afraid of being slashed. They are almost like a torture prop, and remind me of a black and white horror show I watched with my mother late one night. In the show, a monster hunting people on an island holds his victims' hostage in the dungeon of a castle. The monster has these black and brown Doberman Pinschers that he sics on people to make them compliant; after a while, the noise of the dogs howling and barking is enough to make the victims do anything he wants. One of the games he played was making his victims maneuver a long narrow passage way, with nails or blades of some kind sticking out from boards on the walls. They could only navigate the length of the chamber stealthily, slowly, and carefully to avoid the nails. If the person tried to run, they'd be hacked up by the nails. The danger of the narrow pipe room, the jagged edges sticking out and cutting me, this was real to me. I related to this horror movie. If the victims could make it past the nails and successfully exit at the end of the passageway, the monster would sic the dogs on them, so they were doomed anyway. Adamson was always at the entrance of the pipe organ room; there was no other escape. Even if I did get out of the pipe room unscathed, there would be another bad situation coming.

Added to this horror is what God will do to me, being involved in this in his church. This fills me with terror. I have no control of what's going on, but I am defiling God's church, desecrating God's holy choir loft. I can only imagine the retribution God will have on me, but not to Adamson. I never believe that God would ever punish Adamson, along with Father Conrad, Sister Nathan, and Sister Marie. They are all on God's team. Adamson is the enforcer for Conrad, for God. I was on the top of the list *to be punished by God's team.*

I am fourteen years old and have this physical terror with Adamson doing horrible things to me, and then comes the psychological warfare—that God is watching me, that he'll make me miserable for the rest of my life for desecrating his choir loft. I might as well end my life.

One Saturday afternoon, I believe the plan is to tune another pipe organ. Instead, Adamson tells me that we are going to a barn out in the country where people get together to play musical instruments. He picks me up at about four o'clock in the afternoon and I notice that there are sandwiches and lemonade in a cooler, and a large case in the back of the car with what looks like an accordion inside. I guess if he could play the organ that would translate to an accordion.

We drive way out into the country, in the foothills of the Cascade Mountains, about an hour and a half from Seattle. In the early '60s, the land east of Seattle, before one approached the mountains, was mostly farm land and forests, very rural. We turn off a country road and drive across a farm field and down into some woods, across a muddy path, and back up to a dirt road, which ends at this large old decrepit red barn. It looks like someone gutted the top of it where the hay loft used to be and made it into living quarters, with electricity.

Inside, there were several people already playing instruments. I am surprised to see an electric organ in the barn. The owner of the barn is playing the organ. Adamson takes out his accordion and joins in with the band. Someone is playing piano, and another on a banjo. Cars keep showing up—two-door sedans, Chevys, just plain-Jane cars. There are now six different cars, with several older men, each accompanied by a twelve, thirteen-year-old. I wonder if these could be priests from other parishes with their favorite altar boys. I heard the boys talk about St. Alphonsus and other parishes.

These old men are not dressed in priestly attire, just casual clothes, and they seemed very creepy and dark. The common theme is that each one has a boy with him who looks to be subservient, bent over, sad, empty eyes: all the visual characteristics that I have.

When we leave, we drive even farther into the woods, instead of toward the main road. Adamson stops the car and turns to me.

"You know, you could go missing out here and nobody would ever, ever find you."

This is not the first time that I've feared for my life if I didn't go along with Adamson. In the past, my attempts to tell anyone what Adamson was doing were met with denial, and placing the blame on me. There seems no way of going forward to inform anyone about his deeds. He makes it clear this night that I could disappear, die, out here in the middle of the woods, lost and never finding my way back to Wallingford.

At this point, I realize I'm less concerned that I will die from exposure to the elements or starvation out here. Instead, I will die from shame.

CHAPTER 7

EXTRICATION

Summer 1963

My family and I currently live in a dark, dingy apartment building on 46th Street. We move frequently, but it's always in the Wallingford district, so I'm able to stay in the same grade school. My dad's job as a union painter is seasonal; when there is no work at the union hall, he's laid off and there's no money. He is not the type of union worker who will cross a picket line or work in a non-union shop, even when the family suffers. I sometimes wonder if it's an excuse to be lazy. Food is scarce around the house and sometimes the heat is shut off during the lean winters. At times, the car goes missing and my tuition is unpaid at St. Benedict's.

My dad was from an affluent Irish Catholic family, born and raised in Chicago. He was educated by the Jesuits at Ignatius Loyola during his grade-school years and then entered a Jesuit seminary at fourteen to prepare for the priesthood. After three years, he and a friend decided to split the seminary, buy a car, and take to the road for an adventure, with Hollywood as their final destination. His friend made it to Tinseltown and my dad, who wanted to see the Grand Tetons, continued on his way through Montana and hitch-hiked to a small town named Phillipsburg, nicknamed "P-burg." There he met and married my mother, born and raised in Montana, who was probably part Sioux Indian, a seventeen-year-old widow with two children, and non-Catholic. She later converted and agreed to raise their children in the Catholic faith.

Usually, my parents struggled to make ends meet. One exception was in the spring, summer, and fall of 1962, during the Seattle World's Fair. People came from all over the world to visit Seattle, and while we lived at the Burke Avenue Apartments, some of the units were rented as hotel rooms. My dad worked as the maintenance man and painted the apartments, and mother made beds and cleaned rooms, making extra cash. The apartments were run like a bed and breakfast, with pots of fresh-brewed coffee and donuts in the foyer of the apartment building.

Now, as the youngest son in the family, and graduating from eighth grade, I have high hopes of attending Seattle Prep, widely regarded as the best private high school in the city. I took the entrance exam this spring and now there's nothing left to do but wait for the results. My dad, who never had to worry about money, went to the best private schools in Chicago, while I'm worried if my family can scrape together the money to help pay tuition, that is, if I'm accepted. Only one other St. Benedict's student took the test and he had already received his acceptance letter. *Maybe I didn't make the cut.*

Occasionally, I'm doing jobs tuning organs with Pinky, but I manage to get a job at Food Giant as a box boy for a few hours a week. I'm hanging out with my grade school buddies: playing tennis, going to movies and a few dances. I'm also spending a lot more time with my friend Gail, who is now more of a "girlfriend."

One night in late August, I arrive home after working my job at Food Giant. I'm tired and just want to crash on my bed, listen to KJR radio to catch the latest new recording artist on the Pat O'Day show. Instead, I hear my dad:

"Steve, come in here. We want to talk to you."

My parents are sitting at the kitchen table where the "family conferences" are held, drinking coffee and smoking their unfiltered Camel cigarettes. The window is open, though there's no airflow and the room is hazy with cigarette smoke. There's a single light bulb dangling from its cord over the center of the table. A decorative ceramic plate sits on the shelf above the stove; it reads *God Bless this Lousy Apartment.* A letter sits on the table, along with an envelope addressed to, *The parents of Stephen J. O'Connor*, from Seattle Preparatory School. My dad picks up the letter and reads:

"'Congratulations, your son has been accepted to Seattle Preparatory School. Stephen's test results place him in the top 10 percent of all applicants this year.'

"Well, well, well, I find this very interesting. Here's a life lesson for you. You get good grades, keep your nose to the grindstone, work hard, and you get into Prep; you mess around, skip school, don't hit the books, you don't get accepted to Prep. It's cause and effect—so getting into Prep is quite an accomplishment."

I shift in my chair, leaning forward, thinking, *Wow, I did make it into Prep.*

I don't have much time to bask in my success. My mother gets up from the table, walks to the kitchen sink, and begins to wash dishes, distancing herself from this scene.

Dad continues, "Of course, you know you're not going to Prep next year. No chance."

I stare blankly at the table top.

"Where do you think we'd get the money? We don't have that kind of money, Steve."

No sense in arguing with him, trying to convince him, or asking for any help. Without a word, I get up from the chair and snatch the letter from Dad, head for my bedroom, and slowly shut the door behind me.

This is the best news and worst news all in one day. I had hoped that if I was accepted to Prep my dad would find a way to pay the tuition. Or that I could win the speech contest, get a scholarship, or work after hours as a janitor at Prep. Honestly, I didn't have a plan as to how to pay for Prep; I just knew I wanted to go there, so I put all my effort into the entrance exam and the speech contest, never thinking about how to pay for tuition. I could have applied to Blanchet, a much less expensive school, but I was lured by the mystique and prestige of Seattle Prep. I think about the only alternative that is left for me now, the public school, Hamilton Junior High. I've heard from my parents that all the students there are Protestant kids. I might be the only Catholic kid from St. Benedict's, while everyone else heads off to Holy Names, Holy Angels, O'Dea, and Blanchet. *Why me? Why can't they afford the tuition? I made the effort. I passed the exam. Why can't my parents do something, like ask my grandparents to help? Something.*

The following week, Pinky buttonholes me after Mass on Sunday.

"I hear you're going to Prep next year."

"Not quite. I was accepted, but my parents don't have the money to send me."

"No money, eh?"

"Yeah, I'll be going to Hamilton Junior High."

"Public school? You know, I've helped other kids with tuition before. Maybe we can work something out."

I know what this offer means. The unspoken expectation. I push those thoughts aside. I could go to the best school in the city.

"Come down to my place and we'll talk about it. I can make a phone call to Prep and let them know that the tuition payment will be coming from me."

The status and prestige of being a Prep boy might be within my reach.

I'm not sure what to say to my parents, so I say nothing. Pinky visits my dad later that summer and tells him of the arrangement. I'm happy and relieved that I won't be going to a public school next year.

Seattle Prep is the iconic private school. The all-boys Catholic high school is located at the north end of lower Capitol Hill, an affluent section of Seattle. There are fewer than five hundred students in the school, yet we have a record-setting, undefeated football team whose players look like the Green Bay Packers. The first week of school is freshman orientation for approximately eighty students. We meet in the lunchroom with three or four school leaders, members of the varsity lettermen's club, and the student body president. There is also a boy "cheerleader" who instructs us on proper behavior at the football home games held at West Seattle stadium. We hear about the freshman class advocate, Father Small, who is said to be an outstanding teacher, and we also hear about other first-rate teachers and priests.

One of the upperclassmen continues about the faculty: "This guy is OK, Father so and so is OK, and this teacher is fine, but watch out for this certain priest; don't be caught alone in the locker room, bathroom, and bridge to the rectory at night, or *anywhere* with him. Particularly the bathroom. He's a sicko."

This was not a warning about any severe punishment we might receive. I immediately knew what he meant. I felt good about this. *Finally, someone is looking out for you, and they're taking care of each other.*

We also learned how to stay out of Justice Under God (JUG), a name given by students for the disciplinary actions at Prep. JUG was after school detention where you were given a lengthy poem such as "The Raven" or "The Highwayman," which you had to memorize and recite. If you missed any part, you were detained until you memorized it perfectly, which could take you late into the night. There was also the discipline not mentioned in the student manual for failing to 'make a hole' or stand against the wall when a priest or upperclassman passed by, or if an upperclassman didn't like the way you looked at them, or spoke to them.

I learned how to dress at Prep, carefully observing what the guys wore: the starched buttoned-down collar dress shirts, V-neck sweaters, wool dress pants, and spit-polished wing tip shoes. There were no t-shirts, Levi jeans, corduroys, or khaki pants. I spent most of my Food Giant earnings on clothes from Vons Men's Store.

It took three separate bus routes to get from my home to Prep. I took the same routes to my first dance at Prep—homecoming weekend. By myself. I was nervous about going, and paranoid that attending the all-boys school would somehow solidify the danger of gaining a "homo" reputation. My grade-school friend joked about the boy cheerleaders at the Prep football games. When I entered Prep, I believed that I'd never see a girl in school again; I never saw any around the building. I figured that the Prep dances would be all guys dancing with each other. As I walked from the bus stop to the Seattle Prep gym in the pouring rain, I was shocked to see row after row of girls outside with their umbrellas, waiting in line to enter the dance. There were girls from Blanchet and the all-girls schools: Forest Ridge, Holy Names, and Holy Angels. I heard live music booming from the gym and saw the sign advertising a popular northwest band, The Coachmen. I thought to myself, *this is going to be good.*

I tried out for the track team and my running times were fast enough that I made the varsity team, a rarity for a freshman. I ran the ordinary, unremarkable course every day, pounding hard on the concrete streets and sidewalks so much that I got shin splints. The coach would stand at the starting position, stop watch in hand, and then he'd disappear somewhere for a coffee break; he'd return when I finished and say, *now do it again, run faster, go the other way, to the left*. He didn't provide us with much direction or inspiration. I felt exhilarated though, and anxious to prove myself as a freshman on the varsity team.

Gail was at Blanchet and she and I started to pair off more and more during the first six months of our freshman year to go to movies, dances, and the Seattle Center. That winter I asked Gail if she would like to go with me to the CYO Christmas Ball, held at the downtown Olympic Hotel, and she agreed. This was my first formal dance and I had to earn a lot of money to pay for a suit, a corsage, tickets, and dinner at a fancy restaurant.

The following spring, while hanging out with my friend Gregg, he mentioned that he was asked to the Blanchet Tolo by one of our grade-school buddies, Paula*. This is a dance where the girls get to ask the guys to be their date. I'm wondering why Gail had not asked me to the Tolo; we had just played tennis and gone to the movies a week before. I fixated on Adamson, thinking maybe he had said something to her. I imagined the conversation he might have had with her and how she would believe that I committed a mortal sin, being a "homo," and now didn't want to have anything to do with me. It wasn't just Gail I worried about, it was everyone. I found out later that she went to the Tolo with Dennis, our old second baseman. This sealed the deal for me, and we stopped talking at this point and did not go out again, except for one Saturday afternoon later that spring. It was a week before Easter and I had run into Gail at the Serv-U-Drug.

She came up to me and asked, "Do you know anything about the Passion Play?"

"No, what about it?"

"Mr. Adamson said he is picking us up at your apartment and driving us to the Passion Play at Seward Park this Saturday."

The Passion Play is a reenactment of the Stations of the Cross, Jesus' journey in Calvary to his crucifixion.

"I have no idea about this," I tell her, "but OK, I'll be ready to go."

When Saturday comes, he picks both of us up at the apartment and orders Gail to sit in the front seat, with me in the back. There is no conversation on the one-hour drive to Seward Park. My nerves are on edge and I'm terrorized by his keeping tabs on me, and telling me he's keeping an eye on my girlfriend. I believe it's a veiled threat of, *I'll tell your girlfriend you're a homo.* While Gail and I are standing at the park watching the Stations of the Cross, he walks up behind us, stands there with his arms folded across his chest, red-faced, breathing heavily in and out, starring at us, not saying a word.

I'm near the end of my freshman year at Seattle Prep. I'm never detained in JUG, or sent to the principal's office for some infraction; I'm a model student. After school, I work at Food Giant bagging groceries three nights a week, and extra hours when I can. My job here is a new beginning—my baby steps to breaking my dependence on making money by doing jobs for Pinky. I need the money for my $45 blue and white letterman's jacket with the big *S* on the front. After I save and scrape together every dime, I can finally make the purchase. It will hang in my closet until next school year because I'm not allowed to wear the jacket until my sophomore year, following a sports ceremony initiating all new lettermen.

A few weeks before the end of my freshman year, however, Pinky orders me to be at his house the following afternoon. I've been avoiding him and not showing up the last few months when he told me to be there. I'm sick of his hold on me, paying my tuition, ordering me to come to his house. I don't want to have anything to do with Pinky anymore. I want to keep going to Prep—it's the school I've always dreamed of going to—but the human cost I've paid is more than I bargained for. I'm not sure what I was thinking when I accepted his offer. This is the way I work: I don't think, I don't plan, I just plow ahead, going by trial and error. Usually, I know that something will work out. I work with whatever comes my way; when opportunity knocks, I seize it, find a way to make it work, and I run with it. But now I know I've made a bad decision and I need to get out of this trap.

Soon after I arrive, an argument about me not showing up much at his house ensues. Pinky threatens to cut off my tuition. *You're not going to listen to me? You're not going to follow my orders? Then you won't be going back to Prep next year.*

At fifteen, I'm wiry, muscular, and in top physical shape from running track. I am now able to defend myself, and I resist Pinky.

"How would you like your girlfriend to find out you're a homo? I own people, sonny boy, and I'll make sure she finds out. Just to keep an eye on her, I've selected her to train with me to play the organ at Monday night devotions."

I think of how he was when he drove Gail and me to the Passion Play.

Pinky, desperate to have his way with me, points upstairs to the attic. I refuse, shove Pinky against the wall, and rush out of the house. To my twelve-year-old self, I say, *We're out of there. We'll never go to his basement again. Or his attic. This is finished.* At home in my bedroom, I take my letterman's jacket out of the closet, slip into it, and look at my reflection in the mirror.

Another week goes by. Time is running out and I rack my brain for any possible way to get back to Prep next year. I've got to do it myself, stand alone, and be free of Pinky's threats and grip on me. I decide to talk to my boss at Food Giant; maybe he can give me some extra hours this summer. I practically beg him for the extra hours, whatever is available. I'll work anytime.

"I can probably give you some extra hours...what's up?"

"The people who were paying my tuition at Prep will not pay anymore."

"How are your grades?"

"Good."

"How much is the tuition?"

"$1,000 a year."

"Well, if any hours come up I'll give you a crack at 'em."

My boss also agrees to write a letter to the principal, Father Seaver, explaining that I will work extra hours at Food Giant and that he will send my checks directly to Prep for my tuition.

The boys at Prep are not sons of Wallingford working class painters; they're sons of bankers, doctors, and attorneys. I've seen what's in the parking lot at school: brand new Corvettes, Dad's Cadillac, and even an upperclassman driving an exotic foreign sports car. Sometimes a student is driven to school in a limousine.

Armed with the letter from my boss, I meet with Father Small, the freshman class advocate, and convince him to schedule an appointment with the almighty Father Seaver. At the very end of the school year, I finally get my meeting so I can hand deliver the letter.

Father Small and I sit down in the principal's office. I explain to Father Seaver why I'm there and hand him the letter. He reads the letter, sets it down on the desk, glances at Father Small, and stands up. There's no malice or anger in his face, more like pity. His voice is as soft and low as I've ever heard come from Father Seaver, a slow deep whisper.

"Steve, you don't belong here."

He walks to the window overlooking the school parking lot, his back to me.

"When you're in your senior year, what are you going to be driving? What? Taking a bus?"

At first, I'm not sure what he's saying.

"The seniors here at Prep are on their way to Stanford, Santa Clara, Seattle University, and Notre Dame. They're not bagging groceries at a Food Giant store. You don't belong here, son."

He pauses, waiting for it to register on my face. I think of the dreams I've carried with me all year long: running in the state track meet, and eventually winning a scholarship to college someday. *I did everything I could and it wasn't good enough.*

"You don't belong here," Father Seaver says again. "I am doing you a favor son."

I board one of three buses for my hour-long trip home. This will be one of the last bus rides home from Prep. I smell the fragrance of cherry blossoms blooming on the trees that line the street and look out to Lake Union glistening in the sunlight. It's one of those days that Seattle waits for patiently through the gray, rain-soaked days of winter. I transfer from the Ravenna bus to the Ballard/Laurelhurst bus.

I know where I'm going now. I'm going to Lincoln next year, to the public high school. I know where I'm not going: back to Prep. But I'm also not going back to Adamson's basement, the attic, and the barn.

By the third bus, I begin to feel light. My shoulders relax and I lean against the window catching my reflection. I don't turn away in disgust. Gone is that old tape playing in my head: *I sold myself out.*

For what? To go to Prep. How could I do that? I'm in a daydream state, waking up from a nightmare. I know who I'm going to be tomorrow.

Arriving home, I walk directly to my closet, take my $45 letterman's jacket off the hanger, slip into it, and look into the mirror; the blue and white jacket with the big *S* on the front fits just like a glove. *It took so long to make the varsity track team, to scrape together the money to buy the jacket, to be fitted and order the jacket, but I'll never wear this Seattle Prep letterman's jacket.* I make my way out the front door, and walk down 45th street, stopping to admire my "look" in the reflection of each glass store window. As I complete my journey, I turn the corner onto Wallingford Avenue, where I come across a donation bin in front of the Food Giant store. It is marked, *St. Vincent DePaul Giveaway.* I slowly remove the letterman's jacket and reverently place it atop the bin. I make a concentrated effort to resist the urge to look back over my shoulder as I continue to the door of our apartment building. I return to my room where I carefully fold up the letter that my boss at Food Giant wrote to Father Seaver. Then I wad it up into a tight little ball and toss it across the room at the waste basket.

He's behind me. Never again am I going to deal with the threats, coercion, extortion, crimes. Never again. I'm not complying. If that means I have to give up one of the greatest schools one could ever ask to go to, then I'll give it up. I no longer have to look in the mirror and say, *boy you've really given in; you sold your soul to go to Seattle Prep?*

I walk down the hall to leave my apartment house. I stop to catch a glimpse of myself in the mirror hanging just inside the doorway. I recognize that face. I've seen it before: happy, free, myself. I've been that way before. I think, *I am no longer a victim.* I'm free now, out of the clutches of Pinky, forever. I've been released.

CHAPTER 8

MORGAN'S MILERS

September 1964

I think about my future. Yes, I'll be going to public high school, but the trade-off is that I've extricated myself from the grip of Pinky's blackmail and coercion.

I'm not afraid to go to Lincoln High School. It's a good school; they have a cross-country and track team and the faculty are rated some of the best in the city. The school recently built a new gymnasium, locker rooms, parking lot, and a modern addition to the original nineteenth-century building.

I imagine my St. Benedict's grade school buddies are secure, returning to Blanchet, Holy Names, and O'Dea for their sophomore year, but I really don't know. I lived in a vacuum of sorts at Seattle Prep—with no information about where my St. Benedict's friends were going the next year. I anticipate running into the boys from the Wallingford Boys Club, the Protestants from the summer baseball team, and my Green Lake fishing buddies, but I doubt that I'll know one girl there.

On my first day at Lincoln, I enter the two massive oak front doors and am met with a sea of over 2,000 kids standing in the hallways, waiting for classes to start. I see two or three of my friends from the boys club. Next, I'm pleasantly shocked to see a group of girls huddled together in the hall—all from St. Benedict's. I am relieved that I am in the good company of St. Ben's students and not the only one who didn't have the money for Catholic high school.

A few days later, at the far end of the first floor hallway, I catch a glimpse of Gail Gibson, my old girlfriend from grade school and freshman year; she's holding crutches, her leg in a cast. I had called her on the phone a few times this summer to play tennis, or maybe go see a movie, but she always politely just said, *no thank you,* and hung up the phone. I make my way to the end of the hall thinking, *Wow, I didn't know she broke her leg. Maybe that's why she didn't want to go anywhere with me.*

"Hello Gail. I see you too have sinned and ended up in public school."

With a bland, indifferent look on her face, she turns back to the conversation with her girlfriends.

I remember Adamson's threats at the end of my freshman year. *I'll tell your girlfriend you're a homo. I'll get someone I own to do it. She'll find out in five minutes, so you can kiss off your girlfriend.* We cross paths every day in the hall that year as she comes out of French class and I leave chemistry, but she acts like she doesn't even know me. I see her everywhere: at church, school assemblies, football games, over and over. She never talks to me again during our high school years. I believe it's one of the consequences for protecting that twelve-year-old; at least I got him out of that situation, and I'm proud of it. It isn't so much the loss of a "girlfriend," but the loss of a really good friend—at the hands of Pinky—that saddens me.

I have a leg up on my studies after a year at Prep and I pull A's and B's without bringing a book home to study. Cross-country season starts and what a course! At Prep we were running on concrete sidewalks, blacktop, up and down Broadway Avenue but here, this is the most beautiful, first-rate garden. We run down by Woodland Park through grassy fields, past the tennis courts, up into the woods and all the way to the zoo. We continue across the rolling hills we call the *Whoop de doos,* down past chestnut and walnut trees, through the evergreens, then deciduous trees, and down back around Green Lake. It is the best cross-country course; all the teams who come to Lincoln think our course is the most challenging and picturesque. The cross-country coach, David Morgan, isn't like the track coach at Prep; he was into the stopwatch—concentrating on how fast or slow we were going, nothing inspiring us to expand our mental game about *running.*

Coach Morgan is the "Zen Master," and his mantra is, *Long-distance running is not about running.* Mr. Morgan, also on staff as a boys' counselor, looks like a young John F. Kennedy. He has east coast ways and I imagine he went to Harvard, Yale, or Princeton. He is muscular, his hair perfectly styled; he wears a tweed sport coat with a blue oxford cloth shirt and gorgeous silk tie. He has a car that no one has ever set eyes on before in the Wallingford district, ordered straight from the Ford dealership: a midnight-green metallic 1964 1/2 first model Mustang, with black bucket seats and a "four on the floor." He is in a class of his own, and just the type of guy that I want to emulate.

We have a nickname for our cross country team: *Morgan's Milers.* Everyone on the team trains throughout the summer and is in good physical shape at the beginning of the season. There are four runners faster than the rest of the team, and after practice we go to the upper Woodland Park area by the zoo and sit on a hill in a circle with Coach Morgan. It is early fall and the foliage on the trees is crisp, the leaves fluttering in the wind, a spectacular array of colors. As we sit cross-legged on the grass, some lying on the grass propped up on an elbow, he talks about how *Long-distance running is not always about running.*

"Traditionally, you know that in running there's a wall where you start to feel pain as you run faster, and when you hit this wall, it's not easy to break through. When you do burst through this mental wall, it's like you're floating."

I am hungry to experience this, and I do, six months later. Every great long-distance runner knows exactly what Coach Morgan is talking about. He tells us that this is a metaphor for life—our lives.

He picks a leaf off a tree and says, "This is not about running; this is about life. As the leaf dies and the chlorophyll production slows and stops, the green color diminishes and the leaf starts to wilt and turn red or yellow, and then brown. The leaf starts to get flaky at the end, and it always starts from the ends. As the cool autumn nights come, it speeds the process."

With the leaf in hand, he demonstrates: "When you take the leaf and grab it at its end and squeeze it in your hand, it crumbles. But even after it turns red or yellow and falls from the tree, if you grasp the leaf toward the base and hold it softly between your thumb and finger, it's pliable. It's like the human spirit; it can crumble at its outer core, and there are bruises, dents, and shadows, but inward if you still have that flexibility, that core softness, you will survive. You might be holding on to the last little bit of that tiny stem, but if the outside crumbles, that does not mean you give up."

Coach Morgan has us hold a leaf as we run. If we're holding it too tightly, the leaf starts to crumble on the outside. You need to hold it perfectly, between thumb and finger, not tensing up, which restricts your lung capacity. Keep your hands and arms low and relaxed, shoulders down, and get the oxygen to your legs; let your legs do the work.

All through high school, I look at that leaf and often think about this symbol of life, and the human spirit, and how long-distance running has nothing to do with running. I realize that I am running away from something, and as I run faster I feel the air, the wind, the rain washing my body, cleansing me from the basement, the attic, the threats and intimidation. The twelve-year-old feels himself breathing again, and the twelve-year-old is floating, and the twelve-year-old is free.

It's not long before I'm looking for a replacement girlfriend. I know that she must be Catholic or my Dad will say, *oh she's a nice looking girl, but Protestant…she'll be spending the rest of eternity in Hell, and so will you for liking her.*

I seek out dances at parishes that are a safe distance from my neighborhood. I'm determined that my next girlfriend will be from another parish—the farther north, the better. I don't want her to know anything about St. Benedict's, the teachers, or Wallingford. There's an upcoming CYO dance at St. Mark's, located in North Seattle, and my friend Gregg and I make plans to check it out. A short time after we arrive at the dance, I focus on a girl standing against the wall, along with a group of other high school girls. She is about 5'4" and dressed impeccably in a black Mary Jane dress with a white peter pan collar and black strappy short heels. Her blonde hair is worn in a short, stylish bob, the sides swept forward, framing her face. She looks like she just stepped out of a Nordstrom fashion show. I watch her for a while; in her interactions with the other girls, she seems shy and quiet, with a slight smile on her face. I make my move and ask her to dance. She tells me that she is from St. Marks Parish and that she attends Blanchet High School. I proudly profess that I am from Seattle Prep. We hit it off and I ask for her phone number. I don't tell her until weeks later that I'm now attending a public school.

Rosanne* and I date over the next two years, going to movies, dances, and playing tennis. On Sundays, I'm invited to her big Italian family dinners at their ultra-modern, ranch-style house in a new suburb north of Seattle. Everyone in her family is jovial and affectionate, always laughing and hugging each other, and welcoming their relatives as if they hadn't seen them in years. Her father, Joseph Sapanaro*, is sociable. Little kids talk to him and jump up on him and he jokes around and plays with them. Mr. Sapanaro plays golf with the local priest, Father Crock*, who frequents their home for Sunday dinners. They even bought the priest a 1965 Chevelle Malibu 2-door hardtop. This is all very foreign to me. There's no laughing and hugging at my house. I somehow try to fit in and her parents accept me as almost part of the family.

I had saved money for a down payment on a 1963 Corvair Monza Spider convertible but it wasn't quite enough. Mr. Sapanaro offered to loan me the rest. For a school the size of 2,500 kids, there are only four or five cars in the Lincoln High School parking lot. Now, one of them is mine. I know "chicks" love it when a guy sings, and I think I have a good voice. I know most of the lyrics to every song that comes out. I'm not hungry anymore; I eat Dick's cheeseburgers or I'm at the Pizza Haven on the "Ave." It doesn't matter that I'm still living at home in one of those dark, dingy rentals with no food. I'm only home to sleep.

I introduce Rosanne to my mother on a weekend while my dad is away on a retreat at the secluded Palisades Retreat Center located on Puget Sound, a place where Catholics devote a weekend in prayer and meditation. My dad was not too happy when he finally met my girlfriend, even though she is Catholic. He hears she is Italian and he calls her a *wop* and makes fun of her dyed blonde hair. He has names for every different ethnic group, stuck in his dislike for anyone different than Irish Catholics.

What is most important to me, though, is that my new girlfriend has no association with Pinky, nor will he ever know her. I have this new persona with her and I make sure to keep her away from anything to do with St. Benedict's. We go to CYO dances at all the other parishes. I always have another plan for us when there is a St. Benedict's Parish dance.

I've grown more confident and emboldened. It's been two years since I put the horror of Pinky behind me. Yeah, I see him at church or the teen club, but he doesn't come up to me. He's nothing. He doesn't bother me or talk to me. He's got nothing to bribe, coerce, or extort. The girlfriend is gone. Seattle Prep is gone. *What are you going do to me? I got that twelve-year-old out of the basement and he's never going back.*

After track practice on Fridays, I run to my car, take the top down (rain or shine, hot or cold), and drive to Dick's Drive-In. At exactly 5:00 p.m. every Friday, and later that night at 9:00, the King of Seattle music, Pat O'Day on KJR channel 95, plays a new group or a new song that we've never heard before: *I've got a song for you from this new group, the Righteous Brothers, singing "You've Lost that Loving Feeling."* Or another group, Simon and Garfunkel, with "The Sound of Silence," and the Rolling Stones, "Satisfaction," or Eric Burdon and the Animals singing, "House of the Rising Sun."

I memorize as much of the words of what will become iconic songs before picking up Rosanne at 7:00 p.m. I serenade her with these new tunes. When 9:00 rolls around, KJR repeats the show and I turn on the radio. *Voilà*, she hears the new releases of the day...after first hearing *me* singing them while driving around in my Corvair.

Life is good. I'm in my junior year now and shifting into high gear. There's real potential for qualifying to run in the state cross-country meet. I am working at a gas station on 45th, learning how to do brake jobs, front end alignments, and rebuild carburetors. I'm making $70 a week, lots of cash for a high school kid. No more shopping at the Goodwill for my clothes; I'm at Vons Men's Store and the Squire shop in the U District and I wear the best quality clothes.

I learn that if you work your ass off, you get money, and that translates into independence and freedom. On the outside, my image is all put together: the convertible, the preppy clothes, the music, varsity athlete. Inside, I develop and fine-tune my blockers, which help me disassociate and bury my past. That's behind me, another time. *These will forever be the best years of my life.*

Rosanne asks why we never go to the St. Benedict's dances. She's heard from her Blanchet buddies that they are a great time. She constantly asks about the dances, and since I'm treasurer of the teen club, it makes no sense why we don't ever go. Finally, I agree to take her to an upcoming dance in November.

The day of the dance, I go to the school earlier to help set up for the dance and work on special lighting in the auditorium: low, dim blue lights, great for slow dancing. We hook up with some old friends at the dance and the band is great. Pinky is at the dance, lurking in the background, circling around, but he doesn't talk to me or bother me.

At the end of the evening, I ask Rosanne to wait in the car for me while I finish up the treasurer business for the night. I pay the policeman, pay the band, and place the remaining money in a metal box, which I take to a school safe until it can be transferred to the Oblate priests in the rectory. I shut off the lights, walk into the hall with the fluorescent lights blaring above, and see that everyone is gone. As I look to my right, toward the principal's office, I see Pinky with his hand pressed up against the wall, near Rosanne's head. He has her pinned to the wall like a frozen little mouse. He looks at me as I walk toward them.

"Well, I just introduced myself to your new girlfriend."

Outside the school building on the stairs, Rosanne stops. She turns to me and says, "Who is that person? I've never been so afraid in my life."

"That's my seventh-grade teacher."

"What's that guy got on you? He is a creepy person."

For several months, she would periodically bring up that night and ask, *what does that guy have on you?* I never answer her.

I'm caught off guard and underestimate Pinky. I'm overconfident, thinking I extricated myself from his presence forever. Part of me has the urge to flee. Just when I thought it was safe to go back into the neighborhood, he is lurking there and I have to be even more vigilant. I'll need to keep looking over my shoulder.

The next day is Sunday and I'm in charge of the ushers at the 9:00 Mass. As soon as Mass ends, I gather the collection baskets and take them to the closet in the vestibule. I hear the wing walkers pounding down the stairs from the choir loft, past the crying room, to the vestibule. As I walk out the front door of the church, Pinky comes up behind me and grabs my arm.

"Friday is Veterans Day. There's no school. If you want to keep your new girlfriend, you'll be at my house by noon."

CHAPTER 9

VETERANS DAY

My junior year in cross-country is coming to a close. I'm running my favorite course—Green Lake, lower Woodland Park—for the north metro league qualifications. Last year I placed twelfth in the finals, and this year I place fourth. I'm getting stronger and faster. I qualify as one of two runners from Lincoln for the state championship meet, which is coming up this Saturday. It's been a long while since Lincoln has sent runners to the state meet, so as the only ones competing this year, all eyes are on my teammate and me.

The week before the Saturday state meet turns out to be an agonizing one. I dread going to Pinky's house on Veterans Day: I have not been in the place for nearly two years. The threats from Pinky are back and I have to deal with them again, I can't just ignore his threat. My sole focus needs to be on preparing for the state meet, but I'm distracted, even as I go through the motions of practice every day: do my stretches, do my wind sprints, and check my time. All said, I'm more ready for Saturday's meet than I am for Friday's trip to Pinky's house.

I leave my car at home and walk to Dick's for a cheeseburger at about 11:30 in the morning. Then I walk the two blocks to Pinky's house. Down the alley, through the gate, through the back door. The tension is thick as I walk in the door and it's hard for me to breathe. I come to the landing at the top of the stairs, look down to the basement, and see him sitting on a stool in his usual place. The rickety stairs are narrow and steep, still with no wall or hand rail. To the right of the stairs, it's completely open.

Pinky glances up to the landing and sees me standing there.

He yells, "Sonny boy, get on down here."

I refuse and stand my ground at the top of the stairs. I am not going to let that twelve-year-old go down those stairs. Pinky rushes up the stairs like a bear coming out of its cave and an altercation begins immediately. He shoves me against the wall and I push him back, hard, and see him falling down the stairs, no wall or railing to slow him, onto the concrete floor, landing on his side.

Everything moves in slow motion, quiet. I realize what just happened and think, *My God, I'm going to get arrested for assaulting my seventh-grade teacher and go to jail.*

Lying on the floor, Pinky's eyes are filled with shock and rage. I run down the stairs, just about to extend my hand to help him up, and in the next instant he jumps up and pushes me into a narrow gap between two filing cabinets against the wall. Wedged between the cabinets, I am on my butt, back against the wall, legs kicking out in front of me, trying to get him away from me. Then, I don't see it coming, I don't understand what happens, I feel it, an explosion of intense pain. He's kicked me in the groin with his hard-toed wing walker shoes. I get up and out of the way and instantly feel sick to my stomach, waves of nausea, I want to vomit.

Later, I learn the swift kick to the testicles has torn my scrotum sack. The wing walkers have performed their function.

I stagger up the stairs and this time Mrs. Adamson is nowhere around to offer us cookies and lemonade. I push open the back door, open the gate, and head up the alley way. Not more than a hundred yards away, I collapse on all fours on the parking strip and begin to vomit. Within a few minutes, a guy in a white 1955 Chevy two door sedan slowly drives by and stops, pulls up to the curb, gets out, and runs over to me.

"Steve, what's going on?"

It's Mike O'Malley*, an older classmate from St. Benedict's, probably on his way to Dick's.

Still on all fours, "I need a ride home, I've had an accident."

Mike looks at me throwing up, unable to get up.

"No way man, I'm taking you to the hospital."

I don't remember the ride or arriving at the UW hospital, which is a mile away. I have trouble getting out of the car. A nurse brings a wheelchair. Once inside, I am immediately put on a gurney and hooked up to an IV, then I'm moved to a private room in ER. The ER doctor on-call examines me and asks me over and over:

"What happened? How did this happen?"

It's the worst pain I've ever experienced, but in just a few minutes, it lessens. It must be some powerful pain killer they're giving me. Though I feel groggy and drowsy, I manage to answer.

"Well, I was running down a hill at lower Woodland and wasn't looking where I was going and ran into a tree."

The doctor cuts my pants away and treats my wounds with gauze pads and bandages on the right side of my scrotum. He asks about my parents and I give him all my information. I know that since winter is coming on, my dad will be out of work, sitting at home smoking cigarettes and drinking coffee.

The doctor introduces me to the anesthesiologist and says that they are taking me up for *emergency surgery*. He asks the same question. *What happened?* I tell another story. *Oh, I was down at lower Woodland playing pick-up football and somebody accidentally kicked me in the nuts.*

For anyone else who asks, I vacillate between the two stories.

I am wheeled into a pre-op room. It's cold and the anesthesiologist explains how he will place a mask over my face and then I will count backward from fifty.

The surgeon enters the room, dressed in drab green scrubs, a surgical mask hanging down around his neck. He puts his hand on the bed railing, moves in close, looking me squarely in the eye.

"You're going into emergency surgery and I am the doctor who is performing this surgery. I want to know right now what really happened."

I tell him who the person is, where he lives, where he works, and how it happened. He leaves the room and I lay there for another twenty minutes. The surgeon comes in again and tells me that my parents have arrived and signed the consent forms. I wonder if he tells my parents what I have just told him, how it happened.

I don't remember any long explanation from the doctor or nurse about what my injuries are, I just know they are serious. All I remember next is starting to count backward from fifty. I awake in the middle of the night, throwing up, sick as a dog, drifting in and out of sleep. The next time I wake up it is mid-afternoon. Darkness settles in on this Saturday in early November and I know the cross-country state meet is over by now. I assume my parents told my coach I wouldn't be there.

As I lie on my back, I see a white sheet draped over me, fastened by a string on either side of the bed so that the sheet is in a tent fashion and not touching my body. I whip the sheet off and look down at the bandages, stretching from my upper thighs to where my belt buckle would be. I can see no part of my groin area, just lots of cotton packing. Nothing but bandages and cotton packing. I thought they must have removed everything, but the Doctor reassured me, no, but you may end up sterile as a complication.

I spend the rest of the afternoon contemplating:

So much for sex.

So much for the state cross-country meet.

So much for a track scholarship, my ticket out of here, to college.

So much for my replacement girlfriend. I'm sure he's told her by now.

So much for my life in general, my future.

What looks like a great job at the gas station…now doesn't look so great. It looks like my entire future: Pinky's boy, *the limp dick homo*, working at a gas station the rest of my life. Great. Pinky never went away. All the while he's been lying in wait for his next opening, to attack. I thought I did everything in my power to protect that twelve-year-old from going to that basement. I felt I did everything I could, and it just wasn't good enough.

As I look out at the darkness from my hospital window, a squall moves in and rain beats down against the window. A phone is ringing on the desk beside my bed. I answer and hear Coach Morgan's voice.

"How are you doing, Steve? We sure missed you today, kid."

The following day, my dad comes to visit me in the hospital and brings me a portable transistor radio, a first for me. I wonder if he and my mother know what I revealed to the doctor about Adamson— that he's the one who kicked me, assaulted me, and it wasn't me just getting kicked accidentally while playing a game of pick-up football.

The doctor must have included that in a hospital report. But my dad doesn't mention anything to me. We talk about the transistor radio and he tells me that he spoke with Coach Morgan and that I should be ready Friday night because he is coming up to see me in the hospital. The high school athletic banquet is this Friday at the Black Angus restaurant and he'll be coming up to see me after.

My thoughts drift to this one person, Coach Morgan, who I admire and respect and that maybe, just maybe, he will be the right person to tell the truth about the incident. As evening approaches, I rehearse what I might say to him about the whole mess. I still feel bad that I let my school down and could not run in the state meet.

That night, as I look up from my bed and see the whole cross-country team at the foot of my bed standing next to Coach Morgan, I think great, *the whole team is here to visit me.* Guess I won't be talking to him tonight, either. Another missed opportunity to tell the truth.

CHAPTER 10

DOWN BOUND TRAIN

December 1965

If Mike O'Malley had been driving down 45th Street in his dad's 1955 white Chevy in December 1965, he would barely recognize Steve walking up the street. *It's too bad about his accident last year,* he'd think. *Since then, he walks everywhere: unsteady, deliberate, and slow. He doesn't drive his car and his grades went south at school, and he might not be able to run track. He's failing at everything.* If Mike were to run into him at teen club or church, there would never be a mention about the day he picked up Steve on the curbside, bent over and vomiting. Mike would never ask either.

Steve looks like a weary old man now, head down, wandering aimlessly, not the Steve people remember with his impatient gait, the guy who walked fast or ran everywhere: upbeat, confident, and having fun. Just four months ago, he was parked at Dick's Drive-In, sitting on the top of the bucket seat in his convertible listening to music on the radio, peering over his shades, scoping out the scene of cars pulling in. Now, he seems like a different person and people are left to wonder, *what really happened?*

After my release from the hospital, I continue to experience excruciating pain at times, and it hurts when I walk or climb stairs. Worst of all, I can't use my left leg to push in the clutch on my Corvair. Not being able to drive my car is torture, a different kind of pain. At least I have all my parts; after the shock of surgery, I was unsure that I was still whole. Rosanne never mentions anything out of the ordinary, and it seems Adamson never did go through with his threats. Either that or, maybe he "got" to her and she dismissed it outright.

Rosanne and I go to the CYO Christmas Ball at the Olympic Hotel in downtown Seattle. My brother Jerry drives us there and picks us up. During the dance, I have to excuse myself and go to the bathroom frequently and spray on a medicine my doctor gave me to relieve the pain.

Around this time, all Rosanne can talk about is looking at colleges to apply to next year. I've lost interest and don't see how there is any hope of a track scholarship now. I'm not sure I'll even be able to run this spring.

In March, five months after the "accident," I'm definitely not up to my speed and times I ran in track last year. My running times are back where I was as a freshman, certainly not top varsity level. I'm cutting classes at school and my grades slip from A's and B's to D's and F's; I end up on academic probation, and am nearly suspended from the track team. Coach Nixon talks to me about what's going on: *I know you had this accident and you're still recovering and trying to get your times up, but what's up with these grades?* His disappointment in me is clear.

Earlier that year, Lee Olsen*, a track teammate stopped by the gas station while I was working one night and gave me the news that my favorite coach, David Morgan, the "Zen Master," had left Lincoln High School, probably to take another high school or college coaching job. If Coach Morgan were here right now, I'd tell him the truth about the assault on Veterans Day. I am sure that he is friends with influential people in town and maybe he could talk to someone. I regret that I was unable to tell Coach Morgan that I wasn't really being careless—playing pick-up football the day before the state meet, injuring myself, and eliminating Lincoln's chance at competing in the state meet. He knew the importance I placed on the meet. He's gone now, but I'll still retain the skills he taught me about running, and life. He inspired me to strive for more, believed in me, and recognized my natural running ability. He gave me hope for the future. All that's dashed now, the way my life is going.

I'm running at the back of the pack now, and there will be no college track scholarship next year. My grades tank and I fail at everything. My jeans rub against my testicle, a constant reminder of Adamson's swift kick to the groin…those wing walkers. I think about my overconfidence, taking my girlfriend to the dance. I let that twelve-year-old go down to the basement again, and I underestimated the enemy.

I listen to my favorite song at the top of the charts this spring, "We Gotta Get Out of This Place," by Eric Burdon and the Animals, and boy do *I gotta get out of here*. I notice a change in Pinky's personality and behavior. He never speaks a word to me, avoids all eye contact, and is not hassling me. I think he's unnerved about what happened that last trip to his basement and he's looking over his shoulder. He better be looking over his shoulder. Medieval thoughts creep in and I imagine ways to take revenge on Pinky. I constantly hear about the Vietnam War on the nightly TV news. I can escape there, versus annihilation of Adamson, or I can annihilate him and then escape. I try to distance myself from these thoughts: it's not who I really am, not in my character, crazy thinking, and criminal.

By spring, I'm finally able to drive my car again. I'm back working at the gas station. It's twilight, around 9:00 p.m. on a Tuesday in May, and as I glance up from my work, looking out at 45th Street, there are one or two cars that drive by in the space of an hour. It's eerily quiet, with no one on the streets tonight, a ghost town rather than a major street in Wallingford. Quitting time finally comes at midnight and I put the tools away, put the cash box in the safe, shut the garage doors, and turn out the lights. After closing the gas station, I drive around in my Corvair with the top down, in no hurry to get home. Aimlessly, I cruise up and down 45th, onto Stone Way or University Ave., and circle around back to 45th. While driving down 45th one last time, I turn left at Meridian, then another left onto 43rd. I'm creeping along at less than 10 mph. I hear Chad and Jeremy's "Summer Song" playing on the radio as I roll up to the curb on Sunnyside and 43rd. Facing eastbound, I survey the two steep hills. There's a full moon and the gravel-covered alleyway is in full view, illuminated by the moonlight.

I stare down the street at the two hills and thoughts begin to creep in. Pinky is a creature of habit. I know he backs his car out of the alleyway onto the side street facing west and drives to St. Benedict's each morning at 7:45; his brown paper lunch bag marked *Danny* sits on the bench seat next to him. I think about what if…what if as he backs out of the alley onto the street, I gun my car down one hill and down the next, how fast will I be going? I visualize broadsiding Pinky's car and have an image of it exploding like in a Hollywood movie. I walk over and watch him burn in the wreckage.

The next night, after closing up the gas station at midnight, I drive to 43rd and Sunnyside to the top of the two hills again. *Let's do a trial run.* I put my car in first gear, then pop the clutch and floor it down the first hill, then down the second. By the time I cross the alley where Pinky will be backing out into the street, I'm doing 35 mph. *Huh, a human torpedo.* Except I'm not taking into account what will happen to me. Especially since the gas tank is located in the front of the Corvair; I will be toast. Bad idea. Or maybe a good idea? He will probably make it out of his burning car and strangle me and bury me out in the woods where nobody will find me. It needs to be something bold—a bigger car—to get this monster.

Two weeks later, on a Monday, I close up the gas station late at night, and once again I go back and sit in my car at the top of the street. I ruminate about his threats to "out" me as a "homo," about how I've ruined my life by going back to that basement. I feel that I'm physically injured for life, my chances at a track scholarship are gone, my grades are in the tank, and I'll probably be working at a gas station for the rest of my life. I blame myself for all this, a consequence of making bad choices, my dad's voice echoing in my ear. By one or two in the morning, my conscience kicks in….I start wondering about right and wrong.

I have an image of a Catholic storybook from grade school: a picture of a child with a guardian angel on one shoulder and the devil on the other. The church believes children reach the age of reason and know right from wrong at seven years old. I remember the lessons about having our own free will to listen to the devil's voice or to the guardian angel's voice. The choice is ours, to sin—listen to the devil, go against God's will—or listen to the angel of light and know, love, and serve God. The angel/devil image moves from the edges of my mind to front and center as I sit in the early morning hours and contemplate ramming my car into my seventh-grade teacher and doing him in. A few minutes later, my conscience is resonating in my ear. *What has got into you? What are you thinking? Are you crazy? Just go home.*

I do go home. I think about what's next for me. I need to confront my dad. He needs to know the truth about Adamson, from me.

It's a weeknight, 5:00 p.m., close to dinnertime and Dad is in the front room in his favorite easy chair, drinking coffee and reading the paper. As I sit across from him on the couch, I'm not sure why I choose to tell him now, except that I worry about the medieval thoughts I'm having about Pinky. Afraid I might do something I'll regret, again. My dad can do something: go to the Archbishop, or the police, and tell them. They can fire Pinky from his job, arrest him, and put him behind bars where he belongs.

I'm not sure how to start this conversation.

"Dad, I need to talk to you about what's been going on."

"Yeah, OK."

He continues to read his open newspaper held up in front of his face as I interrupt his daily ritual. My dad, the World War II radio correspondent on a CBS affiliate. Well, I have some news for him. It won't be something he doesn't already know, though; he's the one who approves of me going with Pinky across the state tuning organs. Staying in motels overnight with my seventh-grade teacher as a twelve, thirteen, and fourteen-year–old. What did he think was happening? He knows I'm Pinky's boy.

"Well, you need to know that Pinky has been doing things to me, from the seventh grade up through high school."

My dad sets down the open newspaper.

"What kind of things?"

My face flushes red with embarrassment and I make references in vague terms about what Pinky's done to me.

My dad winces slightly and is quiet for a long time. His face darkens.

"Is this still going—happening now?"

"Not that stuff, but other things—harassing, threatening me."

"Where was this?"

My head lowers and my hands cover my face…avoiding his look.

"Basement, attic, the boys' bathroom at school, the choir loft, trips, motels…."

After I drop this bomb in his lap, *this explosive news*, I wait for a response. He snaps his paper, carefully creases and folds it, placing it in his lap, and calmly says:

"I'll look into this."

Will he? *Sure he will….* Why am I wasting my time with him? He fully consented to me going on overnights with Pinky, thinking he's some sort of mentor, or role model, for me. He'll ignore it like the others I've told: Father Conrad, and Father Dillon. He's wedded to the church, that's his life: Irish Catholic, 5:30 a.m. Mass every day of the week, *my church right or wrong*. He believes in the authority of the priests and Dan Adamson, a champion for kids. He gets upset and scolds my oldest twenty-five year old brother when he misses Mass on Sunday and lays guilt trips on us if we even give Protestants or anyone outside of St. Benedict's the time of day. *They're all going to hell, they're doomed.* Will he care what's happened to me? I think about the formal relationship we have, a *non-emoting* emotional way of communicating with each other. The only times I like being around him are when he teaches me to paint, or when he plays the piano while he and Mother sing old favorites, laugh, joke around, and drink a few beers. Now, my news hits him right where it hurts: his beloved church. An arrow right through the heart. What'll he do? I suspect he will do nothing…*I'm sure nothing will happen.* Why will he be any different than the others?

Again, he repeats, "I'll look into it."

Then he says adamantly, "Tomorrow's Sunday. Make sure you're at Mass fifteen minutes early and ready to usher."

I leave him alone to his coffee and paper and walk out the front door and onto 45th Street. Everything seems normal today. The sun is out, people are shopping, and kids out of school for the summer are heading to the zoo or Green Lake. I walk by the Tweedy and Popp hardware store and reminisce about convincing the owner to sell me a fishing pole with $2 down and $1 a month. That seems like a long time ago. I felt so confident.

I keep walking. I'm surprised at how calm my dad is. I've done all I can. *I gotta get out of this place.* Somewhere far away.

I wait to hear something from my dad after dropping the bombshell. I do not hear anything for the next few days, then two weeks go by, and the words, *I'll look into it* become silence. There is no further word from him, and I don't ask, because I know; I know he will do nothing.

That's just like him, doing nothing. *Look into it…my ass.* No action from him tells me everything I need to know. I know what he's thinking: *Let's move to Montana, back to the good old days.* They'll make their move, far away from the Wallingford district and this dirty little problem. I'm in the way, last kid at home. Well, I'm going to get out of the way and out of here, and I know exactly what I'm going to do. I've walked by the U.S. Marine Corps, Army, and Navy recruiting office in the U District many times. I watched the movie, *The D.I.*, when I was about twelve, depicting Marines in boot camp and their tough drill instructor who turned boys into Marines.

The next day I walk into the U District recruiting office and ask to speak with the Marine recruiting officer, but he's at lunch. The Navy recruiter is more than happy to talk to me, trying to convince me to join the Navy, explaining all the exciting places that I can travel to, one place being Hawaii, then describing options for training as a mechanic or engineering school. If I put in my four years of service, I could receive benefits for college tuition and home loans. The Marine recruiter comes back and offers a similar spiel. After they're done, I tell them, *No, I don't want mechanic training, engineer school, none of that.* I knew enough that if I joined the Marines, they would send me right away to boot camp, and then Vietnam. That's what I wanted: infantryman, combat duty. I tell them, *do whatever you have to do to get me to Vietnam.*

"How old are you, kid? You realize that if you are under eighteen years of age, you will need your parents' consent to join the Marine Corps?"

"Yes sir, yeah, no problem. They'll be happy to sign off, get rid of me."

I'm thinking it won't matter if they sign off or not. I'll turn eighteen December 8th and join then.

The next day I greet my parents in the kitchen and carefully lay the consent form on the table in front of my dad. I break the news that I've decided to drop out of school and join the Marines. I ask them to please sign for me, since I'm under eighteen. I let them know that if they don't sign the papers, I'll just wait until I'm eighteen. They respond by trying to talk me into joining the Air Force, like my brother, Jerry, though he only lasted a few months. They know where I'll end up as a Marine infantryman. The nightly news reports more than a hundred Marines were killed this week in intense fighting near Con Tien. Every night the country faced the news on every channel with lengthy reporting on the war. We see the body counts of Viet Cong, and how many American soldiers were killed in action, or wounded; war correspondents and photographer's cover stories with pictures of wounded American soldiers being medevaced, villages being destroyed, and helicopters shot down. The war is also all over the covers of *Look*, *Time*, and *Newsweek*.

There is no other discussion. No questions from them about my abrupt decision to join the Marines. There's a lack of curiosity around the house. Silence. Three days later, they decide this will be fine and they sign the papers. Not one word or inquiry from my older brothers. Nothing. At least no conversation with me.

Everything goes through quickly in the span of ten days. Rosanne and I drive up to Woodland Park and sit in the car. Even though it's cloudy, the hills are still green and lush. We hear a light drizzle falling on the roof of the Corvair convertible.

She says, "I sent in my applications for two colleges this week."

"Uh huh. Good for you."

My left hand is resting on the steering wheel, my right hand brushing off the dashboard, back and forth, making sure there's no dust.

"How are you doing with your applications? What schools are you thinking about? How are you doing with studying for the SAT?"

I quit brushing the dashboard and look away from her, toward the side window.

"I won't be going off to college with you after high school. In fact, I won't even be going back to high school for my senior year. I've made a decision to quit school and join the Marine Corps."

She is quiet, but there is a look of shock on her face, like someone just punched her in the stomach.

Before she can say anything, I jump in again. "There'll be no discussion about this. I'm just telling you what I'm doing."

87

I glance at her sideways. Eventually, she reaches for the door handle of the car. She looks directly at me. She's trying not to cry.

"I'll find my own way home today."

She gets out of the car, shuts the door, and walks away. I see her in the rearview mirror and think, *I'll never see her again. Perfect end to a perfect year.*

I give away my prize collection of Ivy League clothes that I've accumulated over the past few years to my grade school buddy. I give him the keys to my car and tell him to drive it, sell it, do whatever he wants with it, cause I'm not going to need a car. I explain that he needs to get ahold of Rosanne's dad and ask him about the car; he is listed as the legal owner on the Corvair because I am under eighteen. He can't believe it. Me—giving away my car and clothes. Though he seems happy to take them off my hands. He says, *I've never heard you talk about wanting to go into the military before... what about finishing high school, going to college?*

"School's not workin' for me," I tell him. "I'm going to do my patriotic duty."

My dad takes the morning off in early August, during the peak season for painting jobs, and offers to drive me to the Armed Forces induction center. As we drive in the car, nothing much is said. There is no mention of what I told him about Adamson, or why I'm joining the Marines. We arrive at a five-story, cold-looking concrete building located on Alaskan Way South, near Seattle's waterfront. I grab my duffle bag and jump out of the car as soon as we stop. I don't even hear a *Good luck!* or *I hope you make it!* or *Hope you don't get blown away.* No. Instead, he says:

"The Marine Corps is not like some kind of track team. You might think you're tough or know what's going on in Vietnam, but they will spit you out in five minutes and you'll be headed back on a Trailways bus in a week."

He knows nothing about the military except what he learned as a radio announcer during the war. There's no credibility in that. He never served in active duty during WWII or put his life on the line for his country. I will show him what it's like to be a true patriot. I will prove his prediction wrong; I will not be back home in a week. I will finish boot camp and fight for our nation.

At boot camp, I receive the highest score in my platoon for rifle marksmanship. I've never owned or even touched a weapon in my life prior to the military. My drill instructors select me to lead the platoon at the graduation parade where I'll be carrying the *guidon* banner and wearing my dress blues.

About a week prior to the end of boot camp, a letter from my parents arrives announcing that my dad is taking a vacation and my parents are coming to California for my graduation. I think it odd, as my dad never takes vacations; I think maybe he looked into the things I told him about Pinky and is coming to tell me that he finally did something.

But my drill instructor calls us to formation two days before the graduation and orders all of us to take one step forward.

"Private O'Connor, stand fast."

He walks over to me.

"Are your parents James and Irene O'Connor?"

"Sir, yes sir."

"Well, they're dead. You need to report to the Red Cross."

I sit in the Red Cross office for the next one or two hours, but no one has any information for me. I imagine that my parents must have died in a car accident. Finally, there's a phone call for me and I hear my mother's voice on the other end of the line. I'm confused, but relieved that she is alive. Then I hear her crying.

"Dad and I were driving to your graduation and stopped at a motel last night in Redding, California and he dropped dead of a heart attack."

He was forty-nine years old.

I feel no sadness, nor am I distraught by this news. I do feel intense anger. My anger is aimed at the entire world that my Catholic God has created. I'm angry that I had to run away to prove a point, join the Marines to rub it in my dad's face, make it through boot camp. Now I'll never know if he said anything to the Archbishop, the cops, anyone. Or if he went to Adamson himself. And where I'm headed, I'll probably never find out.

CHAPTER 11

DOWN BOUND EXPRESS

October 1966

A few days following my dad's unexpected death, I catch a flight home from Camp Pendleton to Seattle. I arrive at our latest dark, dismal rental house and witness my family in various stages of shock and mourning. My mother spends most of her days in the bedroom, sobbing, and my brothers are sullen. This is the first time I've been home since I left for Marine boot camp and my bedroom looks the same, except the closet and dresser drawers are empty. After giving all of my clothes away to my best friend, Gregg, I'm sure he is the best dressed guy at Blanchet High School. As for me, all the energy and drive from my idea of *I'll show him* is deflated. My dad is missing—*poof*—gone in an instant. I didn't get to show him that his prediction that I'd be coming home in a week on a Trailways bus was wrong.

My mother and oldest brother, Jim, have been planning the funeral service, which will be held at St. Benedict Church the following week. The night of the Rosary service, a Catholic tradition held the day before the funeral, I walk into the local funeral parlor and think, *Oh, boy, it's an open casket.* As people pass by to view the frozen smile on my dad's face, I think my dad's probably not very happy about just dropping dead and wouldn't be smiling. The fact is, I've never actually seen a dead body before. Like a tap on the shoulder, I hear a whisper in my ear: *This ain't the last one you'll see where you're going next, and they won't be smiling back at you.*

The next morning, the casket is at the front of the church just outside the altar railing, draped in a black silken cloth. Although the sun is shining outside, the church is dark, with candles lit on the altar and flower arrangements on either side of the altar. The scent of lilies intermingles with the rising incense and creates a pungent smell that reminds me of Easter. The statues of Mary and Joseph are shrouded in black and Father McHugh is wearing black vestments. The Knights of Columbus (a Catholic Fraternal Service Organization) are lined up at the entrance to the church serving as an honor guard, dressed in black tuxes, white gloves, and capes. They form an arch with their swords for the funeral procession. I am wearing my Marine Corps dress uniform with a black armband around my arm.

My mother, brothers, and I take our places in the pew at the front of the church. I hear the organ music playing a long slow dirge that echoes against the green and tan swirled marble walls and high cathedral-like ceilings. Without attracting attention, I turn my head slowly up to the choir loft and steal a glimpse. It's him all right, playing the organ. I'm distracted now. A slow rage fills my body, moving up into my arm muscles, my chest, and my throat. My head feels like it might explode. I grit my teeth and keep my somber, serious Marine face. *Damn, why am I in the same church as him, again?*

The funeral is a requiem High Mass with lots of incense, Latin prayers, and the men's choir chanting morbid, ancient Gregorian hymns. This would all be just to my father's liking: the devout Catholic being laid to rest in the most ceremonious of Catholic rituals. I remain stoic throughout the Mass, sitting rigid and upright in the pew. Sitting directly behind us are friends and parishioners, including my former grade school friend Gail, Bob, Mike, Sharon, Sister Annunciata, and Rosanne, my former high school girlfriend. I'm anxious to have this thing over with as I listen to my older brother deliver a eulogy. I barely recognize who he's talking about: *Dear old Dad*. The procession begins to exit the church and as we march behind my father's casket there is another long, slow dirge being played on the pipe organ. I look up to the choir loft and see Adamson's red face in the small mirror attached to the organ, the back of his head, and that fat neck bursting out of his plaid shirt collar. I have him in my sights.

It's a sunny but cold day in October and the ground is frozen white at the Holyrood Cemetery. I watch as they lower my dad's casket into the hollowed out frozen ground and hear my mother's cries and the priest murmuring Latin prayers for everlasting peace and union with God.

After the burial we gather at the house for a wake where I envision half the people will get drunk and the other half will be crying in a corner somewhere. The food is typical. There's lime green Jell-O impaled with slivers of carrots, and a mystery meat casserole, all washed down with cans of Pabst Blue Ribbon. To my pleasant surprise, Gail Gibson, who hasn't said a word to me in three years, walks up and expresses her condolences. I ask her how school is going. She tells me she is headed for the University of Washington next fall. I congratulate her, mentioning all of her accomplishments in high school, and concluding awkwardly that I guess I wasn't cut out to make the grade academically, or something to that effect. The conversation abruptly stops, with her last words being, *I don't want to keep you from your "girlfriend,"* and she walks off.

At one point during the wake, my mother stands up and makes an announcement to everyone that the Marine Corps sent orders for me to report to Sandpoint Naval Base to apply for a hardship discharge as the sole surviving son at home. Something about an exemption for staying to take care of my mother.

My mother and Rosanne talk a lot about my *crazy idea to join the Marines* and how I need to get these papers filled out for my hardship discharge. I just nod and listen, walking through the back door to the yard. Rosanne catches up to me and says, *I'm so glad that nightmare is over. God has saved you. Now you can put all this behind you, finish high school, and go away to college on your father's Social Security survivor's pension.* I find this odd. No one is asking me anything at all: not my mother, my brothers, Rosanne. They're just deciding for me. That never did work with me. As they chat away about my future plans to stay in Seattle and apply for college after the discharge, I deliver a command performance, neither caught up in their excitement about a discharge nor telling them what I'm thinking. They have no idea who I am or what I want to do.

My mind drifts back to the sight of Pinky playing the funeral dirge at my dad's requiem Mass. That didn't sit well with me. I'm not sure that I'm college material anymore. The Marines suit my current state of mind—killing, and my desire to be far, far away. I obsess about Adamson playing the funeral. I can't believe he's still teaching, playing the organ at church—no penalties, no arrests, nothing.

Nights pass and I still hear my mother wailing from the bedroom. I lie on the couch in the living room at night, restless, uneasy and unable to sleep. Late Wednesday evening the week following the funeral, I hear the sound of a rubber ball bouncing down in the basement. I've heard this sound before; it's a small red rubber ball that sign painters (like my dad) attach at the end of a narrow stick or pole and it resembles a pool cue. It's called a *Mahl stick* and it's used as an aid in painting to avoid touching the wet surface accidentally and to steady the hand while painting. My dad made his signs from plywood and painted the background and lettering in contrasting colors. Some of his signs around the Wallingford district included Acme Office Supply, Serv-U-Drug, and Food Giant.

I open the door and feel the cold draft and smell the damp, musty basement. As I peer down from the top step, I see text on an unfinished sign that reads *GLO CLEANERS, In at 10, out at* _____ propped up against the wall near the bench. The unfinished part is in charcoal, but the first part of the sign is carefully painted in yellow and orange. The large yellow sunbeams coming out of the center look like a work of art. Wow, is it a strange coincidence that the ball just fell off the bench and started bouncing around? It creeps me out. I feel my dad's presence still here in this house. I don't dare go down those stairs. I close the door and slide the latch to lock it. I return to the couch and lie down, straining to hear anything. There is nothing, only silence.

Several days after the funeral, the incessant drizzle of winter returns to Wallingford, breaking the cold snap we had. My brother Jim drives my dad's car from where it's been sitting in the motel parking lot in Redding. Shortly after the funeral I recall my mother and Jim discussing selling the car. In a week, it is gone. About this same time, I announce to my mother that I will not accept the hardship discharge. There is not a lot of surprise on her face and, making her

93

usual response to upsetting news, she walks away to her bedroom to smoke her cigarettes. Later, I told Rosanne. She just threw up her hands, as if giving up on me. I imagined her thoughts—*You blew your first chance, now you're blowing your second chance*—so I figured we probably wouldn't be talking anymore. From my perspective, it seemed like a mutual agreement, since I knew where I was going and what I'd be facing. At that time, the Marines were getting massacred in Vietnam in the hundreds every week, as were Army personnel, but the Marines were taking an inordinate number of casualties.

The military provided me with a round-trip plane ticket to southern California and so when my emergency leave was up in late October, I returned. I thought about what was to come: *I made it through boot camp and guess what the prize is—Vietnam.* Everyone knew that my eighteenth birthday was coming up, the first week of December. According to the Geneva Convention, the military would not allow ground troops under the age of eighteen; they were shipping you out on your eighteenth birthday, however. So I believed that would be the date I would ship out to Vietnam.

Prior to shipping out, Marines stay with their staging battalion, receiving medical and dental checkups and any vaccinations they may need. There are training exercises on live fire to familiarize you with your weapon and any other weapon you might use in the jungle, as well as mortars and radio operations. My staging battalion had already started their training when I arrived back at Camp Pendleton, so they put me into a temporary transitory duty: cleaning, swabbing, and maintenance of the barracks and grounds. After a week of that, they asked me if I'd like to go to battle tank school for M48A3 tanks—tanks that weighed seventy-eight tons. I didn't know they were using tanks in Vietnam, but found out later they used them in a limited fashion. Tank school was described to me as like going to the Holiday Inn in Hawaii. You were at Camp Del Mar, which is just north of San Diego, right on the beach. The barracks were nice and the food was great.

I agreed, even though I knew that I would revert back to infantry status and not be driving tanks in Vietnam. We first trained on simulators and then actually drove a tank. I learned how to fire the 90 mm weapon. At first, I thought it would be nice to be in a tank in Vietnam, riding around in a bulletproof vehicle; you could crawl into the hatch, lock it up tight, and you might feel safe. Except then I learned that tanks were being routinely devastated by large anti-tank mines hidden on trails and dirt roads, which the enemy had easy access to.

After four weeks in tank school, I received another week of field training with a .50-caliber machine gun. This was also a big weapon, mostly used on helicopters, tanks, and amphibious tractors. Most infantrymen were unfamiliar with it. I learned to change the barrels and set the headspace on this gigantic weapon, thinking I'd probably never use or even encounter them once I got to Vietnam.

Instead of going to Vietnam the day I turned eighteen, in the middle of December the Duty NCO notifies me that the camp will effectively shut down for fifteen days and most of us will be on a ten-day leave, going home for Christmas. *Just be back by January 1st for staging battalion, because then you're headed to Vietnam.* I don't want to spend ten days of leave at the base or just head into San Diego to hang out. The Marines don't offer me travel fare or anything. I thought about calling my mom. At first, I decide I'm not going to waste a dime for a phone call. A day goes by, however, and I go ahead and called her collect, wondering if the phone is working at the house or if she would even answer. She accepts my collect call and I let her know that I have ten days leave and plan to travel to Seattle for Christmas. She said *Great*, but there is no offer of a plane or bus ticket home.

I am on my own with eight dollars in my pocket. It's only a month and half since my father died. My brothers have good paying jobs at the post office and at Boeing; they are not unemployed, or sitting out the winter starving like my dad. But there is no offer from them, and I am not about to ask for help.

I talk with one of the guys in the barracks from Northern California and he tells me about a way he's able to get home without buying a full bus ticket:

First, wear your uniform. Second, get on a milk run bus, not express, buy a one-dollar ticket to the next town and hope that you get an old guy as your driver, with a crew-cut and a Death before Dishonor *tattoo, probably a Marine from WWII. Third, when you stop at the next towns up the road, pretend you are asleep or go to the bathroom. You might get kicked off, though, as I have a few times, but just buy another one-dollar ticket and get back on the bus. You might make it all the way up the coast from San Diego to Los Angeles, Ventura, Oxnard, Pismo Beach, to Monterey.*

I have twelve dollars now, which is a lot of money for the day, but still not enough to buy a bus ticket to Seattle. I borrow twelve dollars from the other guys at the barracks, so I figure that I can get as far as Redding or Medford, Oregon. Assuming I don't eat.

So I buy my dollar ticket and hop on the bus traveling north to Ventura. Each stop, I pretend to be asleep and no one bothers me. The bus takes forever, it seems, as we roll through San Luis Obispo, Pismo Beach, and Monterey. Shortly north of Santa Cruz, I am kicked off the bus in a remote area. It is Christmas Eve, about three o'clock in the afternoon. I see a sign near a gas station pointing in the direction of Highway 17 and San Jose.

Somehow I end up on Highway 9 instead, which leads into the Coastal Range. As I walk alone, without a house in sight, middle of nowhere, in my Marine Corps uniform, a Ford station wagon, junker of a car, full of hippies, pulls over to the shoulder of the highway. I have not seen a hippie before; at this time, they were only in the San Francisco area and the movement had not spread throughout the United States. I was familiar with beatniks and 'fringies', coffee house-type people, but this group did not look anything like them.

They are heading to a party at a cabin in the moutains, and can give me a lift. I look at them and think, *How strange. What a contrast. Here I am with my duffle bag, wearing spit polished shoes, a high and tight Marine Corps haircut, in uniform and they are dressed in bell-bottom pants and tie-dyed shirts.* I find it unusual that a group of five young adults are riding together—not a nuclear family with a husband, wife, and children. There are three girls and two guys packed into this station wagon, with a guitar case tied to the top of the car. It's Christmas Eve and with no other options, I say *Sure* and hop in, smashed between two girls. It's not all that bad. They have a transistor radio blaring some unfamiliar rock music, so there isn't much talk. They ask if I have a coat, telling me it gets real cold at night, and that I'll need one. After a short drive, they drop me off at a side road. They're going to some remote area in the mountains and tell me that there's a small town two or three miles down the road called Ben Lomond.

It's dark and I walk on the side of the highway. With the cold weather there's ice fog, making it hard to see anything. Finally, I see some lights and a sign: *Ben Lomond, Population 750.* There is a parking lot with a hardware store, tavern, and donut shop, but the stores are all buttoned up for the night. I see a phone booth, so I call my mother collect and she accepts. I tell her that I'm still working my way up to Seattle, that I'm running out of money and will be hitchhiking the rest of the way.

The temperature continues to drop and I need to find somewhere to stay for the night. I don't have a jacket or gloves, and I start to shiver. I've got to get somewhere warm. I scope out the parking lot and see that there is a large charitable donation box with a domed top about the size of a small shed. I walk over to the box and reach down, feeling clothes about halfway up the side of the box. I reach in deeper, finally getting my shoulders through the opening, thinking I can find a coat. I scoot into the box, landing with a soft thud. I burrow under the clothes, curled up, trying to keep warm in my weird nightly accommodation. It's very dark.

Christmas Eve. I think about last year, going to the Christmas ball at the Olympic Hotel and the trees decorated with colored lights and glass balls. The soft light of the crystal chandeliers hanging from the ceiling. Everyone dressed to the nines in their suits and formal gowns. Now, here I am in a donation box on one of the coldest nights, in the middle of nowhere, and I won't be home for Christmas. All I want is to stop shivering.

At first light, about eight o'clock in the morning, I sort through the clothes to find a jacket or something warm to wear, and score a plaid wool Pendleton shirt, jacket, and goofy knit hat with tassels hanging down from the ear flaps. I change out of my uniform, keeping my warm winter uniform pants on, and stuff the other clothes into my duffle bag. I try every which way to make it out of the box, scrambling around, and in the process tip the box over on its side. Finally, I manage to squeeze through the bin door and crawl out onto the parking lot. The stores are still not open. It's Christmas.

I stroll down the street looking into the store windows and come across the donut shop. It's always the donut shop that's open, even on Christmas. I see a guy sweeping the floor and knock on the door.

He props the door open slightly.

"We're not open yet."

"I know how to clean stuff really well. I've got lots of experience sweeping, scrubbing, swabbing, and buffing from my job at a gas station in Seattle."

He checks out my strange clothes: half uniform, half civilian.

"Are you in the military?"

"Yes, sir, I'm in the Marine Corps and trying to make my way from Camp Pendleton to Seattle for Christmas. I'm on leave."

"Yeah, I was in the Navy, in Korea."

He looks me up and down again.

"Well, I have these pallet grates with a lot of grease on them, a fire hazard. OK, come on in."

He hands me an apron and gives me a wire brush. I go to work cleaning the grates. I try not to get the grease on my uniform pants, but they're starting to look really bad. The Navy vet comes back and tells me that the baker is due to start work soon to make the fresh donuts for the day, so that's all the cleaning help he'll need.

"There's day old donuts in boxes in the back, which we sell for half price. Go ahead and take a box of donuts and here, take this. Good luck Marine."

He hands me a $5 bill, which is a lot of money. I thank him and head out the door, happily biting into a day old donut that tastes like the best meal I've had in a week.

On the highway again, I'm offered a ride to San Francisco by a family that is headed in that direction for their Christmas celebration. They drop me near a bus station in South San Francisco and I buy a ticket to Medford, Oregon on December 26th. I am kicked off the bus again after a stop in Medford. I ask the bus driver if I can buy a ticket to Portland. The answer is *No*—so I wait for another bus, which comes in later that night, and purchase a ticket to Portland.

We stop in Salem for a bite to eat. When it is time to leave the restaurant and get back on the bus, I'm still waiting for the bill. The waitress has disappeared into the kitchen. I'm afraid that I'll miss the bus. I'm five feet from the door and there are only one or two people in the place. I don't think about it very long, just walk out. This is the first crime I ever committed. It's a big crime to me, and I wonder if the seeds are sown for a possible future of criminal activity. What is surprising to me is that a lightning bolt doesn't strike me, or that nobody ran me over with a car. I expect immediate retribution, but there is none. I wish I would have ordered a bigger meal.

I reach Portland on December 27th at four o'clock in the morning. I sleep in the station for a few hours, then make my way across Burnside Bridge onto Highway 99. I hitch a ride with a traveling salesman who gives me a lift all the way to downtown Seattle. I'm local now and call my mother to let her know I made it to Seattle. My brother Jerry, a mailman, always gets off work at one or two o'clock, so he drives downtown and picks me up. Back at the house, finally, I find my mother has cooked a full meal: fried hamburger, mashed potatoes, and creamed corn. This is a big meal at my house—*special*.

A few days later, I'm wondering how in the heck I'll get back to Camp Pendleton. I spend a dreary, rain-soaked day walking. Where to—I have no idea. I begin around eight o'clock in the morning by walking around Green Lake, stopping on Aurora Avenue for breakfast at the Twin Teepees. With my dad's car sold and the Corvair Monza gifted to my best friend, I have no car, no battering ram, and no weapon to blow me and Adamson to smithereens. I continue to walk about eighty blocks up Aurora with no plan for where I'm heading. For a moment, I contemplate leaving the Marines. What if I did? What would I do, go back to high school—back to Wallingford, St. Benedict's, and my medieval thoughts about Pinky? *You couldn't even make it through high school and now let's quit this too?* No, it's not going to happen. I'm not quitting again. I still need to be far, far away. I think about the funeral and Dan Adamson playing the organ and how I'd told my dad what happened and my dad saying he'd look into it. Maybe he did, and he was coming to my boot camp graduation to tell me what he was going to do. Maybe he knew more than I thought he knew, before I ever told him, and he'd never done anything. *But why now?*

What now? Where am I walking to? It's late afternoon, darkness closes in and I'm soaked to the gills. I have walked all the way up Aurora to Shoreline at 185th and Aurora, several miles away from the Twin Teepees. Maybe I'll walk back down through Lake City by

Rosanne's house. She would be at school today, in her senior year at Blanchet, and going to college next year. She has a future.

Then I hear the sound. Instantly, I recognize it as a muscle car revving up.

I slowly saunter over to the side entrance of a huge new car lot with the sign *Olson's Oldsmobile Dealership* atop the sales building. Oldsmobiles were known to be driven by old people, but now they had joined the muscle car craze with a new model, the Oldsmobile 442. One 4 stood for *four speed,* the next four stood for *four-barrel carburetor,* and the two stood for *dual exhaust.* At the back of the dealership, there it is, the brand new Olds 442, a monster idling, door open, keys in the ignition. It's sitting ready to enter the service bay. Like a race horse with its power harnessed as it's corralled into the starting gate, it's a black behemoth, dual exhaust pipes rumbling, and even KJR radio with Pat O'Day playing inside the car. Door open—keys in the ignition—engine running, ready to go. I creep closer, and closer. The service bay door suddenly bursts open. The technician walks right up to me but then passes without hesitation and disappears into the dealership. No one but me and the black monster, within arm's length.

I'm not sure what possesses me, my mind in a fog, adrenalin in high gear as I hop in, and rev the engine of that black bomb, screeching tires out of the parking lot, flying down Aurora headed to Greenwood. I race to the Sears parking lot less than a mile south on Aurora, leave the car, and run full speed through the Sears store out onto 165th and Aurora and jump on a bus. *What have I done?* I've never shoplifted anything in my life—except for that two-dollar meal I skipped out on—and now I decide to steal a 4,000 lb. car worth $3,000. *Why not go big?*

Two, three days go by and I wonder if the 442 is still in the Sears parking lot. I'm not doing anything except lying on the couch listening to my mother's sobs in the bedroom. The dark, dreary rain outside matches the furnishings in our rental. I decide to jump on a bus heading north on Aurora, and I get off across the street from the Sears parking lot. I walk around the block and check my surroundings to make sure no one is watching me. It's late at night, between 10 p.m. and midnight. *Yep, it's still there, sitting in the same spot that I left it.* I unlock the door, jump in, and turn the key. I have no idea where I'm going or what I'm doing. I end up parking it at the top of the hill between Corliss and Sunnyside on 43rd Street, pointing toward the driveway where I know Pinky will be backing out at 7:45 in the morning. A great spot.

The next few nights, I walk from my house to where the car is parked, start it up and drive slowly around the block, and park it again. Then I start it up again, rev it up, and take off down the two little hills in first gear. This time, I'm not just doing 35 mph when I pass Pinky's driveway, I'm doing 40 to 45 in a giant bomb. I'm surprised that I find myself sitting in a stolen car. I get out of the car and go home, wondering what to do.

The next morning, I get up, walk over to the car, get in and slowly, deliberately drive it by Pinky's driveway. I turn onto 45th Street, find my way onto Densmore Avenue, and park right in front of the Seattle Police Department's Wallingford Precinct. I walk into the station, hold my hands out palms up, so they can handcuff me.

"See that car out there?"

The front desk police officer looks up. "Oh, nice car."

"No, no, no, I stole that car from Olson's Oldsmobile seven nights ago. Arrest me."

I get booked into the King County jail and, since I had just turned eighteen that month, I stand before the magistrate the next morning as an adult. My mother had somehow gotten me a court-ordered defense lawyer. He tells me, *We're going to get you out. Your mother and brother are here and you'll get out on personal recognizance.* My family is ready to disown me. And soon I get exactly one visitor: Father Crock. *I'm here to deliver a message to you, from Rosanne's family. You are never to contact her or the family ever again.* What? No, *'bless you my child'?*

At my hearing, the judge says: *I want to remand you to a trial in March. I understand that you are in the military and you will return in March. I would release you on personal recognizance, with no bail. We have a letter here that states you are not at risk of evading, no criminal history. However, the U.S. Military has placed a hold on you, so you will have to remain in the King County jail until your trial date in March.* So I stayed in the King County jail from January 3rd to March 12th.

March 12th comes. The public defender tells me that my mother and brother are waiting in the hallway to pick me up. The judge gives me a deferred prosecution: if I stay out of trouble for a year, this will be wiped from my record. *I don't think I'm your major problem, however. Your major problem is those two military policeman waiting at the doorway who are ready to take you into custody.*

The court has notice from the U.S. Marine Corps that I am now listed as a deserter and am on unauthorized absence without leave, *AWOL*. The two MPs are here to serve me papers and place a military hold on me. The judge warns me that they are going to take me to Bremerton to the Marine Corps brig, a military version of jail.

I walk out of the courtroom and into the foyer. My mother and brother are sitting on a bench, and they seem confused about my situation. It becomes clear to them as the two MPs handcuff me and throw me in the back of a vehicle. They take me to what is called a *red line brig*, a Marine prison a lot like Devil's Island, a torture chamber where I'm beaten to a pulp.

Within days, I am escorted in Marine Corps custody and flown back to Camp Pendleton. I learn a whole new meaning of double jeopardy. Upon my arrival, I am brought before a special court-martial that includes a captain, a major, and a gunnery sergeant. They charge me with absence without leave for the time I was in jail in Seattle. I receive a sentence of six months of hard labor, six months' forfeiture of pay, and a dishonorable discharge from the Marine Corps.

I soon find out what hard labor means. The brig is actually a group of tents within Camp Pendleton, but out near the desert sagebrush. Dump trucks deliver multiple loads of large boulders piled high, and each of us have a sledgehammer. We spend all day in the sun making large boulders into small boulders for no particular reason, that's just what hard labor is in military prison. We're humping big poles and digging ditches. We're thrown into pits for physical punishment or they put these fire hoses on us, and we're ordered to do endless push-ups and sit-ups.

Within a week, fellow prisoners ask what my MOS is; that's short for Military Occupational Specialty. I tell them I'm a grunt, O311, Infantry. They all claim that I'm not going to be here very much longer. *The Marine Corps ain't going to let you go, they need you.*

About a week later, the MPs come and take me to the same Quonset hut where I was court-martialed. The same cast of characters is there and they inform me that they've decided an appeal in my favor. *We're rescinding dishonorable discharge, rescinding forfeiture of your pay, rescinding your six months of hard labor, and returning you to full active duty with full rank of private first class. Here are your papers, sign here.* At the bottom of the papers are a set of official orders: ten days leave to your hometown; return to active duty; report for staging preparation for your next duty station, Western Pacific ground forces, Republic of Vietnam, First Marine Division; assignment, rifleman. The major said, *We'll pay for your airline ticket home and back, and by the way, don't even think about not showing up for active duty or we'll have you shot for desertion during wartime.*

So I fly back to Seattle, home to my mother's. She and my brothers have nothing much to say to me, the *non-emotion emotion.* So I'm sitting around the house and five days, six days, seven days, eight days go by. The only place I go is to church on Sunday and there is Dan Adamson still playing the organ. It's now Monday, late April, and my high school friends are seniors, getting ready for graduation. I think about Gail, always involved in so many things at high school: Girls Club president, student of the month, Chanters chorale group. Always in our high school paper for some award or achievement.

It's the day before I'm scheduled to leave and I decide to head over to Food Giant and pick up a Coke. There she is, walking into the store. None other than Gail Gibson. I remember that if she was by herself, chances were she was going directly to the freezer section to pick out a Nutty Buddy, a favorite ice cream treat. Today I notice she doesn't have a basket and she's not with her mother, so I know where she's headed. I follow her into the store and sneak around the back way to the ice cream section so she doesn't see me. I'm standing there with my arms folded as she walks up and reaches in for the Nutty Buddy. She knows that I am still in the Marines, and she may have heard rumors that I would be taking the hardship discharge and go to college on my dad's social security. By this time, I had earned my GED, so it was possible that I could apply to a junior college.

"Well, hi. What have you been up to since your dad's funeral?"

103

Momentarily, I think about jail time and the brig.

"You don't want to know."

Together we go to the counter, pay for the ice cream, and I walk her back to her house. She is acting very pleasant to me.

"What's going on at Lincoln?"

"We're getting fitted for our caps and gowns next week. The guys are wearing black, but the girls are baby blue. You won't believe it but there's such a large graduating class it's going to be in the Coliseum at the Seattle Center."

"Say, if I can get a hold of my brother's car—would you like to go out to dinner tonight?"

She said yes, so I pick her up and we go to a Chinese restaurant just north of the Ballard Bridge called Art Louie's. We talk about music, the latest songs, and nothing is mentioned about the Marines or *Adamson*. I'm starting to feel more certain that maybe she really didn't know, that Adamson never talked to her. After dinner, we drive up to Magnolia bluffs to a park, not to neck or anything, just to watch the city lights and listen to songs on the radio. Back in the Wallingford district, we park in front of her house and talk some more.

"What's up?"

"Well, I got my orders and I'm heading back to Camp Pendleton tomorrow morning."

"Where are you going from there?"

"Vietnam. I'll be heading there in a week or two."

We mutually agree to write each other, Gail going off to the University of Washington, me to the jungles of Vietnam. I ask her, *when you write, please let me know about graduation and how college goes and what sorority you join, things like that.*

The next morning, my brother and mother drive me to the airport. There is just a simple good-bye. At this time, my impression is they are happy to see me go. It reminds me of when I was in boot camp; I imagined my mom and dad sitting around the kitchen table saying, *My God, did we dodge a bullet. He's going to Vietnam and he'll probably be dead in a week, a month, or a year, and we won't have to dredge up this issue with Adamson.* This was my impression of how they were thinking.

CHAPTER 12

INTO THE BARREL

May 1967

It is now eight or ten hours into the flight across the vast ocean below me. As I gaze out the window, daybreak reveals the utter openness of the water. No islands visible, no mountains, landscape, or hints of civilization. Just the sea and the horizon. With every passing hour, I am closer to the inevitable: Vietnam.

I feel I am ready. I better be ready or I'll be dead sooner rather than later. At this point in my short life's journey, I am fairly certain it isn't going to be if, but *when*. There isn't much thought about any return flight after a thirteen-month tour in Vietnam. My immediate goal is surviving my first firefight and possibly gaining enough experience to last through the current calendar year.

I reflect on when my metamorphosis took place and my memory is vague. But I do know it was pronounced and permanent.

After refuelling on the tiny coral atoll known as Wake Island, our last leg of the journey across the Pacific deposits me and 160 mutually terrified souls on the tarmac of a gigantic military complex referred to as Danang Airbase, Republic of Vietnam. First, we stand in the wake of the jet exhaust, and it's mixed with a humid mist from the jungle carrying with it smells I would not now, or ever, refer to as exotic. To the west, my eyes gaze for the first time on a rich tropical scene. Myriad shades of green in the distance complement a serene group of points and islands just off the eastern shoreline.

But more remarkable is my next visual of *THE NAM*. Some groups of military look just like me—eighteen years old, in combat gear less any weaponry; we stand out as a confused mob. Then the opposite—*real* combat infantry, eighteen, nineteen, twenty years old in stature and physique. But no other similarities. The *real* grunts are armed to the teeth. They look as though they had been thrown into a giant washing machine that contained mud, dirt, blood, sweat, and whatever, then been turned on to tumble for thirteen months. Jungle boots that had been green and black were now bleached white, tan, and brown by the sun, swamps, rain, and mud of Vietnam.

More striking are their helmets and flak jackets, adorned with graffiti, slogans, names of girls, biblical phrases, you name it, from the lengthy to just a simple word or two. *Fuck it. Born to kill, born to die. Chi-town. Mo-town, Southie.* Then I notice their faces. They don't look at us, they look through us.

One of them approaches, walking past me, stops, turns around. He leans forward with a menacing stature, his M16 pointing vaguely in my direction. I'm uneasy with his closeness, then I hear him utter, barely above a whisper, "You poor fucks, you have no idea."

Shortly after that, another grunt with a different personality, seemingly *happy go lucky*, walks by and lets out a high-pitched, insane laugh, like out of a horror movie.

"Rule number one—remember this—you know that rule."

We look at each other, shrug our shoulders, and think, *what's rule number one?*

He shouts, "Kill 'em all and let God sort them out."

I imagine if they dare to sit down, they will all crumble into a pile of dust. I never, ever, in my life have seen such utter fatigue. The group closest to me has just exited a Marine CH-46 Sea Knight Helicopter. After they pass by me, there are two door gunners walking by. They have an almost *stateside* look about them, wearing their flight gear and com helmets, and then I see the pilots with the same attire, so different from the ragged, dirty, sweaty grunts I had just seen. Airbase personnel rush into the open back of the chopper and exit a short time later, each struggling to drag what I soon come to know is a body bag. One after another, uniformly laid side by side, neatly on the edge of the tarmac. At that moment I wonder how long it will be before I take my place in my own rubber deathbed.

I wonder if the grunts I'd seen shuffle by were in the same unit, or squad, and if they even knew the guys in the body bags, or if death was just hitching a ride.

Several hours of sitting around waiting for who knows what gives me time to reflect back, which I am doing more frequently. I think about the start of my fledgling life living in the idyllic Wallingford district, with Green Lake to fish in, the free zoo, the Wallingford Boys Club, Woodland Park, and trails to ride my bike. I had pretty good ideas about making my way as a young boy—mowing lawns, making sure I was not going to be anything like my brothers. Then the down bound turn of events. *Oh to be Adamson's boy*. Was I really going to blame this latest turn of events—ending up in Vietnam—on a dreary Catholic grade school in Wallingford?

Maybe this theme is just the same theme of the war I am about to engage in. Which war I am not at all sure, but I fear I will not be fighting the Viet Cong as much as I will be fighting myself, my past, Wallingford, St. Benedict's, till the end of my days.

November 1967

As May, June, July, August, September, and October pass, I reward myself by printing each month on my helmet, beginning at the front and continuing up over the top. A line begins to form, and if by chance I am still around to write the last months, the line will hopefully end in the back of the helmet as I mark *June* next year and return to the "world." The side of my helmet is emblazoned in a black mark of bravado: *I came, I saw, I conquered*. Not long ago, someone remarked, "You should put: I came, I saw, I said fuck it." I had to admit that it was a more appropriate description of our situation lately.

The last six months had revealed a lot to me about the Marine Corps. I'm happy that I have earned the right to be a member of the "Real Marine Corps," what would much later, and always thereafter, be referred to by us survivors as the "Old Corps." I witness, firsthand, the absolute heroism of eighteen year olds performing in the midst of the unimaginable. Despite this, I have trouble understanding what the heroism and the suffering are for. A definitive objective, let alone a sense of accomplishment, is certainly lacking.

What had become clear to me recently was that we were fighting bravely for a cause, all right. Not at all the same cause that the "management"—captain and above—seemed to be professing. No, we are fighting for each other. Each and every miserable, unfortunate soul, soaked to the core, starving, homesick, and thirsty. Hoping against hope that someone gives a shit about us somewhere in this vast world.

One thing is certainly clear to the low-level grunts: we sure as hell aren't going to find any sympathy in this little corner of the world. We were low on ammunition, low on drinking water, and restricted to only two C-ration meals a day.

When I first arrived in my unit, the platoon sergeant asked, *What the hell are you wearing stateside leather boots for?* My response was, *They told me in Da Nang that they were out of jungle boots.* He then asked me what size boot I wear. I said size 9 and he threw me a pair of size 12, certainly in "used condition. " He said it wouldn't be long and I'd have my pair of 9s—implying there would soon be more dead Marines. I stuffed the too-big jungle boots with toilet paper; I felt like the cartoon figure, Goofy, walking around with these huge boots. Sadly, no more than a week went by when I found myself stripping size 9 boots off of a corpse hanging out the side of a medevac chopper.

In early November, someone confirms the actual day of the month. I don't establish whether the individual who came to that conclusion took into account that we are way west of the International Dateline, so Monday would really be Sunday back in the "world."

It doesn't matter much. What is announced to all is that it's November 10th, 1967. Every one of us knows what this means. The Marine Corps always makes a very big deal about the date. It's the commemoration of an event which took place in a certain drinking establishment in Philadelphia called Tun Tavern, where on November 10th, 1775 the United States Marines were created. On that date, wherever Marines gather, be it in dress blues at a formal ballroom in Washington DC, or a foxhole in some godforsaken war, the youngest and oldest Marines in the unit gather around with the rest, and ceremoniously "cut" the Marine Corps birthday cake.

I can't foresee how this is going to happen where we are. I know we don't have a cook, or anything to cook if we did. Additionally, it would be suicide for a group of Marines to stand around above ground. We're often told, *Spread out, one round will get you all.* As dusk approaches, I am informed that I am, indeed, the youngest Marine in the unit. And someone has also located the oldest: an *ancient* twenty-four-year-old gunnery sergeant. Wow. In Vietnam, that is old, that is really old!

It is announced that we are going to assemble in the command bunker shortly after dark. It seems reasonable, as the bunker is really an underground cave, covered with sandbags. More like a giant gopher hole. As we begin to gather around two dimly lit candles, I watch the Marines make their way into the bunker. Faces not really in tune with the rest of their anatomy. A look that requires no explanation. These are eighteen and nineteen-year-olds who have clearly seen more than any human can take.

There are now ten to twelve of us packed around the candle. The gunnery sergeant and the recently promoted *Corporal* O'Connor kneel around what is presented as the Marine Corps birthday cake. Someone had decided to open a can of C-rations and produced a small, round piece of pound cake. In the middle is a melted bead of wax from candle drippings and a small piece of shoelace protruding from the wax. As the shoelace is lit, a feeble attempt to spontaneously sing the "Marine Corps Hymn" is made. Somewhere in the back of the bunker comes a voice as pure as a choirboy. Others can only dribble out a few words through their lit cigarettes. I start out singing robustly, but soon the chorus fades off into a hauntingly sad refrain. The gunnery sergeant and I then pull out our bayonets, and I lean over to cut the cake.

I look around at our tiny little group and, at that moment, I am the proudest of any time in my Marine Corps career. I am proud of our filthy, dirt-encrusted flak jackets, some adorned with their own personal motto, some just a sad phrase or a description of their life in the jungle. I am proud of our courage. I am proud that we are ready to die for each other at a moment's notice. I am proud of these men. The real Marines.

And at the same time, from my vantage point, I begin to constantly resent those *in the rear with the gear.* Those who are deciding whether to have strawberry ice cream or chocolate cake for their dessert.

It don't mean nothin', I'd take my stand with these guys any day. I am proud to be here. Fuck it. We are United States Marines, and we can take whatever they throw at us. It was in that little underground bunker, November 10th, 1967, that I was privileged to be a member of what would become legend: a member of the "Old Corps."

June 1968

Thirteen months now. Where'd it go? Thirteen months now, I don't know. Oh yes, I do know. It went nowhere. It is right here with me as I "hump" the three miles to the river, where I will catch a Sampan, which will mark the beginning of my trek back to the "world." As I carefully print *June* on the last space at the bottom, back of my helmet, I realize that any hope of leaving Vietnam behind me is nothing more than wishful thinking. My predicament is, what to do to suppress it? Which ones do I bury in my soul so deep they cannot detonate at some inappropriate moment? What scenes do I try to make sense of? Which ones will my blockers be able to keep out? What about the suffering, dying, and death of most of the people I came across? Was it to be a constant question, *why am I still alive and they are not?*

Deep and haunting thoughts for a nineteen-year-old kid. A nineteen-year-old kid in a forty-year-old mind. If I look like I feel, then I sure won't be getting any "dates" when I return to the "world." Gnawing remnants of recent gunshot and shrapnel wounds are a constant physical reminder of the past thirteen months. Reminders of bullets that wounded instead of killed. The difference between breathing in and out, or ending up at graves and registration (the mortuary) is always a difference of inches.

And as I trek closer to Da Nang airbase, I don't have to think back on the events of the last year. They are riding with me where I know they will remain. From the first death, to the last, they will forever be my constant companion.

CHAPTER 13

ARE YOU EXPERIENCED?

I look forward to driving the car that my mother and brother picked out for me and bought with a down payment from my military pay saved over the last thirteen months: a yellow '66 GTO with black bucket seats. I envision what it's like back home, still the same as in the fifties: men in their suit pants, dress shirts, and wing tips mowing the lawn, one car in the driveway, and women are the homemakers. I know there will be some slight changes: more muscle cars on the market, the evolution of exciting music like the Beatles and the Rolling Stones, but people dressed pretty much the same as when I left. I'd be wearing the same wardrobe if I hadn't given all my clothes away.

I'm not worried about leaving the Combined Action Platoon (CAP) unit behind because of Gail's letters this spring. She's been upbeat about her work on the Robert F. Kennedy presidential campaign at the University of Washington. RFK had done well in the election primaries and was headed to California, where he is even more popular. When I wrote back and asked her what she thought he would do about Vietnam if he won the election, she replied that everybody thinks he will win in a landslide—especially the young people—and they believe that five minutes after the election, *You'll all be coming home.* That seems a little naïve to me, but we heard rumors starting to spread among grunts about going home by Christmas, if Kennedy won. There's real hope that he could extricate us from Vietnam.

Making my way to the rear in Da Nang, I need to register for my transfer home. Before I leave on my trek, I give away some of my prized possessions that I had squirreled away to the remaining Marines in my CAP unit. It's been calm the past two weeks in the area because lots of air strikes are going on and few combat incidents, so I have a bit of a stock pile. I give away my carefully guarded ammunition, magazines, extra fragmentation grenades (always in short supply), blasting caps, detonation cord—all essential during operations and firefights. I have a couple of rolls of Polaroid black and white film, five pictures to a case, which I very carefully guarded so that I could take flicks to send back home. I also have two or three cans of peaches and pound cake from my C-rations, and a few cans of fruit cocktail and beef ravioli that Gail had sent me. I part with these as well.

There were fifteen Marines to start with in my CAP unit but now we have dwindled to seven due to casualties. I wonder who else will soon be dead. As I start down the trail, I hear their parting words— *you'll be back.*

There are more than a few stories of disillusioned Marines who went home at the end of their tour and didn't fit into society, or felt they needed to get back to the jungle to help their buddies, and returned for another tour. I feel I'm different; I'm going back to the Wallingford district where people know me and I have family and friends—people will welcome me back with open arms. Dan Adamson is certainly in prison or dead at the hands of some victim. One of the members of my CAP unit had been back home to Boston; there was nothing wrong there, or in New York, but it was while he was at the LA airport that people became hostile. He warned me: *Your people aren't going to want to hear anything you have to say. They'll be looking at you like you're extremely strange; you'll be shunned and met with indifference. Seattle is probably full of hippies, so look out.* I took all this with a grain of salt.

I walk through *Indian Country* and *Dodge City*, named by the Marines because of their shoot-'em-up characteristics. This area, thirty to forty miles from Da Nang, is familiar ground for the Marines. I catch a ride in a sampan, a flat-bottomed wooden boat used for transportation and fishing on the rivers. They drop me off by a blownup bridge, where I spend the night with Korean Marines.

The next day, I crawl back up the river bank to the main road and jump on the back of a rickety old truck traveling down a bumpy Highway 1 to the 2nd Combined Action Group headquarters in Da Nang. This is a huge installation built in the rear: it's more like a city, with a PX, a runway, F-4 Phantom attack jets, Huey gunships, and medevac choppers.

I am taken back by seeing all of this after seeing only jungle for thirteen months. The first evening, I sleep in a "Conex" box similar to a large metal storage container, which is one of many lined up on the runway for transitory personnel who were used to sleeping in the jungle. They are sand bagged and seem to be a better choice than a tent or Quonset hut, with the chance of incoming rockets. The next morning, I walk to the headquarters of the 2nd Combined Action Group, 3rd Marine Amphibious Force, which was the parent organization that ran the various CAP units. I learn that I'm not going to be processed until the next day, however, so I hang out all day in the supply hooch because it is air-conditioned. It has been over a year since I have felt any type of cool air.

I take off my flak jacket, helmet, M16, .45-caliber pistol, and cartridge belt and lay them on the table, emptying the chambers, placing the magazine with the rounds in a metal bin. The supply people are very safety conscious and nervous around grunts who carry an automatic weapon with *one in the chamber*. But for us, this is what we are used to. The supply sergeant is wearing a pressed uniform with spit-polished jungle boots, bright green with black leather. My canvas boots are pale brown and falling apart from exposure to the elements in the jungle.

"What CAP unit are you with?"

"CAP ███████, or what's left of it."

"Oh boy, no thanks," was his reply." "I'm on my second tour and I'll tell you, it's gravy. I'm making good combat pay, sixty-five dollars a month, all tax free. I've been promoted to sergeant, get three meals a day, have access to a Jeep, live in air-conditioned barracks, and watch movies at night. How long have you been here?"

"Thirteen months, and no, I'm not coming back."

"You want me to save these for you, just in case? I know some of you guys get attached to your own individual flak jacket and helmet."

I stare at him blankly. *Who is this guy?*

"The reason I'm asking is lately I've seen you guys from CAP units up north say you're not coming back. But then they say *I don't know*. The last guy here, I asked him if he wanted me to keep his flak jacket and helmet in a bin, in the back there. He said *OK*, and sure enough, thirty days went by and he came back and picked up his flak jacket and helmet."

I think about this. An M16 rifle is an M16 is an M16; hand grenades are hand grenades. But your flak jacket and helmet are like your personal moniker, your bumper sticker. My flak jacket still has old, brown blood stains on the shoulders after thirteen months. There are a couple of ripped panels, and shrapnel holes. And my helmet…there is a full stripe right over the top crown of my helmet, starting with *May 1967* to *June 1968*.

Your flak jacket and helmet are like part of your skin, and they define you. Walking behind a grunt, you recognize who he is by reading the sayings on his helmet or flak jacket: *Born to Love, Born to Hate; When I get to heaven, to St. Peter, I will tell, 'one more Marine reporting sir, I've served my time in Hell'*; or *Yea though I walk through the valley of the shadow of death, I will fear no evil, cause I'm the baddest Marine in the valley, I am the meanest fucker in the whole valley, the killer elite.* Or the more pragmatic, *Born To Die.*

The tattered, dirty, sweaty, blood-spattered flak jacket and helmet marked a battle, a fight, and the casualty (or death) of one more Marine in the CAP unit; they were like a history of where we'd been, what we saw, what we experienced. Mine has the distinct reddish dust embedded in every crevice, a sure sign of being *up north*. Another distinct feature appears on both shoulders of the flak jacket: dark stains, yellowish brown puddles long dried and crusted by the tropical sun, a reminder of when the incoming got too close for comfort. The concussion can tear the membranes in your ears, and the damage causes tiny balls of dirty wax balls to gather inside, resembling a small wasp nest. It was a common sight to see grunts with these dried-blood wax stains, like tattoos running from their ears, then down their neck. Eventually, large bubbles of crusted yellow wax, blood, fluid, and dirt protrude like a horror movie.

I feel funny taking my flak jacket and helmet off. More often than not, I slept with my helmet on. Once in a while, I'd take it off for photos that I'd sent to the States, cause with your helmet on, you just looked like every other grunt. I feel naked without them, even though I know I'm safe back *in the rear with the gear.*

"No, you've seen the last of me, I'm not coming back here." In the back of my mind, I think, *I've stretched my luck as far I should go.*

"I think a lot of you will be coming back, and it won't be by choice...." Then he added, "Especially since Kennedy got assassinated."

"Look pal," I replied, "I've been here a long time, but not that long. Kennedy got killed when I was a freshman in high school."

He gives me a look like, *oh shit, you don't know.*

"I mean Robert F. Kennedy."

"What are you talking about?"

"He got assassinated in Los Angeles, week ago. Read it in the *Stars and Stripes* newspaper two days ago."

For us who are out in the "bush," it takes ten to fifteen days for letters to get from the United States, and the last one I got was from the first of June. I didn't know. It's a huge shock for me, but by now, I am stoic—nothing surprises me in my frame of mind. This news ends our conversation and he takes my flak jacket and helmet, tossing them into the bin with three or four others. *He's saving them,* I think, *the guy didn't hear me? I'm not going to be back here.*

And then I experience being in the rear with the gear: there are lights, music playing, and a soft drink machine in the supply depot (and if you put coins in, out comes a can of soda). *Money.* I hadn't seen it for thirteen months. Now, I'm face to face with the culture shock of two different militaries. We always knew the rear in the gear had it pretty good. There might be a few rocket craters in the air strip, but when the medevac helicopter pilots, the gunship pilots, and the F-4 pilots make it back to the base, they have a hamburger, a cold beer, and watch a John Wayne movie. There were two worlds: Two and a half million served in Vietnam, but only a small percentage of those troops were in the northern I-Corps, in combat on a continuous basis. The ones in the rear with the gear were vulnerable, too, and though they might be killed, the chance of it was miniscule compared to the combat troops.

I wait for two days and then board a flight to Okinawa. We don't travel with our unit or platoon, we're just individuals thrown together with strangers on a flight back home: Navy pilots, Air Force mechanics, supply sergeants, and Marine grunts. The contrast on the plane between the Marine grunts and others is stark. Lots of stateside uniforms and spit-polished shoes, but not so with the grunts. The guys in the rear with the gear are laughing and joking around on the plane, whereas the grunts don't look right, like a body in an open casket when the funeral home pastes a smile on the deceased person's face, as if they were glad to be there.

I really stick out on this plane as a grunt. Our CAP unit developed strong bonds; I had developed intense bonds with other eighteen-year-olds, some still alive, and some dead. I feel closer to the people who are dead; I carry each person—their psyche—with me, and each is unique as their fingerprints, or their blood stains on my flak jacket. I would not wish this feeling on anyone.

My hope is that we arrive in Seattle while it's still daylight. The darkness is always my enemy. On the three-hour flight to Okinawa, while using the restroom, I look in the mirror and see a forty-year-old man with a strange stare on his face, and an odd grin. It's like having a "tick" of some sort, and I hope no one else will notice; I need to fix it and pass for normal.

There are other grunts on the flight and I recognize that they are just like me. We are wired in the jungle, far surpassing anybody who is tripping on LSD or is high on cocaine. We are self-wired, oxygenated beyond what any illegal substance could do to you. We never walk on anything like a road or trail, always to the side of it. Any sudden movement—even an insect—would send you closer to your bones than you wanted to be. I need time to practice walking on a sidewalk. Maybe all I need is three days home, a Dick's cheeseburger, and a cold beer. Oh, that's right, I'm not old enough to buy beer, also not old enough to vote. What an irony.

When I arrive in Okinawa for a three-day layover, I learn to fake it. On our twelve-hour flight to the Marine Corps air base in El Toro, California, I observe the guys in their clean-cut uniforms who laugh all the way on the trip, as if everything was a joke. As they disembark the plane, they are kissing the ground and saying things like *God Bless America*. I think, *how phony these REMF's are.*

At El Toro Marine Airbase, an officer greets us and shuttles us off to a secluded area, a debriefing room, where no civilians will see us. We should have been met at the airport by psychiatrists, or sent to a mental ward. If we were, we'd be there for years, or decades.

We are instructed to get rid of any contraband: weapons, ears, bad pictures of what we were up to in Vietnam, etc. I don't have any of these; I was fixated on leaving it all behind. The officer continues with his instructions:

If you are going to San Diego, Lindberg Field, keep your Marine uniform on, you're fine. It's a Navy town and there are Marines all over. If you are going to Chicago, Boston, anywhere in the state of Texas, you're good to go, wear that uniform. You'll probably be mobbed by good ole boys offering to buy you a beer at the VFW hall. If you're going to Alabama, Louisiana, or Mississippi, you'll be greeted as a real hero when you step off that plane. If you're going anywhere on the West Coast, north of San Diego, get that fuckin uniform off. Buy yourself some civilian clothes before you board that bus, and I don't need to tell you why, 'cause you'll find out soon enough."

I don't believe him. I watch as some of the grunts run to the nearest PX store to buy clothes. When I get to the Wallingford district, I'll be running into people I know from my high school of twenty-five hundred people; half of those guys, or probably 90 percent of them, are home on leave or in Vietnam, they just weren't in my unit. I won't be the only one walking around with my uniform on. Guys from Seattle Prep and Blanchet must be in the war, so I won't be alone.

While we are in LAX, I see quite a few people in the Army, Navy, and Marines walking around with their uniforms on. Nobody is yelling at them, giving them the finger, or throwing things at them. But then I start to hear something strange. Some familiar songs are playing from the Rolling Stones, and Peter Paul and Mary, but there is also music that I don't catch, with a lot of long guitar licks. Guys aren't wearing tight, skinny pants with white socks and black loafers; they're dressed in wide, bell-shaped pants that fan out at the bottom. A salesman with a briefcase, dressed in a suit, also has long, bushy sideburns like Elvis Presley; he looks like he needs a haircut.

I catch a flight from LAX to San Francisco, with a two-hour layover before my flight to Seattle. Once in the San Francisco airport, I notice a whole new flavor. People have a lot more hair, and many of the black people have gigantic afros, something I'd never seen before. The girls are wearing full-length hootenanny dresses, like peasant dresses, and as I watch them, I am surprised to notice that they are *unharnessed*.

More bizarre than the dresses, Ho Chi Minh sandals, and multicolored beads are the stares as people pass by. It is the same look that we got from people when we walked into their village in Vietnam with our flak jacket and helmet on, pointing our M16 at someone. I can see hatred in their faces, or if not hatred, certainly indifference.

While at the airport, I call my mother and let her know that my flight will arrive at about five o'clock that afternoon. She says, *Fine, Jerry, Frank, or Jim will pick you up, and I might even come with them.* I wonder what kind of new cars my brothers have by now, and what I'd be riding in after we land in Seattle.

At the Seattle airport, I am ushered off to another secret place by what seems like volunteers handing out programs and taking tickets, not security guards. We are now in a closed off area with seats that the USO set up. Everyone is in military uniform and no one is intermingling with the civilians. When I approach the baggage claim, I can see a couple of groups outside, with placards, heckling a few buses that are waiting to pick up Army personnel and drive them to Fort Lewis. The groups walk up and down, yelling at the buses, not anyone in particular. I think it's weird because the buses are all empty.

Up drives a 1965 Mercury Comet Caliente convertible. It's pretty cool looking, white with red seats, and my brother Frank sitting behind the wheel. He looks normal: short hair and wearing a button down madras shirt with cords. Next to him in the passenger seat there is a woman. I hop over into the back seat without opening the door, just like I did with my Corvair, and throw my duffle bag down and say, *Hit it!* As Frank heads up Aurora Avenue, he introduces the woman next to him as Nancy, *his wife*. I'm thinking, *Well, I know your wife and her name is Donna, and she is short and has black hair.* He was married to her when I left, and it hasn't been that long. *Well, we're not married anymore.* I think, *Jesus, if our dad was alive, we wouldn't be having this conversation.* She seems real nice and keeps asking me if I'm OK, like I have some sort of disease. *I'm fine, so far. I'm fine,* and this is the beginning of my performance.

"All I need is a cold beer and a bologna and cheese sandwich, and if Mother doesn't have it, will you go to Food Giant and buy what I need?"

I pepper Frank with questions about the GTO. He assures me that I'm going to like it, and that he pulled it out of the garage, so it's sitting right out front of the house, waiting for me. It's a beautiful July day in Seattle, sunny and seventy degrees, though I'm cold, riding in the back of the convertible dressed in my short sleeve khaki shirt. I'm used to 100-plus degrees in the jungle.

When the car turns the corner down our street, I can see the taillights of the GTO. As soon as we stop, I jump out of the convertible, going over the fender, and make a beeline for the car. My mother and Jerry are sitting on the porch sipping a cup of coffee. As I stand there looking at the car, my brother Jerry throws me the keys. I put them in my pocket and walk up to the porch to say hi to my mother and brother. My family is very formal and there is no hugging or crying or rejoicing. It appears they are glossing over the past, or maybe they have come to terms with the disgrace I brought upon them after the stolen car incident.

My mother makes me a bologna and cheese sandwich, and she has milk in the house. As I sit at the table eating, she walks over to me, smoking her cigarette, and comes out with her ultimate phrase.

"I'm glad nothing happened to you in Vietnam. Now you need to get on with your life."

My brothers nod in agreement.

Although I knew this would be coming, it sounds like the most bizarre thing coming out of my mother's mouth. The sandwich goes down OK, but the milk does not settle. I end up vomiting in the backyard.

Later that afternoon, my brother Jim, his wife, and their five children, which would grow to eight, come over to say hi. It's odd to see children happy and playing games together. My thoughts turn to the children in Vietnam, at the center of some of the most horrific things I'd ever seen. I mention to everyone how it's so different being around people with "round" eyes again. For the last year, almost everyone else I've seen was Asian; I use the slang word, a *gook*, and my mother gives me a look that says, *That's not proper language.* I think, *you better hold on to your hat Mother, cause in the next thirty days, you'll hear a lot worse.*

As the sun sets, I start getting agitated and anxious. I feel like a vampire, coming alive as darkness arrives, staring out the window, checking for things that move in the night. In the jungle, getting set up before night approached was ingrained in my body's cyclical rhythm. I walk around, sit down, then start to talk and jump up and walk around again, repeating these moves over and over. My mother tells me that I'm making her dizzy, that it looks like I've got the St. Vitus dance. That's what had become of me: jerking, moving around, up, down, part superstition, and part reality. I had gone through such a change in the bush, and as night fell, I noticed that my family had no sense of urgency. My mother wasn't "prepping," my brothers weren't getting their gear ready. I think, *Of course they're not, get a hold of yourself. It's not them, it's you. What the hell are you thinking?* But I can't shake it. *Just give me a few days and I'll just chill out...and be fine.*

As darkness deepens, my mother walks over and turns on a switch that controls a lamp in the living room. I go over and turn the switch off, then turn it on, turn it off again, then on again. My mother walks over and turns on the TV. I follow her and push it off, then pull the knob on, and I repeat this a few more times.

I decide to take a shower, still a strange experience after being in the jungle so long. After ten minutes, the hot water runs out, but I continue to stand there under the shower, in freezing cold water, in a trance. I hear my mother walk by the bathroom door, probably thinking, *Are you even in there?* After I come out of the bathroom, she is gone, down the street to my brother Jerry's house a few doors away. I think she's had enough of my strangeness for one day.

Alone now in the house, I turn off the TV and all the lights. I pace back and forth in the living room, between the front door and the large picture window. Soon, I can see my mother coming up to the front door of the house, so I'm not startled when she walks in; but as she sees my silhouette in the dark, she is stunned and jumps back a step.

"What's the matter?"

"Nothing. Why?"

"Why are all the lights out?"

She walks around the house, turning on the lights.

"Are you OK? *Are you OK?*"

I think, *Yeah, that's just what I do.*

They'd seen enough of me. I grab my car keys, walk out to the curb where my new GTO is still parked, start it up, and sit there with the lights off for several minutes. Things sure have changed around the house. The electricity is on, the heat works, there is more food in the cupboards than there ever was before. My mother told me she was able to get a job at the federal building downtown, and had gotten first priority in being hired because I was serving in Vietnam. The thought crossed my mind, *Gee, I wish she had been in charge of running the family when I was growing up, instead of my dad. She certainly seems more qualified.*

This is the first night of many where I drive all night. I head east out of Seattle across Lake Washington's old floating bridge, up into the foothills. I remember the drive to the barn, riding in Adamson's Borgward, wondering, *where we are going? What will happen? Will I ever make it back home?* I continue up into Snoqualmie Pass, reaching the summit and then down the other side. It's about two o'clock in the morning, and still dark. As I come into the town of Cle Elum, I drive down the main street; the town is lit up, but asleep, and I make a U-turn at the end of the town and drive back to the highway. As I reach North Bend, I pull to the side of the road until I can get the sense that the sun will soon rise over the mountains. As the sun comes up, I *stand down.* I relax and continue my drive across the bridge, back to my house. As I walk in the door, the sun flooding through the windows, my mother—a night owl, and usually not up before noon—comes out of her room.

"What's the matter? *What's the matter?*"

"Nothing."

"Where'd you go?"

"Nowhere, just drove around."

"What do you think of the car?"

"It's fantastic."

After being up all night, I'm tired and I walk over to my bedroom and open the door for the first time since my return. I take off my khaki uniform that I've been wearing for two days, pull out the dresser drawers, and find that they are all empty. Not so much as a t-shirt or pair of shorts. The bed has not been lain on for more than a year, and it has the same sheets on it. The room seems sterile. No Lincoln High School letterman's jacket hanging on the wall, nothing in the closet. It's as if my former life was erased.

The next day, Jerry brings over some civilian clothes, circa 1965, for me to wear. I still need to replace my spit-polished Marine Corps dress shoes, so I drive to the University District in search of my favorite stores, Vons and The Squire Shop. I stock up on V-neck sweaters, button down collar shirts, baby blue cords and floaters, a type of suede high-top shoes. I'm set now and return home, still daylight. I shower, shave and change into my new clothes.

Instead of using our home phone, I walk to Lincoln Pharmacy's phone booth and stick a dime into the phone and call Gail. She seems animated and excited over the phone and agrees to go out to dinner that night. I choose Art Louie's Chinese restaurant, the last place we had dinner the night before I left for Vietnam. In anticipation of the night, I go over in my mind what I need to do to be proper: sit up straight, don't be looking around, pay attention to the person you're talking to, and don't stand up when you start to talk. As we order our meal, my hands are holding onto the seat of the chair as I talk to keep from standing up. Gail pays attention to my eating and observes how my habits have changed, odd and out of character.

"Do you think that I'm acting differently?"

"Some of your personality traits are a little different. You seem to have grown up a lot. I've never seen you eat anything with your hands before, like the way you reached into the bowl of sweet and sour pork in red sauce, picked up a piece, and popped it into your mouth."

She seems happy to see me though, and we talk about the UW, and how she's doing in school. There are no direct questions about what it was like in Vietnam, except about the food. After I drop her off at ten-thirty, I drive to West Seattle and look at the city lights, then over to Queen Anne, down to Wallingford and past Lincoln High School, over to St. Benedict's, around Green Lake, and up to Capitol Hill.

There is a structured routine to my days and nights, now. I drive around all night, and when the sun comes up I head home, take a shower, and crash on my bed. I sleep until afternoon, find something pleasurable to do between five and ten o'clock and then, *the night watch*. Sometimes I drive across the Evergreen floating bridge, to what used to be the Sammamish Slough, now Redmond. I stop the car and wander aimlessly around the park, then sit in my car and listen to the radio, turning it on and off, on and off.

My family starts to see my quirkiness and I hear more talk like, *Glad nothing happened to you over there*, and *You need to get on with your life*. It's not really my choice; I am in the Marine Corps so they will determine where I go and what I do. Other questions come up from friends and family: *What's your next duty station? When will you get your orders?* That week I drive over to Sandpoint Naval Station and check in about my orders: *No word yet.*

As I walk around the Wallingford district to familiar places like Food Giant, Dicks, and Dairy Queen, I run into guys I knew and they look different: long hair, and shirts hanging out of their pants. The following week, I attend Mass at St. Benedict's and I'm hit like a lightning bolt at what I witness. About six or eight guys I know from high school, or even grade school, all with a lot of hair. I wonder how they got out of Vietnam. Looking around the church, I take a poll: none of them went to Vietnam. *Did I miss something here and it's all a big joke?*

Later that week, I look up an old friend, Gregg; he's working for the parks department now, doing maintenance. As I walk up to him, I see this white man's afro, his curly hair sticking out two to three inches on each side. He's wearing a rainbow-colored shirt.

"What happened to the clothes I gave you?"

"They're out of style man, gone."

As we talk, I notice the unfamiliar slang terms he uses: *groovy, wow man*, and other hippie phrases. I ask him about societal changes I've seen, and about the new music. He talks about Vanilla Fudge, Janis Joplin is a big hit, and this black guy from Garfield High School, on the other side of Seattle, is the world's greatest guitar player. You'll recognize it, he says because it's real *psychedelic*. That must have been what I heard at LAX.

I ask him if he knows how many guys from Blanchet or Prep had gone to Vietnam. He doesn't know anyone.

"What about Lincoln, how many guys from Lincoln went to Vietnam?

"You…. No, seriously, there's one guy from Prep, Ted Jacoby, he went to Vietnam, and out of 1400 guys at Lincoln, maybe five. One of them, however, didn't come back. He was the center on the basketball team your junior year."

"Oh yeah, John Tate?"

"Yeah, he joined the Navy thinking he would "skate," but they made him a corpsman and he got stuck with the Marines. End of story."

The next shoe to drop in our conversation is about some changes at St. Benedict's.

"Yeah, what's going on there, do they still have the same principal, Sister Marie?"

"No, she left, and now Sister Nathan is the principal. But she'll be leaving soon. So guess who's next in line to be made principal…."

"Yeah, who, another Dominican nun?"

"It's rather unheard of…."

"Who, then?"

"Your old pal, Dan Adamson."

I have no response; I just fall silent.

Gregg changes the subject quickly and tells me that he's staying at a flop house and that they're going to be having a party this weekend. I ask what a flop house is and he describes it as a bunch of people living together, where you pay what you can for rent and share food, make dinners together.

"We're having a party; do you want to come?"

"Yeah, when is it, what time?"

"Well, that's not how parties go anymore. We start on Friday and go till Sunday, or when everyone's done."

I ask him who will be coming.

"It's open door, people come and go all weekend. This is not like the parties that we used to go to, where we'd play records and dance with each other, like a CYO dance. You're going to see chicks and guys pairing off, laying on the floor, or in upstairs bedrooms, a lot of people smoking joints."

"You mean marijuana cigarettes?"

"Yeah, man."

"Going to be any beer there?"
"Sure. Beer, wine, maybe some spiked Kool-Aid.

This conversation with Gregg about all the changes I'd missed, and who St. Benedict's was promoting to principal, was the second blow that week. The first one was at Mass on Sunday. As I returned from Communion and looked up toward the pipe room, I saw Adamson playing the organ—his fat face with his bow tie and red crew cut—looking right down at the altar.

If you'd have told me in Vietnam that he was not in the state penitentiary, or dead at the hands of some parent, or had fled to Canada, I wouldn't have believed that. It never entered my mind that Daniel T. Adamson would be anywhere around the Wallingford district still. I am extremely upset about this, both internally and externally. I start to feel like I did when I was in the jungle, with serious medieval thoughts.

I ask Gail what she knows about Pinky being promoted to principal. She says there are some rumors to that effect, but she knows for sure that he's still playing the organ, and teaching. *Yeah, you should go down and visit him, he still lives in the same place.*

I'll go down to see him all right, but not to say hi. My '66 GTO weighs about as much as that 442 Oldsmobile, and it's faster. So I begin my nighttime vigil at the top of 43rd Street, waiting for him to come out of the alley way on his way to school or church in the morning to work on some project. I drive by St. Benedict's and see that his Chevy station wagon is parked in his usual spot outside of school, sure that his mommy had packed his lunch.

I sit in my car at the top of the hill near Adamson's alleyway two, three nights a week, sometimes with a Dick's cheeseburger, and I think that I have literally killed for less—a lot less. In Vietnam, I had obliterated anything that moved in the jungle, just because it made noise in the dark. That's how I lived. I set traps to ambush the enemy, using dental floss stretched between the trigger guards, tugged on like a fish on the line when the lead person on a patrol came down that trail and snagged the line. That was the signal to blow the hellboxes on the Claymores. It was intensely choreographed.

In my mind now, that's what I'm doing, waiting there for the sun to come up and for Adamson to back out of that driveway. I expect my conscience to kick in. Instead I hear a little voice say, *come on, get serious, it's almost daybreak and you're going to have to fit in.* This time, however, the little angel and devil on my shoulder, representing right and wrong, good and evil, are gone. I don't hear, *turn yourself in, what are you thinking?* or, *Go back home.* No, I just think, *when…when are we going to do this?*

This time, I won't ram the car and hope he hits his head on the windshield. I'm going to just tap it with enough force so it jars him, and maybe he'll get out of the car. If not, I'll pull him out of the car and pour gasoline on him and light it, then stab him in the throat. I'll head down the alleyway to his house, climb the stairs, and step into the kitchen to the right of the landing, not the left that goes to the basement, or to the attic. Mrs. Adamson will be baking cookies, and I'll slash her throat, drag her down the stairs, up the alley, and pile her on top of the burning inferno. Then go back and get the old gardener. I'll bet he'll have something to say then. Drag him onto the inferno, go back again and empty out the koi pond and stab every fish, throw them onto the fire. If the neighbors come out and ask me what I'm doing, maybe I'll throw them on too for knowing about the horror chamber next door to them, but doing nothing.

This can't happen to one more child; they must be protected. My rage and anger is now out of control. But I think, *this is what I would be expected to do in Vietnam, for less cause, and far less idea of why I was fighting, and killing.*

This is the most petrified and afraid of my thoughts I've ever been, and I've only been home about ten days. Doubting what my actions might be at night, I think I best be out of my house when it's dark. I might revert back to kill anything that moves. My control is hanging by a thread and it's slipping, dangling, sliding through my fingers and what it is, is my life, my personality, my whole mental being.

This happened to me before in the bush. If you go crazy in Vietnam, in a Marine Corps grunt unit, and you tap a lieutenant on the shoulder and say, *I'm going absolutely crazy,* he'd say, *Cool.* It's the most sought after state of mind. In the jungle, we needed that—deranged, psychologically unstable—in order to function. Now, here I am in an environment where there are rules: stop signs where you are expected to stop; speed limits to obey; no overnight camping in the park; no firearms allowed.

A few days go by and I decide to take my friend Gregg up on his offer to go to the party. As I arrive, there is a guy who's lying next to the curb on the street in front of the house. Approaching him, I see that he is half conscious and throwing up on himself. I recognize him as someone I possibly went to Seattle Prep with. I walk up the stairs and enter a world where everything is *psychedelic*. The girls look like they just crawled out of a sleeping bag, their hair uncombed, no makeup on. Guys without shoes on. Actually, no one is wearing shoes, and they are staggering all over the place. Someone in the kitchen is drinking out of a big bottle of pink Bali Hai, shit wine.

I'm thinking this looks weird, because I've seen some people on the streets who look normal, dressed Ivy League. When I went to Gail's sorority, they were dressed like in the fifties: wearing dresses, hair pulled back with a hairband. Looking out the side door, there is a commotion and I see guys meeting the description of Ivy League, maybe football players, unlike anyone in the house, and they are yelling that they want their claw foot bathtub back. My high school buddy Gregg seems to be the *den mother*, in charge of the group of people in the house, and instructs them to go get the bathtub in the backyard and haul it out to the parking strip, which they do; then the Ivy League guys haul it away. Not only do I think the bathtub thing is strange, but I am witnessing two very different cultures. I don't fit in with the guys with the crew cuts, because they're going to college, and I certainly don't fit in with the psychedelics, so I fit in nowhere.

I ease down slowly onto what looks like a flea-infested, decrepit couch with springs poking through. Next to me sits a hippie girl with a homemade cotton flowered dress, elastic at the neckline and wrists, beads flowing around her neck, and handmade leather, beaded bracelets. She is smoking a joint and seeds are popping out of it…*ditch weed*.

Holding the joint between her thumb and forefinger, she passes it over my way,
"Want a hit?

"No, I don't smoke." She gives me a look and giggles, as if to say, *it doesn't have anything to do with smoking.*

I recognize some of the music playing at the party, like the Temptations, and Tom Jones, but then something plays that is the longest song I've ever heard and it seems to lighten up the whole crowd. People are up dancing, not with each other, but alone, moving around in circles, with their arms waving up to the sky and gazing up at what might be the sun, moon, and the stars. I look up and think, *There's nothing there, except the dining room chandelier.* The girl sits back down.

"What do you think of that song?"

"Well, I never heard it before in my life."

"I thought that you were from Seattle."

"Yeah, I grew up in the Wallingford district."

"Are you experienced?"

I laugh to myself and think, *Are you jokin' me? How much time do you have and I'll explain how experienced I am.*

"That's the name of his latest album," she continues.

"Whose latest album?"

"Jimi Hendrix. He's from Seattle, he went to Garfield High, and the song is 'Purple Haze'!"

"Oh, yeah, I did hear something about *Excuse me while I touch the sky.* Is that what you were doing when you were looking up and dancing in circles?"

"No, you just do your own thing, man."

I had asked Gail to come to the party at about four o'clock, so I call and tell her, *you need to come over and see what this is.* She is a member of a sorority where they wear dresses and patent leather shoes, or white polished pumps, their hair neatly coiffured with lots of hair spray and they walked like professional models and eat properly...nothing like this group. Gail's look was softer than most of her sorority sisters, less chiseled, and her hair was long, not sprayed, but gently flowing off her shoulders. *But not flowing like these people!*

I figure there wouldn't be much at the party for her, but I go ahead and pick her up drive her to the party. As she walks in, she expresses no surprise at what she sees. She says a lot of the people here might be going to junior college or maybe even the U. There's a mixture on campus now—it's a bit like a melting pot. It's a short stay at the party and we leave, going to Dicks for a hamburger and then I drive Gail home.

That night, I don't drive by Adamson's place. Instead, I just drive around, trying to absorb what I had witnessed at the party.

I feel sad and lonely, despondent as I realize not only do I not fit in, I don't think that I ever can. I don't think I can fix myself, and the thoughts I'm having. Medieval thoughts, if acted upon, will end with me being on death row. I need to go somewhere where there are no laws, and rules, where someone will pat you on the back and say, *it don't mean nothin', it don't mean nothin', it don't mean nothin'*. Where you can be a little crazed and go a little off, or a lot off, where you can have a high-level mental breakdown, you can go crazy, and it's just cool, he's just having his time. *O'Connor's just doing his thing*, a little *famfire* again moving through the jungle. Maybe let off a couple of hellboxes, too. Maybe just have a little walk down the trail, see what comes up.

I need to go back, because back is my present and if this is future, count me out.

So ten days turns to twenty days, then twenty-five days, and every conversation with Gail, my mother, and brothers includes, *where you going to get stationed? Where you going to get stationed?* Over and over. So I drive to Sandpoint Naval Station again and ask if my orders have come in yet. The answer was, *No, you'll be notified at your home via Western Union. Don't be surprised if it takes more than thirty days, you won't be considered AWOL, we have all of your information on 3x5 cards. You'll be getting a good duty station.*

After two more days and nights of deep, terrifying medieval thoughts at the top of the hill, my funeral pyre is getting bigger. I think I might need the same kind of kerosene, like the coaches used on the baseball field, that ugly black smoke billowing up from the inferno. Or maybe even better yet, Napalm. I learned how to make homebrew in the bush with laundry detergent and gasoline; it's called *jelly gas*. I think about including the parishioners and nuns, people who thought, *My God, it's fine for Steve to go on overnights at motels at twelve years old, and if he's one of the priest's favorites, maybe he'll become a priest. We can sacrifice one of the kids and we can all go to heaven. We don't want to know what's happening in the basement or in the attic, Adamson's torture chamber.*

Impatient, I go back to the Naval base and ask about my orders.

"Hey, man, what if I want to just do a *replay*, put the tape back in and send me back to the 2nd Combined Action Group, my CAP unit, Vietnam!"

"I can get you back *there*. We can get orders from Washington D.C. via courier or Western Union in forty-eight hours. Yeah, if you want to go back to the bush, no problem."

Within three days, a Western Union telegram comes to my house. My mother seems excited and hands me the yellow envelope. I go to my bedroom, open it, and in among all of the coding, I see *West Pac Ground Forces, 2nd Combined Action Group, 3rd Marine Amphibious Force. Reporting date: ASAP.* I place it in my dresser drawer and start to pack my stuff.

I take Gail out to dinner that night and don't say anything.

A day later, I share the news with my mother and brother.

"Hey, I got my orders."

I read the telegram with all the abbreviations. They don't understand.

My brother asks, "What state is that in?"

"DEPART CONUS" is the key phrase. It means, Depart Continental United States. Proceed to Western Pacific Ground Forces, 3rd Marine Amphibious Force, 2nd Combined Action Group, Republic of Vietnam."

My mother stumbles a bit. "That's the same address you had in Vietnam."

"Yes, that's because it *is* the same place, and I'm going back to the bush."

There is no sadness, or crying, or hugging.

"Jesus Christ! My idiot child." And the cigarettes are coming out. *My idiot child*, again and again, puffing on her cigarette, staring out the window, or looking at my brother, not speaking to me directly. My brother shakes his head in disgust and walks back home.

My mother had changed a lot in the last twelve months; she had gotten her driver's license, bought a car, and worked a job with the federal government in downtown Seattle. Now she was heading to

Spokane, to the Fairchild Air Force base to work as the base librarian. She had come a long way from the wailing, sobbing housewife in the bedroom; she hit the floor running and never looked back. I continue to send her money each month, but I don't worry that I need to take care of her. She's now independent.

Then I take Gail out to dinner at Art Louie's the next night.

Sitting in the booth, there is a paper Chinese lantern giving off a faint light.

"I got my orders."

"Oh great," she says optimistically, "where are you going to be stationed?"

I read the telegram to her.

"That's the same address I wrote to you for thirteen months."

"Yes, I'm going back to the same place. I'm going back where I belong. I don't belong here. I need to find out what happened while I've been gone. I've thought a lot about the Marines I left behind. No one replaced me and they're doing double duty and some may be dead by now. I just need to go back."

I get a stoic, head-down look from Gail, as if to say, *what have you done with your life? You've ruined it, there's no hope for you.*

Then, out of character, she gets excited. "Who is driving you to the airport tomorrow?"

"Jerry is."

"Can I ride along with you to the airport?"

"Sure, we'll pick you up at five in the morning."

The next morning, Gail and I sit in the back seat, holding hands. Jerry is driving with the windows up in the car, chain-smoking, and you can cut the haze with a knife.

Saying good-bye, Gail says, "I'll write you and send some ravioli and cookies."

She gives me another look, as if to say, *I hope nothing happens this time that drives you insane.*

It's a little late for that. I don't have the heart to tell her that I'm damaged way beyond that. And it's permanent.

CHAPTER 14

THEY LOVE US IN SAN FRANCISCO!

August 1968

I am back in Da Nang at the CAP unit headquarters, picking up an M16 and .45-caliber pistol from the supply sergeant. I ask if my flak jacket and helmet are still there from thirty days ago. I remember how he said he'd store my things for thirty days even though I said I'd never be back. *Yeah*, he said, and after a while, lo and behold, he finds my flak jacket and helmet. As I look at my helmet, I laugh to myself. I ask if the supply sergeant has a felt marker. He gives me one and I carefully cross out the last line on the side of the helmet, the line that says *conquered*. I print the words, *I came, I saw, I said FUCK IT.*

I turn the helmet on its left side and begin another line with the month: *August*. This line that would eventually pass over a previous line of months, to form a 'cross' of months. Geared up and ready to go, I hop on a Huey gunship back from the staging area. I'm taking the exact same journey, except for my ride on a sampan is going up river instead of down. As I come up to the last stretch of the trail, I see my CAP unit all sitting around chewing on their C-rations. They aren't surprised to see me; no one says, *hey we told you so*, or *we knew you'd be back*. I'm thinking, *I made it back with my people, and they're all still alive. I wonder how long I'll be alive.*

Christmas 1968

Long gone are the letters I sent home during my first few weeks in Vietnam. The ones that told about how we were *winning the hearts and minds of the locals,* or *keeping the domino theory in check,* or *fighting the good fight.* Gone too are the upbeat letters from the end of my first year; *hope I don't get blown away before I get home to drive my new Pontiac GTO,* or *when I get home we're going to have a great time together Gail!*

My correspondence with Gail or my family in the winter of 1968 is matter-of-fact and to the point. I write things like, *hope I am not the last Marine to get killed here for absolutely no reason.* Months ago, reality set in and I don't reminisce anymore about returning to the "world," the land of the "round eyes," Occasionally, I'd interject some feeble attempt to sound positive about my situation in my letters to Gail: *hope you are doing well at the University of Washington,* or *have you had a Dick's cheeseburger lately?* In reality, what I want to write, and sometimes do, is—*hope all my parts end up in the same body bag. Hope part of me isn't left hanging in a tree. Hope the NVA don't dismember me and stick me up on a bamboo pole somewhere.* Although deep in my soul, I wouldn't have blamed them in the least.

March 1969

The Vietnamese holiday celebration of the Lunar New Year, affectionately called *TET,* is coming up. To me, it means everyone in Vietnam celebrates by massacring each other. If it's anything close to TET of 1968, then *Mr. Charles* is going to *Pee* all over us again. The TET of 1968, one of the largest military campaigns launched by the Viet Cong and North Vietnamese, was one of the worst periods for casualties during the war. The only difference this time, this year, is my change of heart about the whole situation. It's fatalistic and my thoughts are *let's just get to it and get it over with.*

The *death wish* is my constant companion. No more Malaria, or C-rations, no more humping through the jungle—at this point I'm just wishing for something nice and clean. My favorite flavor is like the John Wayne war movies. *Oh, I'm hit.* Of course, I know that isn't the reality. How about one right through the running lights? I've seen that one plenty of times. Dead before he hits the ground. Not bad, unless you happen to be right behind him when the back of his head responds to the effects of sudden impact.

I certainly didn't need to be reminded of when one first gets to Vietnam. It's an excellent time to get blown away, most desirable to get it over early. The worse of the worst is to suffer for a whole tour, or as in my case, almost twenty-three months, then get it as you are distracted thinking stupid thoughts like *when I get back to the "world."*

No one bothers to let me know when my flight date is; a quick calculation from my last incoming letter told me that with a March 5th postmark, it must be around March 15th now. This means that my present tour of duty is about up, or very close to it.

I have to admit that my mind isn't 100 percent on the task at hand. I'm aware that NVA troops are amassing on the far edge of the village we are near. Also, reports have come in from the locals that during the last week, NVA patrols are coming into the village, sometimes setting up ambushes. Boy, things have changed from the days of General Westmorland who said, *If we can just get them (the NVA) to come out in the open, we will destroy them.* The original strategy from the *great* general that never happened. Instead, it was the NVA going out on major search and destroy operations. Searching to destroy us.

Not much remained of our fifteen-man Combined Action Platoon. If I recall, none had left on two legs. So it was that morning, that the remaining six Marines set out to *snoop and poop* the village of Dien Ban. Walking point, I first notice nothing, as we approach the village. Not a good sign. No people, no chickens, no pigs, no water buffalo. The silence is deafening all right. But not for long.

As I walk toward the edge of a rice paddy dike, the air is filled with lead, immediately followed by incoming mortars. That means they came in during the night and had time to set up likely avenues of approach.

I don't remember who got hit first, I hear a voice, a high-pitched wail. Next, the rest of us fling ourselves over the side of the rice paddy dike and begin to return fire where the muzzle flashes originate. As the NVA fire begins to kick up clods of mud from the road, bits of our meager berm wall begin to show signs of collapsing. Mud flies through the wall, occasionally accompanied by a tracer bullet.

To my left, I hear other voices, groaning, moaning, and wailing. A quick peek over the paddy dike reveals the source of our quandary. There are more NVA then I had seen earlier, firing in a skirmish line, and heading right toward me. Strangely, I also hear the sound of Huey gunships and the sound is getting closer. At that point, I swing my left leg onto the top of the dike. This is immediately welcomed by the feeling of a swift punch to the inside of my thigh, followed by a searing heat that is actually causing my leg to smoke. Along with this heat, I see a spray of blood, and a leg that is now bent in a direction it wasn't made to bend. With my left forearm cradling my leg, I attempt to roll to my right and suddenly number two comes whizzing by me, taking the muscle below my kneecap with it. Now my knee is not connected.

It doesn't look like it's going to matter anyway, because a quick check to my right shows the landing zone for the bullet that has just ripped my knee has hit Sharpe* and gone *through and through left to right*. He's breathing in, but to no avail, as the air is coming back out his chest in a foamy pink froth. As I look to my left, three Marines huddle together on the ground that is quickly turning reddish brown. Again, I hear the sound of gunships, and they are on top of us swooping back to front, raking the NVA to our front. I'm thinking, *probably too little too late* as we await the next mortar barrage.

Miraculously, one of the Hueys hovers right in front of me and Sharpe, spraying support fire from the opposite doorway. A crew chief jumps out, grabs me by the flak jacket, and literally throws me into the chopper. Next, he drags Sharpe in, and the gunner and I position him toward the back of the doorway. My helmet falls off, landing upside down on the ground, looking like a turtle upended, rocking back and forth. I wonder, *did I forgot to mark the month of March?*, as the prop wash from the Huey blows it into the rice paddy out of sight. This inanimate object with my calendar of time in the bush etched upon it, is gone.

Before I know it, we are airborne, circling one last time, spraying the paddy. I can now see the ground as the warbird heads aloft. What I see at first is encouraging, as I count two additional Hueys getting into the fight. What I also see is NVA still moving toward what is left of my CAP unit, three or four Marines, all wounded. I presume another Huey will swoop down and snatch them also. I don't think it's going to matter for a couple of them, however. Sharpe is on his side and has the *death grin* going to the max. All teeth gnashing at the prop blast, hoping for some air. The gray pallor is setting in on him as we land at 1st MED Battalion hospital helipad near Da Nang. I've been here before, when I had malaria, but this time it is total chaos. Every now and then, a stretcher will open up as the previous occupant is transferred to graves and registration. The tourniquet on my leg causes excruciating pain, but the blood is starting to dry up as I am thrown onto a rigid table. I see the IV drip, then, *lights out*. An inglorious ending to an inglorious war.

I don't see Sharpe again. All I know is that he is far from OK when they lift him off the helipad. Days go by and I keep asking if any more Marines have come in from Dien Ban that day, but the answer is always no. My time at 1st MED Battalion is short and uneventful, but the day I arrive at the Naval hospital at Cam Ranh Bay, on the southern coast of Vietnam, is paradise. It looks like a beach in Hawaii and there are lights, food, nurses in uniforms, doctors in uniforms, no helmets, no smells, and no flak jackets. A whole other world. Within a day, a Navy doctor is at my side when I awake. This is my chance.

"Hey Doc, is there any way you could keep me here or send me to Hawaii or somewhere until my leg heals? I've still got malaria pretty bad."

His response is something I'll always remember: "Fucking Marine Corps. You were supposed to be in the rear getting ready for your flight home three weeks before you got shot. Needless to say, you missed your flight."

I thought about the timing. I would have been home in Wallingford if I had caught my flight; instead the Marines kept me there, no word about when I was to get back to the rear. Now I've ended up with multiple leg wounds and I can't walk. At least I'm out of there alive, physically alive. And what's happened to Sharpe, the others?

"It says on your chart that you are from Seattle, Washington, right? Well tomorrow, you are headed to the States, where there is a bed waiting for you at Bremerton Naval Hospital."

My joy is short lived, as the patient next to me yells.

"Fucking Marine Corps, right. Don't you guys have maps?"

"Me, why?"

"We're Army, and we're here because we walked right into one of your ambushes. I guess you "Jarheads" just shoot till it doesn't make any noise, eh?"

"Pretty much."

I must say, the Navy doctor is true to his word, and within a few days I am one of eighty or more stretcher cases sandwiched onto the trays lining a bulkhead of a huge gray plane known as a C-141 Star Lifter. I will soon learn that all stateside medevacs are handled by the U.S. Air Force medical staff. They tell me we'll travel to Yokosuka Japan for interim treatment, then depending on our final destination, be transferred by plane to a permanent hospital.

I get letters to home off, trying to let my family and Gail know that I'll be coming home, wounded. Four days later, I am again strapped to the bulkhead of another C-141 with the final landing being Travis Air Force Base which, they tell me is outside San Francisco. I think, *great, they just love us in San Francisco!*

The twelve-hour flight is anything but a scene of happiness. There is one small porthole on each side of the plane and they're covered by pillows stuffed up against the glass. In the front of the jet, I see several ambulatory patients sitting in rows of two or three seats across. In the back, ours is a different ride. Strapped like a tourniquet to the stretcher, my view is the bottom of the stretcher above that is separated from me by less than six to twelve inches. There is no conversation or talking, only an occasional, feeble moan emanating through the fuselage. More than once, a nurse and an aid slip down the aisle, body bag in tow, flop it up onto a stretcher, then the final *zzzzipppp*. And a tag placed on the bag.

My closest companion residing directly above me continues breathing through chokes and coughs. I see the bottom of his stretcher is beginning to show signs of a wet, dark, puddle at the center of the depressed portion. Near the end of our flight, I am surprised that my stretcher mate is still breathing as we make our descent into "the world." Landing instructions are blunt and to the point. "When the doors open, all ambulatory patients hustle to the buses parked to the left of the plane. They will take you to the hospital on base. All stretcher cases—you will be laid out on the tarmac and they will get ambulances to you and pick you up as soon as possible. And, by the way, the nurses will be covering you with a blanket, as you will in no uncertain terms get shit thrown over the fence at you."

The medevac flights are routinely met with war protesters throwing stuff over the fences at the stretcher cases. Fruit, garbage, you name it. Consider it "freedom of expression. The medical team says, *Xin Loy!* This is common slang used in the bush, Vietnamese for *sorry 'bout that. Then why park us near the fence?*

Soon, we are not disappointed. But as the protestors lob junk at us, we begin our own chants.

Thank you for sharing!

Two of us are strapped into the back of a gray military ambulance and as I look out the window, I see we are crossing the Oakland Bay Bridge. The ride terminates at one of the most beautiful places I have seen in a long time: Letterman Hospital at the Presidio in San Francisco. White sheets, television in the room, and a constant attendant who introduces herself as a Red Cross volunteer, one of the few remaining humans on our side.

The next day, after the redressing of my wounds, I am loaded onto a smaller military jet with more seats and only eight to ten stretcher cases bolted to the side walls. My next destination will be McChord Air Force base outside of Tacoma, Washington. Ironically, I visited there as a ten-year-old child. My older brother Frank, in the Air Force, had landed there on his way back from duty at Aviano, Italy. I have a distinct memory of my parents packing an elaborate picnic lunch and chatting all the drive down about what a hero he was and how proud they were of my brave brother who served his country. *Proud, proud proud!* Fleetingly, it crosses my mind that maybe there will be something of that sort waiting for me.

Two hours after leaving San Francisco, I arrive on the tarmac at McChord. I am not met by either protesters throwing garbage or by a tearful family beaming with pride. Instead, a steady torrential downpour greets me. Minutes turn to an hour as we wait, not knowing how long we'll be waiting. Still on stretchers, another Marine and I are notified we'll be remaining here, out in the rain, next to the terminal until an ambulance arrives. Two hours later, the two of us are strapped into a military ambulance and driven to

Bremerton Naval Hospital. It soon becomes obvious that the Air Force is better funded than the Navy. But hey, I am home.

Bremerton is one big *shithole*. The hospital is an old, dreary, damp, moldy brick building. That's how I describe the personnel too. I am unceremoniously moved from my cot onto an old metal frame bed in the middle of an open squad bay holding twenty to forty Marines, equally miserable and wounded. I'm not sure if the corpsman tending to me doesn't like his life, or the Marines, because he is beyond indifferent, a sarcastic asshole. As he pulls the packing out and I grimace from the pain, he looks at me and says, *You can always chew on your crutch. Oh, you Marines are so tough, it's no problem for you guys.*

Later a Navy nurse issues me a pillow, no case, just a stripped gray-colored pillow with feathers poking out and a wool blanket stamped, *U.S.* I'm escorted to a squad bay that is filled to the brim with fifteen beds lined up on each side. There are people in various stages of agony and pain, from total body cast, to amputees, to men lying on their stomachs because their back is full of holes. Then there is the ominous packing and unpacking of wounds. It begins to feel just like a torture chamber. My bed has no sheet, mattress cover or anything.

The next morning at dawn, I hobble to the phone down the hall and call my mother. My voice is met on the other end of the line with a sense of shock by my mother who isn't expecting me. I guess my letters never arrived. She and my brother say they'll come over and pick me up from the hospital today, however. I let the corpsman know that I have people who are coming to transport me home. He says, *Sorry but we have a rule that we need to keep you here forty-eight hours before you can be released.* My personality has changed a bit in the last several months and instead of saying something like, *sir, yes sir,* I tell him, *As soon as my people come to pick me up, I'll be hauling my ass downstairs and out of this hospital. What are you going to do? Shave my head and send me to the Nam?*

I arrive at my house on a Saturday with nothing more than a pair of blue hospital pajamas, slippers, and crutches. It's my first weekend out of the hospital. For the next few months, I will split my time between the Bremerton Naval Hospital during the week for treatments and physical therapy, and home on the weekends.

My brother Jerry brings me civilian clothes the next day and after changing, gives me a ride to St. Benedict's for Easter Mass. I know that Gail will surely be attending Mass today and in fact probably helping out with the music. I arrive close to the end of the nine o'clock Mass, late, but decide to continue down the aisle and slip into a pew. My eye catches a glimpse of my old friend Gail. As we exchange glances, I can only muster a feeble shrug while leaning on my crutches and in the next second, glance up to the choir loft.

There is *Pinky*.

Sitting at the organ in a time warp.

Same silly clothes, same sickening stature.

My reaction is—*he's just one of many criminals, like crows sitting on a fence.*

I am going to be too busy seeing how light switches work, relishing my bologna and cheese sandwich, and watching people walking in the streets.

Everything is flooding my senses and there's no room for *hatred*. I've lost all ability to hate. Possibly lost the ability to love, to feel.

Back in the hospital after the weekend, I notice the nurses seem preoccupied with sweeping, swabbing, and buffing the floors. And washing the windows. One day, the nurse asks me what I am doing as I stand there gripping my crutches.

"I'm waiting for them to change the packing in my leg."

"Well, while you're waiting, grab a mop and start swabbing the floors."

"How the hell am I supposed to do that, Sir?"

"Come over here and I'll show you."

So I hobble over and she looks at my leg, grabs my left crutch, and fastens the mop handle to my crutch, attaching them together with an ace bandage.

"There now, you can swab the floor like that using your left crutch."

My response is like, *Are you kidding? Get out of here lady....*

The doctors have about the same attitude toward us patients.

The place is a *real* shithole when it rains. I hobble over to the tall windows knowing that if you open one up, chances are it will come slamming down on you like a guillotine. At the base of the window is a line of black mold and as it rains, the inside of the window is dripping and fogged up.

I overhear people talking about the lice that's all over the place and the beds are infested with bed bugs. After being deloused for the third time, I buy myself sheets of clear plastic drop cloths at the hardware store while home for the weekend, bring them back, and wrap my mattress and pillow.

I try not to eat at the hospital as the food is not good. It seems to me that the whole place is like a dingy, dark old castle rather than a hospital, with people's attitudes matching the bleakness. My perception is that the Navy corpsmen did not have the experience of ever being west of California, nor were they the ones who spent time up north with the Marines, where most of them got killed. A corpsman who spent time in the Marine Corps infantry would never have an attitude like these guys.

The town is also a shithole. It's nothing but bars, tattoo parlors, and drunken sailors stumbling around at 2 a.m. in the morning like homeless people. But it is a Navy town, with a shipyard, a Marine barracks, and naval hospital. The locals are proud of Bremerton and the contributions they made during WWII operating a huge shipyard.

The walk down to the ferry terminal is twelve to fifteen blocks from the hospital up on the hill. I routinely limp down to the ferry on my crutches in my uniform. Many civilian cars pass me by and not once—whether I'm returning on the ferry and hiking on crutches up the hill to the hospital or making my way down to the ferry—do I get an offer for a ride. Not one time does someone stop and ask, *Hey Marine, do you want a ride to the ferry dock?* No, I don't have anybody roll down their window and throw garbage at me like San Francisco; there's just this indifference. I am just another wounded Marine, in the way of how the world is going by.

Even with my trips on the ferry from Seattle to Bremerton hospital for treatments on my leg, I manage to see Gail and take her to dinner or a movie. We have many late-into-the-night talks, about our future. After exchanging letters for two years, we are close, attached. We talk about how it would be if we got married, how different we'd want to be from our parents. I wouldn't have to worry about the

Marines sending me back to Vietnam, at least for a while. I could stay in the Marines and we'd move to a new duty station, probably a good one, based on how grunts are rewarded after their tours in Vietnam. We dream about California, and our future, that will be filled with sunshine, beaches, and a new car—another convertible, for sure. And in the short term, we talk about teaching her to drive the GTO since my leg was in a cast.

One day toward the end of May, Gail comes to my house to let me know how the wedding preparations are going. She talks about the sorority sisters helping out and how the bridesmaid dresses are being sewn.

"Oh by the way," she says, "Dan Adamson got a hold of me after Mass last week and said he saw the wedding bands for our marriage published in the bulletin. He offered, *please, I'd love to play for your wedding—no charge.*"

I am lying in bed with my hands clasped behind my head, my leg elevated up in a sling, and I look at her standing at the foot of my bed.

"What did you say?"

"Dan Adamson wants to play the organ at our wedding."

"Oh yes, that's perfect."

I see that the significance of what I just said is lost on her; she doesn't have a clue. Adamson means nothing to me now. Just ten months earlier, home after my first tour in Vietnam, my hatred was intense and I was planning and scheming ways to massacre him.

Now I think *he'll not come up in any situation that will impact my psyche, ever again.* Not only had the Nam shot my wad of hatred, anger, and vengeance, but also other human emotions such as love and compassion. I lost the power to hate anymore. Adamson is beyond worth spending one minute contemplating. The war has not cleaned me out, but has, it seems, made me incapable of any feeling whatsoever.

After the wedding in Seattle and honeymoon in San Francisco, we move to Seal Beach, California where I am to be stationed. While I'm back in the hospital, still receiving treatments for my leg and malaria, Gail is busy. In the period of a week, she finds us an apartment, contacts my commanding officer and gets her military

ID, signs up for her allotment check, then starts a new job with a local medical clinic. I'm amazed at all she has done, and excited for my new duty serving in the military police.

It's about as normal a life that I can hope for, now. I plan to get as far away from the tragedy of Vietnam and forever bury the memory of St. Benedict's.

CHAPTER 15

OUT OF THE BARREL

Twenty years now
Where'd they go?
Twenty years
I don't know
I sit and I wonder sometimes
Where they've gone.

—Bob Seger, "Like A Rock"

August 1989

Today is the day of the Stanwood-Camano Fair, in the first week of August. Notes from my log book: *Beautiful summer day, very festive, the whole community turning out for the fair, which rivals the annual tulip festival, without the tulips.*

The fair includes carnival rides for the children and food for grown-ups and kids of all ages—hot dogs, cotton candy, ice cream and pizza to name a few. I'm signed up for the dunk tank. It's one dollar for three balls, and how they love it when someone hits the target and the police officer falls into the water.

People hold parties and barbeques before and after the fair, and at night there is a dance for high school students and square dancing for adults. The start of the day is a long parade to begin the festival.

This is my first year leading the parade. It is an upbeat, memorable day for everyone. I feel proud of my role and being a part of this community.

August 1994

Notes from my log book: *This summer has been hot and dry and now we're into the first week of August. I arrive early on this Saturday morning to prepare for the parade to kick off the Stanwood-Camano Fair.* It's grown over the years as one of the largest community events in the region, with the carnival, exhibits, dances, and activities for the entire weekend. I'll be leading the long parade again this year in my patrol car, throwing candy to the children up and down the parade route. Later, I'll report for my annual round in the dunk tank at the carnival in the park. They'll be lined up to hit that target and if they do, there will be eruptions of laughter to see me knocked off my perch.

This year though, I feel on edge for some reason. I've seen enough as a police officer to know how wrong things can go, even on a day of festivities like today. These past couple of years, there have been very few days when I could say that I loved my job, especially working as an undercover narcotics detective for Snohomish County. I'm ready to be back in the community this year.

At the end of the parade, I open the route to regular traffic then drive to the Thrifty grocery store. There is a long line of kids stretching out of the store, waiting to get their free ice cream cones, compliments of a local Stanwood company. I recognize a lot of the D.A.R.E. kids who were in my classes; some are older now, in high school, or off to college—all fifth graders when I knew them. I feel proudest of my work with D.A.R.E., having a small influence in shaping kids' lives. I think of my own children, Stephanie, Robyn, and Christy, now out of high school, and Ryan in fourth grade. The fair is a lighthearted weekend, a time for family events.

It's around four o'clock and I'm mingling with people and doing a lot of community policing. Saying hi to some of the teachers I know from the grade school, and stopping to talk to a number of families like the Mancini* family. He's an attorney and his wife, Cathy*, is a school teacher. I saw her at school over a year ago when she was holding her four-month-old baby boy, telling me they named him Lucca*. Today, I run into them at the grocery store, where they are picking up hot dogs and marshmallows. They live a short distance from Stanwood on an acre in a large house with a deck, garden, and a fire pit out at the back of the property.

They say, "Hey, if you get a chance, stop by our place later for hot dogs and marshmallows."

"Thanks, yeah, if it's still slow, I might stop by."

I ask her about Lucca and she says he's ten months old now and back at home with her sister, brother-in-law, and their kids, who are staying with them for the weekend.

The day's atmosphere is light and sunny, and people are happy. It's one of those days when it's fun to be a cop, where you are extremely proud of your uniform. You can look around and see many people you know and they give you a positive, good feeling. Sure, there are others you might recall for bad reasons, but this weekend, everyone is getting along, *waving with all five fingers.*

About a half hour after seeing the Mancinis, I am back in my patrol car when I receive a call on my radio. From the dispatcher's voice, I know it's bad. Just as the dispatchers can recognize from voice inflections what kind of crap an officer is involved in, I sense something bad from the dispatcher's tone.

"1433, Stanwood unit 1433 child not breathing, no fire or emergency personnel, no medical on scene— ███████████ Road!"

Again. "Any Stanwood unit, child not breathing, 1433 fire and aid notified."

I respond, "1433, I'm going code."

How did I get to this place? I recall my training at the police academy. Some officers would brag about forgetting everything they were taught in the academy; these guys make terrible cops. For me, the time at the academy were exciting days. We were a big class at seventy-five members: dedicated, fresh-faced, and eager to prove ourselves. We learned about probable cause, search warrants, continuum of force, criminal procedure—these were all good things we took with us into the field. I thought back to our instructor at the academy, a wily old veteran, talking about his peers, his cop friends, and to the recruits before him. On the first day of class, as he wrote

146

on the chalkboard, outlining our day's coursework, he stopped and swung around to face us.

"So how many of you have a beer once in a while?"

About 30 to 40 percent of the class of seventy-five cadets raised their hands. He went back to the chalkboard, then turned back to the class and waved his hands, speaking with resignation and sarcasm:

"You'll all be alcoholics."

He looked at us as we grappled with this information, and then he said, "How many of you are married?"

Some hands went up.

He stared at us. "You'll all be divorced—mark my word."

Everyone looked at each other—*is this some kind of joke?*

He started writing on the board again, returning to the lesson plan.

"How many of you have friends?"

By now, we knew better than to admit that we had friends.

No matter; he turned and waved toward the door and said, "Hit the fucking door if you want to keep them!"

This all became clear to me later; nobody is comfortable around cops. Cops only relate to cops. Police officers don't come across well to civilians, who might ask you how your night went and if you tell them, you find out that they really don't want to know. Almost by osmosis, cops bond together, not out of love and respect for each other, more like survivors packed into the same life raft.

A few years before I joined the Stanwood Police, there was a ten-year-old boy who was playing outside during recess at Stanwood Elementary School. The playground had no chain-link fence. A car pulled up and a man snatched the kid, took off, and kept the child for two days. After joining the police force, I happened to be listening in on a discussion of the case between a Snohomish County detective and a local Stanwood Police detective. They thought it was really weird that this kid said he couldn't remember what happened or where it happened. I thought, *yeah he remembered, he just doesn't want to tell you. Maybe he's just trying to block it. It'll come back to him when he's twelve, twenty, thirty, forty, and fifty years old.* I'm sitting there listening—and visualize placing my hands over my mouth. I can't say anything. They thought it odd that he remembered only one thing, and repeated it over and over. He said that when he sat in

147

the car's front bench seat, there was a chrome plate on the dashboard that read, *J Model*. The first overnight trip I took with Adamson, I don't remember anything except staring at that chrome-plated script on the dashboard, *Borgward*.

Other incidents came up as a police officer that brought me straight back to Vietnam. One day, when I returned to duty after a recent fatal shooting event that I was involved in, the chief called me into his office. He thought I was regressing back to my Vietnam personality.

"Steve, you need to understand to keep police work in perspective. It has no correlation with your experiences as a Marine in Vietnam."

Internally, I smiled. He'd never been a Marine, didn't know anything about the bush.

"Thank you for sharing," was all I could say.

I returned to my wall locker, leaned my forehead up against the cold steel door and with both hands, I pulled my bullet proof vest out away from my chest exactly like I would do in Vietnam. The hot steam spewed up through the top of the vest permeating my nostrils; the stench took me right back to the bush—I was there.

So, Vietnam returned and I was tipping, and tipping, and didn't know if I crawled down that rabbit hole if I'd ever come back. Things continued to come up for me as a police officer, beyond Vietnam. While investigating sexual crimes against a child, I would be haunted and go back to my vulnerable twelve-year-old self. I was spending more time guarding myself from memories of both Vietnam and St. Benedict's.

I head home at five a.m., take my bullet proof vest off, unfasten my gun belt, sit at the dining room table, lean my head back against the chair, and instantly fall asleep. It's not a sound sleep though; any noise would wake me up. Other physical problems start to interfere and slow me down. My gun belt rubbed against my waist and irritated an old shrapnel wound, which required surgery the year before. A few years earlier, when I scrambled down a cliff over the Spokane River to rescue two people whose car launched from the road into the river, I crushed a disc in my back that meant more surgery. I think about a part of Chief Kane's letter nominating me for the Medal of Valor for saving those two people:

Your actions reflect highly upon yourself. Your personal pride, integrity, physical condition and courage were all tested and not found wanting.

I consider the physical issues that are now problems for me, and the thought of resigning is creeping into my mind. But as I let my mind drift, it lands here—what is really happening is I'm starting to feel like I did in Vietnam, and things are becoming more than I can endure. I know that when you get to this place, you either stop or go through a wall. I went through that wall in Vietnam and it's not a good place to be—a catatonic state. *You're not going to show me anything I don't know or haven't seen.* You lose all ability to emote and are numb to everything. This is my greatest fear now.

Early in my career as a police officer, the chief said to me, Steve, you wear your emotions on your sleeve. I am proud of that, and I guard against going back to where I was in Vietnam: *don't mean nothin'.* I don't want to get to that point.

Soon after these incidents, another experience would bring Vietnam back up again, in an intense reconnection with fellow Marines. I call it *the ghost phone call.* I came to the department's office from court late one afternoon and my counterpart, Dave Backstrom*, gave me a message.

"Hey Steve, the departmental 'den mother' received a pretty official call for you today from somewhere in Indiana."

"I don't know anybody in Indiana."

"She left a note for Chief Kane that says it's from the Attorney General's office, and that it's important to contact you. They asked for your home phone number."

I thought maybe they had the wrong guy; I didn't know anybody in Indiana or at the Attorney General's office. I went home and didn't think anything more about it. I ate dinner and at about six o'clock on this summer night. I'm going over my notes and preparing for a case in court the next day. The phone rang and it was Dave Backstrom again. He said the guy from Indiana called once more at the station and they sound pretty official.

"Is it OK if I give them your phone number?"

"Yeah, go ahead. Call back and give it to them."

I just wanted to find out what this thing was about.

Within an hour, the phone rings and the person on the other end of the phone asks me if I am Stephen J. O'Connor and I say, yes. He asks me if I am Officer Stephen J. O'Connor with the Stanwood Police Department and I say, yes.

He says he is with the state Attorney General's office in Terre Haute, Indiana. They have been trying to track me down over the past month. Again he repeats, *I want to make sure this is Sergeant Stephen J. O' Connor from the Marines, 2nd Combined Action Platoon, 3rd Marine Amphibious Force, service number 2251129.*

I am getting a bit apprehensive and impatient.

"Why are you asking me this?"

"I just want to make sure this is you before I put someone on the phone. Do you remember the following names: Lance Corporal Radke*, Corporal Beudroit*, Lance Corporal John Sharpe, and PFC Plummer*?"

He was listing the members of my combined action platoon that were on the patrol with me on the morning of March 17th in the village of Dien Ban.

I knew that Sharpe was alive when I last saw him because he was on the medevac helicopter with me. I knew he was in bad shape, but thought he might make it. As far as the rest of them go, the last time I saw them, it was from the air about fifty feet off the ground. They were huddled behind a rice paddy dike, and several were wounded. About sixty to one hundred North Vietnamese were coming toward them from the tree line. So I thought that was probably the last day of their lives. Even if it wasn't, I really didn't want to know the outcome, had no reason in my mind to try to find out the outcome, except for my attempts to locate them the first few days after I was airlifted. In my mind, I hoped they were still not out there.

It would have debilitated me for a month if I went there—to Vietnam. This was a path I didn't want to go down. Maybe someone did survive.

"I want to put someone on the phone first and then we'll go back over that after you talk with someone here."

"I'm not interested in talking to anybody. Why don't you tell me now what this is really all about."

"OK. Did you ever know a person named Marvin Bieghler?"

"Yeah, I did. Early on he was a member of my CAP unit."

"What do you remember about Marvin Bieghler?"

"He went crazy in Vietnam. You'd have to have been there. No one said, *oh my god he's gone mad!* It was a pretty common situation for us."

"Marvin Bieghler is on death row in Indiana. He killed two people execution style, twenty-three years ago, and we're involved in an appeal of his death penalty sentence. We're trying to get the court of appeals to reverse the death penalty and give him a life in prison, instead.

"Who are these people you keep talking about?"

"Well, four of them were with you, your last day in Vietnam."

"And they're at this place, sitting with you at this hotel? Well, that's a pretty good trick, because they're all dead!"

"Bear with me, I'm going to put someone on the phone."

Next thing I hear: "Grumpy, this is Grit."

He had a strong southern accent, for sure. Radke had written *Grit* on the back of his flak jacket and that's what we called him. Everybody in my CAP unit always referred to me as Grumpy. So this was all very unsettling—I still didn't believe it was Radke, didn't buy it. He started with a dissertation:

"Grumpy, sorry to throw this at you, I know it's a shock to hear from us all at once, after all these years."

I said, "Last I saw Radke, he was bleeding pretty bad. You can't be alive."

"No, we're all here, we're alive and I'm alive!"

The next person on the phone is Sharpe.

While we're talking, he places me on speaker phone, so the others are listening in. An incident comes up that I ask about.

"I remember when there was that explosion in the bunker and I woke up and saw a guy dead right next to me, but I also remember there was another guy beside him, but I don't remember his name. The bunker had collapsed on him and he was covered, except he had one leg sticking out from the debris and he was missing his boot, covered in red ants."

The phone goes silent on the other end.

"Hello, hey, are you guys still there?"

It's Sharpe's voice. "Yeah, Steve, we're here. You know that other guy, covered in the bunker collapse, with his leg sticking out—that was you, Steve. We were part of the reactionary platoon that came out the next day. The CAP unit had been overrun, all the bodies stripped. We pulled what we thought were two dead Marines, tangled together, but when we uncovered you—you were alive. We were the ones who untangled you and carried you to the medevac chopper. Three weeks later, you came trotting back up the trail to our CAP compound, back from the dead once more."

After this phone call, I sit at the kitchen table. The kids and Gail are in bed for the night. I decide to clean my duty weapon. I never do this when anyone is at home. I would never unholster my weapon or leave it laying around. I sit there all night cleaning my weapon with a towel and swabs, field strip it, reassemble, put a round in the chamber, take it out, lay my weapon on the table, repeating this all night long, until five o'clock in the morning when Gail walks in and says, *Steve, what are you doing?*‡

"1433, I'm going code!"

I hit the lights and the siren and race down the road.

I know that the entire fire department and medical emergency personnel from the Stanwood-Camano area are voluntary, and most are at the fair today, or working at Twin City Foods. There would be a delay; they'd have to go home and get into their gear or get their truck, or ambulance, before responding. I was familiar with being the first responder as a police officer, having frequent experiences conducting CPR on the scene before anyone else arrived.

I'm waiting to hear the address from dispatch as I'm flying down the highway. Finally, it comes in and it's familiar—on the same street where the Mancinis live, maybe two houses away. Driving at top speed down the road. their house and driveway come into view. A boy about twelve or thirteen years old is standing in the driveway flagging me down.

I make a sharp turn into the gravel driveway and see several adults gathered around the house.

"1433 I'm 10-23, close the air."

"All units, air is closed for 1433."

‡ Having exhausted all appeals, Marvin Beighler was executed by the state of Indiana in 2002.

I bail out, throw my sunglasses off, and start running to the back. There is a wooden deck and a large, sunken hot tub. The jets are still going, signaling to me that someone had been in the hot tub in the last few minutes. I immediately see a child face down on the deck, and two people are pushing on his back; they don't know CPR…not that it would have helped.

"1433 to dispatch, male Caucasian child, toddler-age, drowning victim, CPR in progress."

Most of the people go into the house and I hear them talking to dispatch as I flip the child over. It's Lucca Mancini.

The aunt and uncle are there. It's a bad situation, chaotic. There are other children around, including the kid who had flagged me down. I clear the child's airways and attempt CPR. I know if a child goes into water and it's very cold, sometimes their body will shut down and they can survive—but warm water, hot water, there is no hope. This child, Lucca, is dead. There is nothing I can do.

"1433, child is DOA, notify coroner. 1433 to dispatch, open the air."

In our log book entries, we are required to keep everything official, registered, dated, certified, and then it's placed in a safe and archived for twenty-five years. So we're taught, *don't put any funny or weird comments in your log book.* Looking at some of mine, I had a habit of writing in the margins: *did everything I could, wasn't good enough.* That was right next to the last entry I made that night: *DOA, child toddler-age, notify the coroner.*

Police are required to stay on the scene until the coroner comes, and ours is traveling some distance, so it takes over an hour. Unlike the movies, you don't cover the body with a sheet, you don't touch it. I make everyone go back into the house, then I hear wailing coming from around the side of the house. It's Cathy Mancini's sister, who is pregnant, and she seems to be having a medical problem. The aid crew take her to the hospital. Shortly after the parents of Lucca arrive, our chaplain, Don Hanika, a former St. Benedict's parishioner, now a deacon at the local Catholic Church, is there to console them.

Don and his wife, along with friends from the Mancini's law firm, assist with getting the Mancinis away from the scene to their friend's house. By six o'clock, everyone is gone; it's just me and the child.

The coroner arrives and snaps photographs, takes the body temperature, then places the corpse in the back of the hearse, and I close up the house. As I walk toward my patrol car, the boy next door comes over and is obviously distraught. He hands me my sunglasses, which had been stepped on.

"Here sir, you dropped these in the driveway. My parents and I were so hopeful when you drove up. I told them that you were my D.A.R.E. officer—Officer O'Connor."

I'm not so resilient this day. It's as if every good thing I had done in the past—staying with the woman injured in a traumatic car crash as she took her last breath; performing CPR at Midnight Mass and saving a life; helping someone out of a domestic violence situation; teaching the D.A.R.E. kids about making good choices—all were overshadowed by today. All that time I stood over the uncovered dead body of baby Lucca, I thought, *just wasn't good enough.*

The coroner leaves, and I sit in my patrol car for a minute, then go to the back of the car and lean against the trunk. A sheriff's car pulls up next to my patrol car. Out comes Dalton Smith*, a Snohomish County Sheriff, and Dan Smith's* brother. Dan had been my partner when I was a narcotics officer, and he had committed suicide.

Dalton had heard about the deceased child on the police radio exchange.

He said "Steve, I know there's nothing you could do. I thought I'd swing by, see if you are you doing OK."

"I'm pretty far from OK."

"Yeah man, you know I've known you for a long time. I could tell by your voice you weren't taking it too well."

He asked if I wanted to be relieved.

"No, I'm just fine, it don't mean nothin'."

I finished my shift and four days later I had my resignation letter ready to go.

Summer, 2002

After retiring from the police force, I return to a semi-normal life of a family man, moving closer to my eldest daughter, son-in-law, and grandchildren in Spokane, purchasing a fixer-upper home and plunging into remodeling projects. I also make sure that my three grandchildren are safe at their Catholic grade school. Each year I volunteer to run the Summer Faith Camp at their school, and help implement new policies to ensure a safe and fun environment for all the kids. My super-vigilance is now focused on my grandchildren. I'm busy with other activities: I fish, play golf, buy another boat, take many trips to the auto wrecking yard for parts to repair my cars, and at my favorite time of year, I sit by my large living room window and watch the snow fall at Christmas.

Several years go by and I manage to keep my blockers in place, even during the times when I cautiously share a few of my Vietnam experiences with others. Some people think this sharing is helping me heal from the past. I'm not so sure about that.

The one thing that I never talk about or reveal to anyone is the tragic abuse I suffered while at St. Benedict's, nor do I ever reveal or answer questions about why I really signed up to go to Vietnam and fight in a war. People would say, *it's so uncharacteristic of you to quit school and join the Marines or have anything to do with the military.*

Then in the spring of 2008, the invitation to the St. Benedict's 100th anniversary celebration is mailed to us. I definitely do not plan to attend. But then things come up such as a special phone call and invitation from the anniversary organizers for Gail and me to be interviewed for a video about our memories of St. Benedict's. And, knowing that I'd want to drive Gail to Seattle so that she wouldn't be stuck on her own in a dangerous snowstorm predicted for the mountain pass, I reluctantly agree to attend this anniversary celebration at St. Benedict's.

October 2009

I am back sitting on the bench, staring at Green Lake, my cell phone in hand and Michael Pfau's phone number on the screen. If I dial this number, I'm making a decision to fight for myself. I know the choice will lead me into a different kind of war, one that will eventually, hopefully, release me from the secret suffering and demons of my past. I want to feel again, but then if I bring up all of this, chances are that I will lose my ability to feel any emotions and go numb again. It's a risk with no guarantee of the outcome, but I need to try to make it right and find justice for the twelve-year-old. And for all the unheard voices of children who are victims. The time for purpose is now.

Second grade pictures of Steve O'Connor and Gail Gibson.

The author with his father, 1955.

Daniel T. Adamson

Father Henry B. Conrad

Author as an 18-year-old Marine, Northern I Corps, Vietnam, 1967. (opposite, top)

"Letter writing time" outside a foxhole. (opposite, bottom)

Marine Corps "RECON" patrol. (aka *snoop & poop*). Sergeant O'Connor at 20 years old (the "old man"), 1969. Author seated on the oil drum. (top)

Author in the "hootch" with Marvin Bieghler. (bottom)

DEATH AND HOPE

CHRISTMAS and the NEW YEAR are coming!

But you will not be at home by the fire, enjoying these traditional festivals will your dear people.

You will be killing people here and sure you will be killed too. A great many of you will never be back home, they are absent for ever, they were dead here in a remote country, far from sweet home, from their beloved families.

Many of you have much trouble here, you have to lead a life of privation, to sleep on the ground you are exposed to dangers in thick jungle, in mud and swamp, with painful wounds, with Death as a faithful attendant.

Why ?

Why have you to enduro all these misfortunes and sufferings ?

There is but one answer, that is because of the dirty War of aggression

Propaganda leaflets left by NVA soldiers found on and around bodies of dead Marines after a battle near Hoi Anh, Vietnam. May 1968.

provoked by " Johnson, Mc Namara and Co », a dirty desperate War.

By now, hundreds of thousands of people in all the States are joining manife tations, meetings and rallies for an end to the Vietnam war. Norman Morrison, Roger Lapote, Celine Jane KoWski, John copping and other American have burnt themselves to death as a sacrifice and a protest against the aggression policy of Johnson, Mc Namara and Co

Will you like to live in peace and quiet ?

Will you like to have happier and more significant Xmas and New year?

THERE IS BUT A SIMPLE WAY : Join the American people as a Whole, join American youth to claim :

— THE WITHDRAWAL OF ALL US TROOPS FROM VIETNAM.
— THE LIBERTY FOR THE VIETNAMESE PEOPLE TO SET THEIR OWN AFFAIRS,

That is the only way for you to be able to resume a peaceful happy life and for the States to come off with honor.

Envelope containing letter to Gail.

26-March-69

1ST MARINE DIVISION (REIN). FMF, VIETNAM.

Dear Gail
I really don't have much to say except that I miss you alot. I've really been thinking about you alot. Especially now that the time is getting shorter and I'll see you before long. It looks as though my leg is going to be healed pretty much by the time they let me go home.

They clean out my leg 3 times a day with peroxide and a round brush. You'd think they were cleaning the bore on the barrel of a rifle the way they do it. It does sting just a bit.

Hey, you want to hear a good one? I'm growing a mustache. Just out of something to do. They'll make me shave it off before I go home. It really looks weird - you wouldn't recognize me. About another 2 weeks and I could take off my shoes, put on an old field jacket and be right in the crowd around the U-district HA HA. The way they've been shooting me up with needles, I feel like a regular "head".

I was just thinking of something

1ST MARINE DIVISION (REIN). FMF, VIETNAM.

to say and the corpsman came in with a letter from you. So now I've got something to talk about. Yah you're right Gail my leg isn't working right now but not because I've been decapitated.

I wouldn't have said anything to you or my people about it but right after I came out of surgery they shoved a pen + paper at me and said I better write home and tell them what happened because they sent a teletype to the Marine liaison section at Sand Point and that a Marine would be out to notify my parents right away. Maybe they came up when my mom was at work. I hope so. Otherwise she probably would have opened the door and had a heart attack or something. It probably would have been better if I didn't mention it but I'd rather have told you myself than have my mother walk up, say did you hear any about Steve's leg. Then you probably would have gotten all shook

Last letter written from Vietnam, March 1969.

1ST MARINE DIVISION (REIN), FMF, VIETNAM.

I to really gotten to be more of a
KATHUMP KATHUMP lately. HA. HA. I can tell
your in a better mood.(By all the TEE HEE'S)
Like you said, I did luck out. & The
Gook that shot me hadan (AK 47
RUSSIAN-ASSAULT RIFLE) If hed had an M-16
like we use, it would have torn the
lower half of my leg off below me.
My knee isn't bad at all. Instead of sewing
it up, they cuta circle around it and it'll
just leave a circular scar. The back of
my thigh hurts the worst but it's getting
better.

Gail-the first word I forgot the
meaning of when I became a Marine
is "QUIT." I never give up if it's worth
trying-more of us do. That's why were
the best. Well like I said - if I would have
given up or lost hope - I'd be dead now.
And I've got too much to live for as long
as I have you. I told you I'd be back
I had to crawl through hell. Well there
were times when it felt like it but
I still have you and I'll be back like

1ST MARINE DIVISION (REIN), FMF, VIETNAM.

browning you). These last six months
have really been doing me in. Getting
my arm wrecked then catching Malaria
and now getting my leg shot up. It
really bugs me when I can't walk.
Just laying here all day-I'm going crazy.
One thing tho- Why the hell didn't
you go to Portland? I figured you'd already
be down there otherwise I wouldn't have
told you. See I wanted you to get a
chance to use your luggage. You should
have gone down to Portland. It bugged
me that you didn't go after all. These
no sweat on my leg - it'll just take awhile
to heal. But there's no problem. I thought
I told you not to worry- Boy you sure
don't follow orders very good (Just Kidding you)

Well if I messed-up your going to
Portland I'll think of something to make
up for it when I get home. What do
you say.

So I better watch out for you
when I get home eh? Now you're talking
(TOUCH!)

1ST MARINE DIVISION (REIN), FMF, VIETNAM.

I promised you Gail. I've beat Charlie
at his own game. Maybe I'm lacking a
few wounds but I won. I'm still alive.
I'm quitting while I'm ahead. I want
to come back and try living like a human.
I just want to forget this place.
And I want to be with you - more
than anything.

I'll see ya real soon,

Love you always,
Steve

P.S.
IF They send any of my mail back to
you then put under my address
"1ST Med Hospital."
Danang.

Wedding day, May 24th, 1969 in front of St.
Benedict Church, Seattle.

Officer O'Connor, Stanwood Washington Police Deparment.

Author, 1990.

Stanwood School District D.A.R.E. students, 1994.

Snohomish County

March 29, 1994

Sheriff's Office

James I. Scharf
Sheriff

Officer Steve O'Connor
Stanwood Police Department
P O Box 127
Stanwood, Wa 98292

- M/S #606
3000 Rockefeller Ave.
Everett, WA 98201
(206) 388-3393
FAX (206) 388-3805

Dear Officer O'Connor:

On April 28, 1994, the Lynnwood, Alderwood, and Marysville Rotary Clubs are
sponsoring the third Medal of Valor Ceremony. Also cosponsoring this event are
Lynnwood Police Officers Assoc., Everett Police Officers Assoc., Snohomish County
Deputy Sheriff's Assoc., Snohomish County Fire Chiefs Assoc., Everett Firefighters
Assoc., Mr. John W. Paxton, Litton Industries, Intermec, Boeing, The Herald, Seafirst
Bank, Stevens Hospital, GTE Northwest, CityBank, and Olson's. This ceremony will
honor citizens and public safety personnel who have performed extraordinary acts of
bravery and heroism.

Your name was submitted for nomination for your involvement in an incident in Spokane
on September 18, 1992, where you witnessed a car go over a 400' cliff along the river.
You went over the cliff to assist the ejected occupants giving life saving first aid. Upon
review of the incident by the nomination committee, it was determined that you receive a
Medal of Valor. See attached sheet for clarification on criteria for the award. The
ceremony will be held at the Everett Holiday Inn, 101 128th St. SE, Everett, Washington.
The event will begin at 6:00 p.m. with a social hour so that you may have the chance to
get acquainted with members of the sponsoring agencies, other recipients, and various
dignitaries attending the ceremony. Dinner will begin at 7:00 p.m. followed by the awards
presentation. Bayview Arts String Quartet, who are members of the Everett Symphony,
will be providing music. It is requested that you wear your Class A uniform for the
ceremony, if possible.

You and a guest are invited to the ceremony as guests of Rotary International and the
cosponsors of this event. If you have any questions or if you need to make reservation
confirmation for you or your guest, please call Karen Cook at 388-3342 Reservations for
additional guests can be made for $25.00 per person.

On behalf of the Rotary International and the sponsors of the Snohmish County Medal of
Valor, it is my pleasure to invite you to the ceremony. I look forward to meeting you on
April 28th.

Sincerely,

James I. Scharf
Snohomish County Sheriff

JIS/kc

recycled paper

Medal of Valor letter of notification
and event program. (opposite)

SNOHOMISH COUNTY
MEDAL OF VALOR

MAY, 1994

GUIDELINES

DEPARTMENT PERSONNEL

MEDAL OF VALOR:

Extraordinary bravery, above and beyond the call of duty, where risk of life actually existed and the officer was aware of such risk; where failure to take such action would not justify censure.

MEDAL OF MERIT:

An act of heroism, beyond that expected, performed at great personal risk with the intent of saving life and/or property; an act of outstanding service or performance, requiring extreme tenacity and devotion to duty.

Snohomish County
Medal of Valor

April 28, 1994

STANWOOD POLICE DEPARTMENT

BOB KANE
Chief of Police

10220 270th Street NW, Stanwood, Washington 98292

Police: 206-629-4555   206-652-9090   City Hall: 206-629-2181
EMERGENCY: 911   FAX 206-629-3009

TO: Steve O'Connor   October 27, 1992
FROM: Bob Kane

SUBJECT: Official Commendation

It has been brought to my attention by members of the Spokane Fire Department
that on September 18, 1992, you were involved in action that most probably
saved the lives of two men involved in an auto accident.

On September 18, 1992, at approximately 1700 hours while off duty and driving
through Spokane you observed a car go off a cliff. You responded to the area
of the crash and after some difficulty located the crash scene.

At great risk to your own well-being, you descended the steep embankment to
render assistance to the two unconcious men you found ejected from their
vehicle.

As you attempted to get bystanders to help, you provided aid to the victims.
One unconscious victim was having great difficulty breathing. You cleared
the blood and dirt from his mouth and created an airway with your hand.

After arrival of paramedics you searched for additional victims and then
assisted with the transport of the victims back up the cliff.

Your response required knowledge of first aid, repelling techniques, personal
confidence, concern for the welfare of your fellow man and a great deal of
courage.

Your actions reflect highly upon yourself. Your personal pride, integrity,
physical condition and courage were all tested and not found wanting.

You are hereby officially commended for a job well done. We are very proud
of you and the manner in which your actions reflect upon this city and
department.

STANWOOD POLICE DEPARTMENT

Bob Kane
Chief

BK/jam

Official letter of commendation (one of 28
commendations received by the author).

PART TWO

It ain't over 'til it's over.

—Yogi Berra, New York Yankees

Legal terms highlighted in italics appear in a glossary as Appendix A.

CHAPTER 16

BACK INTO THE BARREL

Early-October 2009

The decision to contact the law office of Michael Pfau was the simplest of choices, for there really was no alternative. I could not go on and do nothing. Maybe another path would emerge, possibly Michael Pfau would refer me to another approach or—he would dismiss me from any consideration.

My thoughts are pessimistic, creating a scenario of Pfau's rejection. In doing this, I avoid being hopeful that he can, or wants to, take on my case. I believe that the more plausible result of any meeting would be, *Gee, what a heart wrenching, sad tale; however, sorry, I can't help you. Statute of limitations applies—too many years ago, the perpetrator was not a member of the clergy, he was not an employee of a religious order, or he is dead.*

I did not need to be an attorney to clearly understand the hurdles that would be presented to me in this case—if in fact, I had a case at all. To my mind it is very clear: *I will most likely fail, but if I don't attempt this, failure is guaranteed.*

As I review all the reasons there'll be no help for me, I listen for a live voice on the other end of the line. A receptionist answers and after a short description about why I am calling she transfers me to another person in Pfau's office. So far so good.

"Jack Kennedy here."

I think, *wow, they go by secret code names.* The seriousness in his tone dispels my theory, however. I begin my explanation for calling by briefly and generally describing that I know of a situation that occurred at St. Benedict's grade school in the 1960s, which was the absolute worst of the worst of any crimes committed against children in the Seattle Archdiocese. When he asks why this is, I respond that not only did it involve horrendous sexual abuse of multiple children, but that most, if not all of the people in authority knew about it at the time it was happening.

Kennedy now seems curious. "When did this happen?"

"Approximately, between the years of 1958-1974."

"What was the abuser's name?"

"Dan Adamson. He was the seventh-grade teacher and director of the Seattle CYO. He volunteered to run St. Benedict's teen club, the boys' choir, and played the church organ at Mass on Sundays. He was eventually promoted to principal of the school."

Jack Kennedy replies, "OK, I don't think we've heard about any cases coming out of St. Benedict's, or heard Adamson's name before. But I'll pass on the information to Mr. Pfau and—don't expect an immediate response, however—he will get back to you."

My perception is, *don't waste your time sitting by the phone waiting for a call back today.* He must be an extremely busy attorney.

In Spokane, I continue to spend my time mulling over why I'd been so inept at making progress in this venture. My initial presentation to Pfau's law firm was feeble at best. As I review the phone call in my mind, I realize that my description of the events may have been easily interpreted as telling a story that happened to someone else. Like I was a witness to the events, instead of the person it had happened to.

The next few days, I spend reviewing any and all press reports of cases such as the Archdiocese of Spokane bankruptcy, cases involving the Archdiocese of Seattle, and similar newspaper articles on the *Catholic Sex Abuse Crisis,* as referred to in the media. I read about Fr. Patrick O'Donnell, the state's most notoriously abusive priest who was transferred from parish to parish in Eastern Washington, ending up in the Seattle Archdiocese. The former Bishop Lawrence Welsh of the Spokane Diocese failed to inform Archbishop Hunthausen of the Seattle Archdiocese about Fr. O'Donnell's history and he continued being assigned to other parishes with grade schools.

What stands out with many cases in the news is a stark contrast to my allegations of a lay teacher committing sexual abuse; these all involved Catholic priests molesting male children mostly twelve, thirteen, fourteen years old.

What kind of case do I have, if a case at all? The perpetrator is not only dead, but he wasn't a priest at all, but a civilian employee—a teacher and principal at the school. What is my recourse? Do I even have legal standing to file a lawsuit, if in fact it comes to that? I have no idea if, or when, I will hear from Pfau, but I am sure he will answer the question for me in the first five minutes of the conversation, if there is to be a conversation at all.

I decide to write my story about what happened to me as a child, just the facts—who, what, when, where, and how—and did so on three by five cards. I go over and over it in my mind, practicing how I will give this information to Mr. Pfau, making sure everything is sequential and factual. I keep my three by five cards close by at all times, just in case he might call me back.

Mid-October 2009

Sunday evening comes to a close with me reading the book, *A Civil Action*. I remember a reference in the movie to the civil legal system being based upon negotiation and compromise. The book makes it clear that most cases rarely see a jury verdict. To go to that extent takes years, preparing for trial. In the final episode, one side or the other is going to get hurt, *real bad*. The author implies that only a fool would risk the costs and possible outcome of a trial. No, by far a negotiated settlement is what is desired by both parties.

Well—shit I don't want a settlement, I don't want someone to write me a check, I want justice. Justice through exposing these terrible events. Justice in revealing the people who knew and did nothing. Justice for those who could not come forward. At least I want a letter from the Archbishop admitting that they covered it up. That they knew and failed to protect the most vulnerable. With that self-righteous proclamation, I throw the book to the floor and roll over to go to sleep. It is 8:30 p.m. pacific time. A few minutes later, I am startled by the landline phone ringing. Normally, in those days I'd answer the phone even without caller ID.

My *hello* is met with, "Is this Steve O'Connor?"

"Yes, who is this?"

"Michael Pfau here. You contacted Jack Kennedy a week or so ago. Sorry I haven't gotten back to you, but I've been busy on a case in New Orleans for some time."

Where to start—*Steve, don't ramble, take a deep breath, be precise, and get back to the police days—who, what, when, where, and how.* I scramble out of bed and grab my three by five cards. I start to read my story to him over the phone, my voice formal and stilted as in relaying testimony in a case.

Pfau interrupts. "What are you reading from?"

"I wrote some things down on three by five cards."

"Put those down and just tell me what you know."

So I begin to relay what happened and what I know.

Pfau listens. Then, "I'll look into a few details when I return to Seattle and if I need to talk to you or have questions, I'll call you back."

That was it, the phone call is over as suddenly as it started. Then the waiting. One autumn week turns to two, two turns to three. This is not working. I have my doubts about hearing from Mr. Pfau again. I rehash everything I said to him and I'm sure I represented myself to Pfau as someone who knew about or was a witness to the events, instead of the person it happened to. My blocking mechanisms are still protecting me.

I have no idea how badly I will need them in the near future.

The snow is returning to Snoqualmie pass on my recurring treks to Seattle. I will figure something out. I will find a path to pursue this—with or without Michael Pfau. As I walk around Green Lake, the pelting rain pierces my clothing, not only drenching me, but it begins to feel as if I took a dive into the icy waters of the lake. The cellphone rings. It's a 206 area code: Seattle. It is 3:15 p.m. on the first Saturday in November 2009. One year beyond the 100-year anniversary.

"Michael Pfau here. You're familiar with downtown Seattle, right?"

"Yes sir, I am."

"Tomorrow morning, Washington Athletic Club, 7:30 a.m.

"Yes sir."

Click.

Why didn't I bother to ask, *how do I get in?* It's a private club. Tomorrow is Sunday. *Did he mean Monday?* He must have. I will be there both days just in case. The next five to seven hours are spent reviewing and trying to compress my entire life into a cohesive series of events. No, I only need to address the pertinent facts of the case. By the end of the evening, I have visualized a clear, consecutive description, along with a short 'pitch' about why he should look into my case.

After spending the night at my daughter Christy's house on Camano Island, she offers to drive me for my "appointment" this morning in downtown Seattle. It's a driving rain storm and the wind has picked up. As we travel the sixty-five mile drive, I'm silent about the nature of my appointment, telling no one the reason for this meeting. I wear my best dark gray suit with a clean, pressed white shirt, tie, and polished black Bostonian dress shoes. I want to make a good first impression. Christy looks worried and curious. She breaks the silence and casually pumps me with questions about the meeting. I don't respond to her questions and give her a look like, *don't ask.*

I tell her abruptly, "All you need to know is that it's a very important meeting."

She follows my specific directions to pull up in front of the Washington Athletic Club.

"I'll only be about twenty-thirty minutes; you can circle the block a few times and pick me up out front."

Downtown Seattle is eerily silent at this time on a sleepy Sunday morning. Surely he meant Monday. I remember hearing a little about the WAC being an old, traditional club for professionals with a gym, swimming pool, restaurant, and lounge. I approach the entrance and am surprised to be met by an impeccably dressed waiter who seems to be expecting me. He directs me to what looks like a large dining room, then to a table far back in an empty corner, where he gives me a perfectly brewed hot cup of Starbuck's coffee. My wait is short-lived, for out of nowhere appears someone from the entrance to the room who seems to be making a beeline for my table. It surely is Michael Pfau. He looks as though he just stepped out of his office after a long day and I wonder about the fact it's 7:30 on a Sunday morning in the depth of a winter downpour. Does this guy just live in his office? Does he just work seven days a week?

We begin by exchanging introductions. He is directly across from me, and pulls out a tablet and pen from his well-worn leather briefcase. He looks polished and professional, but also seems approachable, which relaxes me greatly. He begins to lay out the ground rules for the meeting.

"Tell me your entire story, slowly, accurately, and from the beginning. Do not go into graphic detail about any of the physical events."

"Yes, sir, I understand."

I adjust myself to a more upright position and start to open my mouth, but nothing comes out. After several awkward seconds of silence, I *unlock* and almost get something out, but it's more like a click or a cough in my mouth, no words. I try again and Mr. Pfau asks if I'm all right. *Nerves.*

Then as I begin to tell my story, stuttering the first few words, they begin to flow and I continue in a quite clear explanation that I am the person who experienced the events. I want to make sure that he understands this is not *some guy* that I know. From the other side of the table, I notice he is writing in some sort of hieroglyphics, or code, or abbreviated text. Maybe it's just his handwriting. He asks me a few questions, like how long I've been married and when I met my wife, and *are you still married?* This guy is amused now, or surprised, that I've been married that long and first met my wife in the second grade. I can see his brain working like a rocket, *bam!* He's probably thinking, she knows him—*Adamson.*

From the beginning of my narrative, I sense that I only have five or ten minutes of his time. Occasionally, he will ask me to clarify locations, or time of year, or what years. Thankfully, as the morning progresses and one hour turns into two, I realize that not only is he listening to every word, but in some miraculous fashion, I get the feeling he'll remember every little detail.

I take a bathroom break and call Christy to let her know that we'll be about another half hour. She says OK, it will take her that much time to walk back to her car from the only Starbucks she can find open in downtown Seattle on a Sunday morning.

As I complete the narrative, Pfau asks me a few final questions and thanks me for my time, as I do his.

"I'll be following up with a phone call in a few weeks."

He hesitates before leaving the room, as if he wants to say one more thing. Since he's the first person I'd confided in, pretty much the whole story, I wait for a sign from him, a reaction—was it the worst thing he's ever heard, or was it just one more story in a line of many, and nothing new? I get no signal. Still, some of the questions he asks lead me to think he's very interested in what I had to say. But I am still left wondering, *will he take my case?* And then, exactly as he had appeared, I turn back toward him and he is gone. *Poof.*

Leaving the front door of the facility, I am immediately met with a blustery gust of wind, carrying with it buckets of rain that soak my coat and hair.

Walking down the street to meet Christy, I think back to the conversation we just had. *Who is that guy?* I can't tell much about him, but my impression is that I just encountered the most intellectual, confident professional that I'd ever met. Next, I ponder a question— or more like a statement to myself: *I would not ever want to be on a witness stand with him cross-examining me.* I have the feeling that three years after this conversation, this meeting, he will pop up and say *Steve, I need to stop you right there. You said 'July 1961,' and it was August 1961.* This is my perception after the meeting. That, and the weird sensation that I just came face to face with some *avenging angel,* which is exactly what I need right then and there.

CHAPTER 17

A DECLARATION OF WAR

Several weeks later, Mr. Pfau files a lawsuit for tort damages against the Archdiocese of Seattle, the Oblates of Mary Immaculate (OMI), and the Adrian Dominican Nuns. Yes, a complaint is filed and as a layman I describe it as a *declaration of war* or *the shot across the bow*. The Archdiocese, a Washington State Corporation, has twenty days to respond, as do the Adrian Dominicans of Edmonds. The OMIs, a multinational corporation, have sixty days to respond. We have a response from the Archdiocese within the twenty days, but no word from the OMIs. Calls are made from the judge's office to the OMIs, encouraging them to respond.

Finally, in February of 2010 the OMIs respond with a letter denying they have anything to do with the abuse I experienced at St. Benedict's. My observation of Pfau's reaction to the letter is that he's not surprised and is familiar with this type of response, which is fairly standard at the beginning of a complaint. I detect that Pfau considers the letter to be "arrogant" in tone, however.

In April, the Archdiocese contacts us to schedule a meeting with their attorneys—a sit down and an opportunity to meet me. Nothing like a deposition with a court reporter transcribing—*we just want to meet and ask a few questions.*

It's a Thursday and we meet in an Archdiocesan office in Belltown, near downtown Seattle. This is the first time we are meeting one of their attorneys, Karen Kahlzer. She is very cordial and professional. I notice that she has a stack of blue-colored papers on the desk in front of her. For the past three months, I remember signing documents for a release of records—health records from doctors in Seattle and Spokane. In particular, I recall signing a release for all medical files from the Veterans Administration.

Prior to the meeting, Michael Pfau had prepared me for responding to other attorneys. He explained the importance of waiting for the person to ask a question and waiting before you answer, in case your attorney wants to intervene or object. After about two hours into the meeting, we take a break in the restroom and I mention the large stack of papers to Michael Pfau.

"There must be two hundred plus pages, pale blue. All the rest were white."

In dealing with the VA for a determination or qualifying for disability, I remember that all of their records were on pale blue paper.

Early on in my meetings with Michael Pfau, I voiced my concern about having the trial in Seattle. He was probably five years old when the Vietnam War was happening and in addition to being raised in the Midwest—he did not have my experience.

"Mr. Pfau, I don't think you'll get a very favorable jury here."

"Why?"

"People don't like cops and people really, really don't like Vietnam vets!"

I conceded that after 911, the police have a better image.

"No, I think you're mistaken. Maybe in the 1970s or 1980s, but now it's different."

Maybe he's right. My experience in Spokane was certainly different then the west side of the State. When the cable guy came to our house, he right away commented on my Purple Heart license plates, and asked about the years that I served in Vietnam. We walked into the family room and he looked over at the bar I created with parts from my favorite second-hand building supplies. He sees the backdrop—custom made mirror—and notices a picture of me in police uniform and my badge hanging next to it. *You were a police officer too!*

When he said, *Thank you for your service,* I believe he was sincere. Not the sarcasm from Seattle about being military or a cop. So my three-hundred mile drive from Spokane to Seattle was like going between two different worlds—politically and culturally—a divide often referred to as the *Cascade Curtain.*

I keep thinking, they're going to Vietnam and they're going there in spades. I mention this to Pfau.

"No, they wouldn't touch that with a ten foot pole. They'd be crazy!"

My response: "Yeah, they will."

Seeing the blue stack of paper at the meeting with the Archdiocese attorney, Kahlzer, was my first realization of what we are up against.

During the spring and summer of 2010 there are a volley of interrogatories back and forth. I'd sit down and fill out nearly three hundred various questions, sometimes taking days to complete. The answers need to be exact and perfect and I strive to do justice to each one. Some are easy, but others go on and on covering the same subject: *were you married? how long were you married? where did you get married?* and every little detail about your marriage. Through this process there is no clock ticking, no trial date, or deadline. But soon the Seattle Archdiocese schedules a mediation.

This is a chance for the other parties to attend all day and observe, get to know the attorney and the client, hear what they have to say without actually being in court. It was a courtesy to extend an invitation to the Adrian Dominicans and OMIs. During the meeting, the mediator hands a letter to Michael Pfau from the OMIs. Pfau looks it over and turns to me.

"The letter says thank you for the invitation, we will not attend, and basically *come and get us.*"

The gist of it was pretty arrogant and I'm thinking, *whoa, those guys must not know Mr. Pfau.* I've been familiar with him long enough to recognize I would not be sending him a letter even implying *come and get us.* I think that's like inviting the 1st Marine Division to land in your foxhole.

He is very calm, looks at me, placing the letter face down onto the table—

"Oh, we will."

That was the smoothest, most professional stature I'd ever witnessed. If this guy ever gets into a courtroom— I'd love to watch him, such extreme confidence. As we walk outside to a rare springtime sunny day, he sounds sure of himself, upbeat as he says,

"Not bad for day one, eh?"

There was a cash settlement offer on the table.

As I wade into this legal process against the "church" I learn how they "deal" with the victims. Make them sign a piece of paper and give them a check. All I want is a written apology stating that they knew about it—the Archdiocese knew about it, St. Benedict's knew about it, that there were many victims, and they covered it up. I express this to Mr. Pfau,

"What I want is the Archbishop to talk to the principal, the deacon, the priest, everybody who arranged the anniversary about the worst things that happened at St. Benedict's, then direct them to quit covering it up and tell all their parishioners the truth."

Mr. Pfau responds. "I wish it were that easy. Yes, in a certain way that seems reasonable: call the Archdiocese, explain the facts, and ask for a letter of apology. But that isn't how it happens. They apologize with their check book when they're cornered. If you're waiting for them to come and say, *Steve, it was terrible and we covered it up*, don't expect that."

I know if we go to trial it will be three to four years down the road in King County Superior Court. Continuances can be approved, delaying the trial; proposed summary judgments from the defense; more discovery; depositions; and this could drag on for years. In addition, there is the possibility of it being referred to federal court, which could take even longer. I am in this for the long haul

I begin to learn about all the ways that attorneys and clients prepare for trial. I pick up on the reason for interrogatories, which I fill out meticulously as they can be used at a later time to impeach my testimony. Literally, if you say that you wear a size 35 shorts and you wear a 34, you're going to be asked about that.

During the discovery period, I wonder if Mr. Pfau is busy traveling all over the world looking for that person I told this to --- a therapist, person at a bar, some baseball player, someone at work, a police officer, anyone that could possibly change the starting time/ trigger for the statute of limitations. *Oh, I am looking forward to hearing the results of that futile search, cause you can look all over the world and you're never going to find anybody I told this to. I never told anyone.*

In December 2010, everything shuts down until January 2011. Over the past year, I have received lots of documents from Jack Kennedy and others to sign or review. Jack also starts asking for things like my high school yearbook, pictures of me as a St. Benedict's student, a picture of me in Vietnam, and as a police officer.

He says, *just send them in a mailer, snail mail,* but I don't do that. I jump in my old black Jeep Cherokee and drive over to Seattle and hand deliver them. I don't care if it is snowing in the pass, or if I have other plans or appointments. I really want to be at the Columbia Tower. This is where the action is, and when I arrive with paperwork and pictures in hand, with any luck, there's an impromptu ten minute conversation with Jack Kennedy or Mr. Pfau, if he is around.

I feel close to what's going on and it gives me a feeling into the case. When I'm back in Spokane, I'd wonder what is going on with my case in Seattle. Being in the Columbia Tower, I feel alive, things are happening, and my senses are heightened.

Afterward, I treat myself to a Dick's cheese burger and milkshake, walk around Green Lake, drive by St. Benedict's, drive up and down Wallingford and get a cup of Starbucks coffee on the upper floor of the old Food Giant store. Each time I repeat this ritual, my focus becomes razor sharp—I am back there and I can remember everything. There are no years separating the past, it's not 2011—it's 1961, 1962, 1963, 1964, 1965. It is intense and at times debilitating—very unsettling. However, I remain steadfast and with my sharpened sense of purpose, I commit to *this must be done, this is what's going to happen.* It is black and white in my world. Then, I drive back to Eastern Washington, sit in my old colonial style house and wait another month and wonder—*is anything happening?*

Then March 2011 happens. I am in Seattle, delivering paperwork to Mr. Pfau and planning to stay overnight with my daughter on Camano Island. During the day, I start to feel physically agitated—my pulse is racing on and off. I try to ignore it while on my way to Camano Island and decide to stop off at the Everett Marina to check on my boat and walk around the docks. As the rain pours down on me, I'm not cooled down, but burning up, I feel hot—120 degrees. My pulse rapidly fires off and then stops for four-five seconds, then I can't get my breath. My pulse is real erratic. *BBBBBBmphfph,* then nothing, then *BBBBBBmphfph* again. I decide to drive up to Providence hospital. I park my car, walk in the door and nearly collapse. Next, I ride the lightning—they jump start me—and then keep me in the hospital. They say I had a mild heart attack caused by atrial fibrillation— massive atrial fibrillation. So they conduct an echo cardiogram and all sorts of other tests. I'm there for three to four days and they explain the results of my echocardiograms, my scans, and my arteries— all look OK. There are no blood clots, no deterioration of arteries, no problem with valves; it seems to be some kind of electrical malfunction. Outside of the fact that everything else looks like I'm a twenty-five year-old, I can drop dead from this. The mild heart attack has caused some small amount of damage. They prescribe some medication that doesn't seem to do anything for me.

While in the hospital, I'm thinking, *I'm just getting into this project and now I might drop dead, especially if you look at the history of my family, no joke, it's a given.* So I contact Michael Pfau.

"As soon as I get out of the hospital, I'm going to settle with the Archdiocese."

At the time, I'm worried about my demise, so I should take what the Archdiocese offers me and give it to my kids. At least they'll get something out of this after having to live with me all their life.

In April 2011, against Mr. Pfau's strong recommendation (he was adamant that we not settle) we get in touch with the Archdiocese and settle their part of the case—I have to sign an agreement. I did not get an apology. I give the check to my wife and tell her to distribute it among the family. Tuition for the grandkids and any other ways to help them out.

I still have the feeling that I might drop dead at any moment and ironically, this gives me purpose to not only hasten things, but a stronger will to do this. The medicine isn't working very well, but what I do notice is that when I get these attacks of atrial fibrillation, I can almost fix them by myself, quite often through physical exercise—climbing up and down stairs, walking briskly, running around Green Lake, racing up and down the street to the Columbia Tower and it goes away. Usually when I am sitting down or lying down, I'm lethargic, so it is just the opposite. So I am able to manage.

Historically, I've always owned a boat. This summer, my twenty-five-foot boat is docked at the Everett Marina. Instead of driving back and forth from Spokane to Seattle and up to Christy's, or staying in a hotel, I sometimes stay on the boat. The times when I'm not at the Columbia Tower working on the project, I consciously isolate myself from my family by working on the boat and spending the night there. I don't want to be around anyone I know, don't want to bring the *dirt* of what was happening on to anyone.

Other times, while staying in downtown Seattle, I feel very comfortable at the Sip and Slide wine bar in downtown. I would walk into this place with my briefcase and dressed in a suit, and someone inevitably sits down across from me, usually a woman. They ask me what I do for a living.

"Oh, I'm in Seattle working on a project at the Columbia Tower."

"Oh, you're an attorney."

"No, I'm not an attorney."

"Oh sure you are!"

"No, no I'm not."

It's interesting to watch all of these professionals walk into this place, and I began to enjoy surrounding myself with people I don't know. So when I am not downtown, I'm on the boat, and I am rarely in Spokane anymore.

As the case progresses, I need to be very close to the scene of the crime. In the winter of 2011, I gave my first deposition. There had been two continuances given by this time and also *summary judgments*—appeals to the court by either side as to why this case should not move forward. Michael Pfau made arguments against and the defense argues to drop the case.

This is when the high-stakes poker game begins. Every time summary judgments come up, I think, maybe we should just call the OMIs and settle. One weekend as I wait until Monday to hear what the decision will be, I continue to dwell on a settlement option rather than sweating over and over the outcome of a summary judgment, though chances of my case being thrown out are slim. It has veracity and it is a direct evidence case.

You can corroborate my story again and again, it is not a he said/she said case. Yet, always in my mind I worry about the statute of limitations, or the borrowed servant doctrine. The Oblates argue that they are only borrowed servants and that they did not run the parish, it was the Archdiocese that was responsible for managing the parish. The other issue is the *statute of limitations trigger*, which has not been tested in a trial such as this in Washington State. For this reason, we keep avenues open for mediation and negotiation. This is about to be tested in a court of law—no different than Miranda vs. Arizona, or Terry vs. Ohio—this is going to be precedent-setting for case law, re: statute of limitations.

So every time Mr. Pfau receives notice about a summary judgment, this is the topic that gets real close to your bones; don't even try and go to sleep, *tick tick tick*. It's like a time bomb waiting to go off.

During times such as these, I stay on my boat and work on it. I keep away from anybody I know. Near the end of 2011, there is another argument for a continuance before the judge and the judge rules against—*no, this trial is going to move forward and start on June 4, 2012, and there will be no more continuances.*

CHAPTER 18

THE VARSITY

As 2011 comes to a close, it is time to head to Spokane and act normal for the upcoming holidays. Now is a good time to remove myself from the confines of my self-imposed isolation ward. The last three weeks of incessant rain and wind at the marina made it much easier for me to envision a large living area with a warm fire, normal people to talk to, and maybe the enjoyment of some football games on television. And so, I return to my regular existence for the remainder of December. January, and a return to *the project* would come soon enough.

It is now mid-January 2012, and as I plod through the snowy mountain pass on my drive to Seattle, I am keenly aware that 2012 is *the year*. The trial is pretty much set in concrete, and barring any unforeseen court decisions to the contrary, June 4th will remain as the opening day. The last continuances have been granted and expired. More depositions are being scheduled. My family members are beginning to be subpoenaed for depositions and I am preparing for interviews with the expert witness for the defendants, Dr. McGovern. Additionally, I am having interviews with Dr. Conte, our expert witness on child abuse victims.

For the last two plus years, I have primarily interfaced with Michael Pfau, almost exclusively. Eventually, I come to discover that Pfau was not a single individual who accomplished everything from making the coffee at the firm to bringing cases to trial—to taking out the garbage, typing all the documents, and everything else involved with the practice of law.

In the back of my mind, I'm preparing for a time as events progress when other people in the law firm will likely be involved, or are already working on my case. Some I know, others I see passing by me in the office now and then, without any introductions as to who they are. There is, of course, Jack Kennedy, and yes, it really is his name and not some secret code name as I whimsically pondered when I first met him.

Then there is Jessica. I was not at all aware of how much, if at all, she was involved with my case, but I got to know her, not by discussing my case or any other legal matters, but by her being how I will always think of her: *A Calm in the Storm*. I look forward to coming through the door of the law firm early in the morning and stopping by her desk to waste her time with my idle conversations, like what the weather is doing or how the drive over the pass was. She is unique and kind, and listens to my fragmented ramblings with great patience. I hope that she knows nothing—and would never know anything—about the case. She's just too nice to have it "spilled" on her.

Eventually, I would learn that this was another of my total misunderstandings about how Pfau's' firm operated. In reality, the entire team had been involved since day one.

Another player I refer to as the *Den Mother* because I didn't know her name. She seems to do everything that I originally thought Pfau did: make the coffee, make arrangements for travel and hotels accommodations, and she is a silent rock that holds everything together. Mr. Pfau is traveling all over the place and other attorneys in the firm are going all over the U.S. and somehow she takes care of all those logistics. She works silently in the background which results in an efficiently run law firm.

Then there is *mystery man*. I only see him occasionally pass by on his way in or out of his office. He seems to operate somewhere down the hall. I frequently have the urge to walk his way and take a peek at his office wall. He looks like he might have a plaque that reads, *Secret Agent Smith* or something. The guy is very intriguing to me. I don't think he is an attorney, or law partner, but somehow I sense that he is involved in the case. Maybe he is the investigating guru who travels all over the United States tracking down witnesses and interviewing them? No—maybe he is a *James Bond*. No—I got it, he is a former FBI or CIA guy. But why do they have him around? He seems pleasant, but I never once hear him talk. He has a muscular, athletic build, like an NFL defensive back. Clothes that fit perfectly. No doubt, the best looking, most squared away appearance of any at the firm.

Years later, when I asked Pfau to arrange an interview with him for the book, his response was, *No, you can't, because he doesn't work here. He just rents an office.* So much for my evaluating the players.

It was in the early part of 2012 that I frequently began with this greeting to Jack Kennedy as I arrived at the Columbia Tower:

"Hi Jack, you working on any exciting, important cases?"

The answer would always be the same.

"Yeah Steve, yours." Only later did I begin to comprehend and realize the teamwork, skills, and assets of people in the firm who worked tirelessly on my case.

In early spring, what I had dreaded, came to be. I've always had a concern that one day I'd walk into the law firm and Kennedy would say something like, *Michael Pfau is moving on to another case. Here is Mr. so and so, who will now be representing you.* Of course, in reality, this was never going to happen, but it is tucked away as a worry of mine. As I wait in the conference room with my morning coffee, Jack sticks his head in and announces, *follow me to another smaller conference room down the hall.*

When I open the door there is no Pfau. What greets me instead is someone I've seen many times entering and leaving the office. I know he is a member of the firm, but we've not been formally introduced. In passing by him periodically, he looks very pleasant but he also looks to me as if he is right out of high school. He is tall, thin, nice looking though at times, unshaven. When he interfaces with others, I notice he is the kind of person with too much *touchy, feely* for me. I think he is certainly not a *dragon slayer*. And at this point in time, preparing for trial, I need a dragon slayer.

As I enter the small room, he stands and steps across the room— way too close to me, shakes my hand, places his other hand on my shoulder and introduces himself.

"Hi Steve, my name is Jason Amala—last name rhymes with Pamela."

I am not amused. I'm aware that the law firm consists of Pfau, Cochran, Vertetis, Amala, however, I am only familiar with Pfau. I want to talk to no one but Michael Pfau. Besides, this guy can't be the "Amala" of the firm. He proceeds to explain that he will be working with me the next few weeks. He talks about what we will be doing in the upcoming days. I immediately interrupt him, not in a polite way.

"Where did you go to school?"

"University of Washington," he replies with a smile. The guy is always smiling.

"No, I mean where did you go to law school?"

"Oh, yes. Seattle University."

At this time, I almost ask, *when do you graduate?* Instead, before I can get ahold of myself and refrain from becoming obnoxious, I blurt out in a loud voice, "I want the guy from Boston College!"

I slap my hand on the desk, storm out of the room, slamming the door behind me, and drive back to my boat.

Eventually I would learn that over the past decade, Jason, a law partner of Pfau, Cochran, Vertetis, Amala, has recovered millions of dollars for his clients. He has also been one of the lead appellate lawyers on a number of important issues that have expanded the rights of his clients and others. Since 2010, Jason has been annually recognized as a "Rising Star" or "Superlawyer" by Washington Law and Politics.

He was raised in Salem, Oregon, but moved to Seattle to attend the University Of Washington Honors College. After graduating with distinction, Jason enrolled in the Seattle University School of Law, where he graduated second in his class, earned top honors in ten of his law school courses, received the Faculty Scholar Award at graduation, and was twice elected president of the student body.

CHAPTER 19

AFFLICTION

After I settle with the Seattle Archdiocese, there is a lull in the case. I am busy with my home in Spokane, remodeling and making improvements. There is nothing to keep me over on the west side so buying another boat that needs tons of work is the perfect solution to get me back over there, near the case.

During the fall of 2011, I bought a forty-foot fiberglass, California trawler and christened it, *Affliction*. This boat will keep me busy for years to come.

It's located near Everett on a river/slough in the backwaters off Puget Sound, tied up to an old wooden dock that is falling down and decrepit. There is a highway and bridge to the east with a steady stream of traffic day and night. It's a very different marina than the Everett Marina. Whenever I walk across the bridge down the rickety stairs I hope the dock will not sink. There is an electrical wire near a metal railing, while another is in the water, which I always avoid as I fear being electrocuted. Each night, coal trains pass by and leave a layer of black dust on the boat. A boat tied up in front of me is half-submerged; rats swim in the river and run around the dock at night. It all suits my mood at the time. For me, this boat is perfect: neglected for about twenty years, the inside walls are all rotten and caving in, an accumulation of mold all around. The bathroom is not working and there is no waste-treatment system. But the Caterpillar diesel engines are functional.

I spend months painting and cleaning that summer, fall, and winter and on into the next year. As my legal battle with the Catholic Church continues, the *Affliction*, becomes a new formidable opponent. I use all my physical strength and skills to try transform this boat to its original grandeur. Scrubbing and scouring the outside, I then move to the inside and determine how I can repair what is broken and falling down.

The exterior of the boat has fourteen-foot long sections of teak railing, exposed to the weather for twenty years with no attention or maintenance. My friend who knows a great deal about boats said, *don't throw those away—teak is the hardest wood and once you start sanding the top layer of wood, it will change from that tannish-grey, checkered pattern to a beautiful rich finish.* Knowing that teak is worth over thirty dollars a foot, I decide to take on the challenge of sanding and uncover what is hidden on a five-foot section and make this my project. When the intermittent rain comes and I can't cure it outside, I place a couple of heaters in the aft cabin, which is huge on this trawler, and place the railing inside. Overall, my boat looks pretty good after a few months of dedicated work.

During a particularly difficult time for me, after completing a few more depositions and the only communication from my attorney is *well, things are going as expected; there is another summary judgment,* which I refer to as the high-stakes poker game. I get a call and yes, we survive another one and the case hasn't been thrown out on statute of limitations and we're still scheduled for trial in June.

So I keep sanding this teak, rub it with a tack cloth to remove the dust. I repeat this over and over, until the color shows through. I take some cherry stain, mix it with walnut, and rub that into the wood. I come back the next day and see that it looks richer, darker and the teak grains begin to show through. My boating friend tells me to put six coats of spar varnish on the wood and *you won't believe what it looks like,* and it will last in the weather for five years. I brush the first coat of varnish onto the railing which is about three inches round in diameter. Then another coat of stain which looks nubby and sandy, so I do as he recommends, sand it again with steel wool, put another coat of varnish, wait for it to dry and sand again. After three coats of spar varnish, it is deep and you can stare into the wood, seeing the teak—yeah I'm in here. It is like bandaging scar tissue and when the new tissue forms, the stiches come out and it looks better, like my leg, healthier and beginning to grow new muscle. It is whole and strong.

While working on the *Affliction* that spring, Mr. Pfau calls me and I meet him at the Columbia Tower. There is not a lot for me to do at this point, so I decide to drive back to Spokane and stay home for two weeks. As usual, I become anxious to get back to the west side to be near any developments in my case and to work on the *Affliction*.

It is a beautiful sunny day and I continue with my teak project. I move the railing out to the deck and apply coat number four, let it dry, and then apply the fifth coat of spar varnish. When finished, I carefully move it back into the cabin of the boat to cure. I notice there is a big old horsefly buzzing around the cabin. I have my headphones on listening to music and watching my teak railing dry, when I see the fly land on my teak and get stuck in the spar varnish. Well, I'll just flick it off, then wait for the teak to dry, sand it down again, and re-apply the varnish. That's the logical, intelligent, adult thing to do to fix it. But at this time—after two and a half years into the lawsuit, I'm not an intelligent, well-rounded, logical adult—far from it.

I'm not sure why, but as I watch the fly's wing get stuck and it struggles to break free, I think, *don't let it suffer, just put it out of its misery*. I look around the boat for something to hit it with. I spot a big, fat, short-handled sledgehammer lying in close proximity to me. That's a good way to kill the fly. So I reach over, pick it up, and with all my strength, come down hard and hit the fly. As I lift up the sledge hammer and look down at the railing, it is a real mess with big huge dents in my beautiful teak. I grab one end of the railing with my right hand and hit the teak with the sledgehammer, again and again, at the same time thinking—*teak is a really hard wood, it did not crack, did not break, there are just dents and I've ruined my finish*. But I just keep going, hitting the teak until suddenly the sledgehammer flies out of my hand and crashes through the side window, sending shards of glass into the water (followed by the fly swatter).

I look at my teak and my broken window and calmly walk off the boat, drive two miles to the Everett Marina, walk into Anthony's

Homeport Restaurant, order a happy hour burger and a Coors Light. I feel really calm. Afterward, back at the *Affliction,* I sleep like a baby. The next morning, I wonder if that's how my case is going to go, cause I've been hittin' a lot of teak, hittin' it for one year, two years, and wonder if it will ever budge. So the *Affliction,* is my "affliction," and in another way, my escape. I'm really not so sure it's about the teak railing at all—but teak is a very, very hard wood—a beautiful wood and it can be revived. From old, grey, and weathered wood it can become whole again. Maybe the teak is like the human spirit. Teak is a very hard wood.

CHAPTER 20

ALL ABOARD
(SPEECH ON THE BEACH)

We still have the Adrian Dominicans of Edmonds to settle with. As this case goes on, and as cases went on across the state, there was the same theme, and it made me angry and perplexed. That theme in Catholic schools all across the nation was the Catholic nuns who were teaching in the schools, probably knew about 90 percent of the abuse cases. Many people come to their defense, however. *Oh, the poor nuns were subservient or did not have any power.* But I believe they got off scot free. It was also evident that if we dragged them into a trial they'd come in their walkers, neck braces—and people would think, *oh, the poor nuns, they look like our grandmothers.*

When push came to shove, however, it didn't take the Dominicans a New York-minute to come up with a very hardline, expensive, and experienced trial lawyer. He was not cheap, and he was not a nobody. So they responded right away with the first stringers.

Mr. Pfau and I want them out of the way so that we can concentrate on the real caretakers of the parish, the central ones who covered this up, not someone on the periphery like the Adrian Dominicans.

Depositions wound up. In late April and early May, Pfau contacts me and says that Judge Shaffer has ordered one more mandatory court mediation and makes it clear on both sides in no uncertain terms that she wants to give us one more chance to settle this, because if not, someone is going to get hurt real bad at trial. Michael Pfau and I prepare to walk over to the offices for mediation, ten blocks up the street. At this time, we are joined by Darrell Cochran from the firm. He shows up and mistakenly, as I did with Jessica, I hope he doesn't know anything about this case. *Why is Cochran here, he's not been involved at all?* Well, that is ridiculous, he knows all about the case, as did Amala, and Jessica— they knew for three years. It seems to me that Cochran and Pfau go way back, possibly graduating from Michigan Law School together and that he is a trial lawyer, a first stringer.

I think it's odd that he's coming with us today, for the mediation. I'm familiar with the process by now—one individual, the mediator, goes between the two entities who are sequestered in separate rooms. Neither side talks directly to each other. The mediator asks what you want, then meets with the other side and tells them, and negotiations go back and forth. At one mediation with the Archdiocese, we started at eight o'clock in the morning and ended at five p.m. We usually ordered sandwiches at noon.

So as we walk up the street, Cochran makes small talk with me. Once we reach the offices, we sit down and the mediator enters the room. Mr. Pfau asks who is coming for the Oblates, and he responds, *I think it's Boris Gavaria.* Michael Pfau looks as if he isn't impressed—a third stringer. Mr. Pfau tells the mediator, *don't bother ordering sandwiches, we're not going to be here very long.*

We are willing to go through the mediation procedure, but I'm fixated on going to trial. There is a possibility that the Oblates will come up with a gigantic figure—four million or three million— which would make the decision more complicated. I just can't think of a number that will work; maybe three years ago when I was in the hospital. But with the Oblates, there is never a figure on the table. I think if Pfau calls them, they might come over with a check. But maybe not. They are just so bullheaded and arrogant, determined to just go to trial.

The mediation session lasts forty-five minutes, then we are done and packing up to get out of there.

Mr. Pfau says, "Well, that makes the decision for you to go to trial real easy."

I am not privy to what went on. Maybe they offered a dollar—

I'm not sure. As we walk down the street, Mr. Pfau again remarks on how that mediation makes it easy to go to trial. I look at Cochran and ask him what he thinks about going to trial.

He almost shouts, "This case must go to trial, must go to trial!"

I think that's pretty arrogant for a guy who doesn't know me and knows very little about the case.

Shortly after this, Mr. Pfau explains to me that from now to the end of the trial, Darrell Cochran is going to be here with us every day. *Ok, so he's going to be at the trial. I don't know what he's going to be* doing *at the trial.*

In my mind, when the trial starts, everyone is going to sit down and be quiet, and Mr. Pfau is going to run a one-man show, and Darrell, Jason, and everybody else is going to just sit there with their hands folded.

I return to my boat for a week or so, and as Memorial Day weekend approaches, I drive back to Spokane. I'm having some doubts. Judge Shaffer's implication that *somebody is going to get hurt real bad* comes and goes in my thoughts. And I think of that similar statement in *A Civil Action*, "only a fool ends up proceeding to actual trial." One of us is going to lose, and I just have visions of this case going world-class and the jury finding in my favor but then the judge says, "*oh, by the way I'm overturning the verdict on the statute of limitations, or I'm reducing the award,* or something would go wrong and there'd be a mistrial. There are so many ways that a mistrial can happen and I think about that. This is another factor.

The risks are just too great. I have visions of this case going all the way, the jury finding in my favor. Then, the worries take over. The risks consume my thoughts. Could there be time constraints causing a mistrial? Could there be nothing for the sacrifice? The possible outcomes are daunting.

All the way back to Spokane, my thoughts veer to my four children. Is there going to be nothing that I can somehow do, to make up for my quirkiness and hardship during their lives? My family went through so many struggles as they grew up with me, always determined to figure things out. No matter how hard Gail and I worked, it was always difficult to make ends meet. So, it wasn't like my kids had it easy. For example, turning sixteen did not mean going out to the driveway to find a new car with a bow on it. It was more like me visiting the wrecking yard and finding a shipwreck of a vehicle and turning it around with some welding and a homemade paint job. It wouldn't be new, but it's transportation to school and jobs.

They all have kids, spouses, house payments, health care costs, braces, and school tuition now to handle and they are doing whatever it takes to make ends meet. At the same time, they witness me constantly on the verge of a high-level nervous breakdown for three and a half years. I'm always gone while Gail is running the whole place and working all the time. I am rarely present. Everything is just uncertain.

If I go to trial and walk out of that courtroom, having lost, I've lost three and a half years of my life. At sixty-three, that's—a lot of wasted time. The thought of putting my family through this even longer is weighing on my mind. I've had to tell this story and I imagine it has not been easy on my family—confusion and worry.

On my drive across the state, my mind delves deeper into what is the right thing to do—the best course of action. I start to have rash thoughts of calling Michael Pfau and telling him to settle for whatever we can get.

I arrive in Spokane and head to the family room with my rock fireplace. I cocoon myself in, watching a golf tournament, going through my depositions, reviewing my stacks of paperwork, and thinking of the case a hundred different ways in my mind.

It's a Saturday afternoon and Gail comes downstairs and announces that my eldest daughter just called. She wants to know if she can come over and have a beer with me and cook some hot dogs. This is one of our traditional ways of getting together. I'm thankful for the diversion and agree.

Around dinner time, she arrives. It is still light outside this spring evening. I see her show up through the window in what I like to call a thoroughly used *grocery getter, a family vehicle*. I notice that she needs new tires. She interrupts my thoughts.

"Hi Dad, what are you watching on TV"?

"Just some golf tournament."

She rallies back with, "Are you up for a movie?"

"Sure, what about *Bullitt*?"

She gestures *no*, then heads out to her car and comes back with a six-pack of Coors Light and her own DVD choice. She walks over to a wall in the family room and unrolls a poster.

"Do you have any tacks? I think it should hang right here where you spend your spare time. As a reminder."

As she unfurls the surprise, I recognize the distinct outline of the fighter and character from the Rocky Balboa movies. He is celebrating the struggle of life at the top of the stairs—to be at the top, with his fists pumped into the air. She smiles and holds up the DVD, *Rocky III*.

I remember when Stephanie was just starting high school and testing her skills as a cross-country runner for the first time. It was not uncommon for she and her teammates, including sister runner, Robyn, to get together and watch the Rocky movies as inspiration and preparation to endure the grueling distance and pace of the races.

As we start to view the movie, she quickly asks, "Can we fast-forward to, 'The Speech on the Beach' part?"

"Sure, OK". *I wonder why we're not starting at the beginning.*

As any Rocky fan knows, this beloved character starts out with a lot of struggles with not much to lose and eventually ends up successful by the time this movie installment comes around. Perhaps that is why he is so determined. Once the character finds himself in a position where he must fight and risk losing everything—once he has a family to think about—he begins a period of major self-doubt and begins to give up. He is on the beach, training with Apollo Creed, who is really pushing him in all directions—and it is all confusion.

There are lots of flashbacks of pain and suffering during the scene for the fighter. He is lost in his thoughts on the beach looking out over the ocean waves as the sun is starting to fade. A family member has to intervene after watching his despair, turmoil, and the loss of confidence. They realize Rocky needs some encouragement and a tough reminder. They ask the fighter if he just wants to give up or do what is right, no matter what the cost. They remind him that it doesn't matter if he loses everything in this world, he will never be happy if he doesn't just go for it. He has already lost a lot; there is nothing else to lose.

Just as I realize that I am the fighter that is starting to worry about what I will lose, I am caught up in the similar thoughts as the athlete on the beach, Stephanie pauses the movie after that scene.

"I hope that was not lost on you," she says.

"Well, yes, I get it and while I've got you here, you need to know the trial starts in eight days."

I explain to her my frame of mind—and my dilemma—and how easy it would be to pick up the phone and call Michael Pfau, telling him to settle instead of going through the next grueling phase. I express my concern for how hard the law firm has worked and that it's a precedent setting case. I explained that no dollar-figure in the world would help me with this issue. By now, I know the Catholic Church will never admit their guilt, is never going to apologize.

"Forget it, we're going to trial," she says suddenly.

I think, *who's we?* All my children are under subpoena and it was made real clear that they could be dragged into the courtroom and testify, if asked. At times, I think it might be a bluff on the behalf of the Oblates; however, they are on the witness list, ready to be called to the Columbia Tower and wait—their workplaces already notified.

Stephanie persists with her argument. "You should go to trial, you've gone through all of this. That is why I showed you that movie and I why I brought you that poster."

"Well, that is pretty arrogant of you. Don't you think you need to at least talk to your siblings before you go speaking on their behalf?"

"As a matter of fact, I've already reached out to them and made sure everyone was in total agreement, so they could support my efforts."

She goes on to explain that basically the sentiment from all of them is that I should just remember that this is for the principle of it all, and that any check or settlement offer that is on the table should go right back at them.

"We kids are prepared to go through whatever is needed. If we have to testify at trial, whatever it takes, we're there. I've been talking to my siblings and Ryan thinks you are looking so distraught and not well. He's been worried."

"OK."

"I told Ryan that you would not be able to survive if you had not at least tried. That if anyone can endure this like no one else can, it will be Dad, and we need to support you. It's been a difficult, scary decision to rally for you to go for it! It is much easier to watch in a movie scene."

"Yeah, it would be good to have your support."

They want to leave me with the constant reminder of the guts it takes to go to trial, and you can lose everything else on this earth, but they cannot take away the courage and the support of family.

As Stephanie walks to the door to leave, she gets a call. The ringtone is unmistakable.

"By the way—we all changed our ringtones for the upcoming trial."

It's, "Gonna Fly Now," the movie theme from *Rocky*.

This is the wrap. The last real event for me, prior to the trial. A huge burden is lifted off me. Like leaving on a jet plane for Vietnam is terrible, arriving in Vietnam is dreadful but once you're in the firefight, you're stuck, you're already there, you're in the jungle, *so let's get to it.*

That's how I feel, the anticipation is a psychological roller coaster. Now that I have the family thing out of the way, things are clear, and what I need to do is black and white. I jump in the car that following Monday and go straight to the Columbia Tower with my Rocky ringtone.

We're going code, we're going to trial.

(Left to right) Jason Amala, Darrell Cochran, Michael Pfau, and Thomas Vertitas of PCVA Attorneys at Law, Seattle, Washington.

The *Affliction*.

PART THREE

To everything there is a season,
And a time for purpose under Heaven

—Ecclesiastes 3:1

CHAPTER 21

THE RECKONING: A TIME FOR WAR

June 4th, 2012, 6:00 a.m.
Columbia Center, Downtown Seattle

We have arrived for the truth to finally be told and a slim hope that justice will be served. It has been almost three years of high-stakes poker, summary judgments, depositions, statute of limitations, borrowed servant doctrine, and they all swirl in my head as I sip my coffee at the Starbucks on the ground floor of the Columbia Tower. My black oversized briefcase, constantly by my side since the first moment I met Michael Pfau, is dutifully laying on the table. It is a testament to a period of uncertainty, fallibility, fear, and lately, my life spent on the edge of a high-level nervous breakdown. I never browse through the briefcase. I only add each document, each letter, each resulting court proceeding, each memo from my attorney's desk.

It seems the briefcase has joined the twelve-year-old as they become the audience to the drama about to unfold. Will I survive this latest war? Will I come out fatally wounded? Will I again fail to be the voice of the child? I cannot answer, but I do know this: it will take every bit of courage I can muster, and no matter how strong I am, justice will be determined by twelve humans whom I have never laid eyes upon.

I have no regrets. I have never been able to conceive of any other way. I must complete this journey.

I think back to my speech at the Seattle Police Academy graduation, where I quoted Theodore Roosevelt:

"The credit belongs to the man who is actually in the arena; whose face is marred by the dust and sweat and blood; who strives valiantly...who, at worst, if he fails, at least fails while daring greatly; so that his place shall never be with those cold and timid souls who know neither victory or defeat."

I am proud that I held out against the Oblates of Mary Immaculate. This had certainly been a heroic endeavor so far. But another quote from long ago comes to my mind. *Show me a hero, and I'll write you a tragedy.*

My disjointed thoughts are interrupted by a conversation taking place near the counter. A man is discussing whether to buy a particular roast of coffee beans. I see he has a pound of French roast coffee beans in hand, and I sadly smile to myself. *French roast.*

I drift back to the awe inspiring Annamite Cordillera Mountain range in the fall of 1967, my eighteenth year on earth. To the hills above the village we would come to know as Khe Sanh, and then to the Frenchman, Felix Poilane, and his coffee plantation, which rested in a rich and beautiful valley surrounded by myriad shades of green.

This valley, tucked into the northwest corner of Vietnam, soon became the deathbed for many a Marine. And the final resting place for over forty thousand North Vietnamese. Only *North* Vietnamese, to us. To them, they were just Vietnamese, trying to extricate themselves from yet another in a long line of foreign invaders.

As for Felix Poilanes' coffee plantation? Well, it would soon lie in rubble, resembling burnt matchsticks. Poilane would explain to me how those beautiful dark green bushes with their delicate white flowers took ten years of loving care to produce. Those hardy vanilla-colored beans encased in a brilliant red pod that are eventually dried and shipped to a roaster.

Early in the first few months of my tour in Vietnam, while my classmates in high school were graduating and getting ready for college in the summer and fall of 1967, we Marines had come down from the "hill battles" to Khe Sanh. It was a time before the buildup; there were no large Marine battalions there, but the Seabees had built an airstrip and bunkers. There was a PX, showers, and hot food. It was relatively safe during this period of time.

Part of the mission was to "win the hearts and minds" of the Vietnamese which became a crude saying: "feed them, then bomb them". A Navy Corpsman was charged with working with the village people by providing them with some basic hygiene instruction: handing out toothbrushes, de-licing, and basic medical exams to determine if there were any early warning signs of malaria and help with treatment. Two Marines would accompany the corpsman and post guard.

One day the Corpsman said he'd gone down to the coffee plantation past the French fort. I distinctly remember the first time I went down there: the roads, or rather, the *trails*. You could tell if anyone had been up north near Khe Sanh by looking at their flak jacket, helmet, canteen, or cartridge belt; every crease was caked with this red dirt, and dust. I didn't know much about farming, but the red dirt looked very fertile. I came across the first coffee plantation, which turned out to be owned by Felix Poilane's mother, located down the road from Felix's own plantation. The Poilane family had lived in the area for a long time, beginning with his father arriving from France.

His father was a botanist and he wanted to prove that coffee could be grown in Vietnam at this latitude. At the time, in the early twentieth century, the universal belief was that coffee was ideally grown in a 'belt' that is 15 degrees north of the equator and 15 degrees south. This part of Vietnam is nearly at the 17th parallel, north. What I saw were rolling hills with dark green bushes that meandered over the mounds of red dirt, not in tight little rows, but random and wild. Immediately I thought of Western Washington and how they resembled the lush dark green rhododendron plants which grow wild and can be seen in many yards in the northwest.

I met Felix Poilane in his compound one day. He ran the plantation by using some of the Bru tribesman, like a sharecropper agreement. He invited me to sit with him in his house that was surrounded outside by a combination of grass and red clay. The grounds were meticulous, as the Bru swept them daily and made everything look neat and orderly.

It was not as hot, since we were up higher and fall was coming. The first time I talked with Felix was when he invited the corpsman and I to have coffee with him. I'd never had coffee except for c-rations (instant coffee) in a canteen cup. He served it in tiny cups and it was black, the color of old motor oil. It was strong, but he added some type of cream, maybe crème de menthe, as it had a minty flavor. Definitely gourmet coffee.

During one of our visits, I asked him, "Don't you feel safe, because there are a whole lot of Marines coming here. The word around the campfire is that the Vietnamese are coming down the Ho Chi Minh trail—which is one trail away. They are coming from Laos."

We were probably about five to ten miles from Laos, in the far northwestern corner of Vietnam. This was early in my tour, so I continued, expounding with my Marine Corps spiel—"We'll need to fight em in the jungles so we don't have to fight them in our cities and towns."

"No, it's not a good thing about the Marines coming."

He shared how his dad had a pretty good relationship with the Viet Minh (the precursors to Viet Cong). They got along OK, but after World War II, the French wanted their colony back and they and the U.S. decided to split Vietnam up. The Viet Minh were not very happy about this and one day Felix said they ambushed his dad and another plantation owner on the road and shot them dead while still seated in Poilane Sr.'s Citroën.

The French left in 1954. And there was a fairly peaceful existence until the Americans came. Their history has been marked by colonization, take overs, wars, and foreign invaders. The Chinese and the Japanese came, then the French. To Felix Poilane, we are just another invader, coming to take over their country. I never did convince Felix that it was a good thing we were showing up.

Felix was a tall, lean man about forty years old and had very weathered skin, probably from working outside all of his life. He wore a wide-brimmed hat made of tight woven straw. His clothes were light-colored to deflect the hot sun, a hand-sewn white linen shirt with long sleeves pulled tight at the wrists to keep the mosquitos away and wide-legged, almond-colored pants, dirt-spattered from working in the fields. On his feet he wore what we called *Ho Chi*

Minh sandals made of pieces of rubber tires. They would take old discarded tires from a tire factory, cut them about twelve inches wide with a hacksaw—the contour of a bow—u-shaped and tied off with parts of inner tubes through slits in the side. They were aerodynamic and when they walked the shoe rocked back and forth. If tires lasted forty thousand miles, these *Ho Chi Minh sandals*, would last a lifetime.

Felix spoke with a definite accent, from the Bru area. He also spoke French. Due to the French influence, many Vietnamese mixed in French phrases or words into their language, like *beaucoup*. I was intrigued by Felix explaining the process of growing the coffee plants for ten years and then hand-picking the pods, drying them in straw baskets, then packing them in burlap sacks that were transported on the backs of water buffalo (or some other animal) to the headwaters of the Mekong River. Later they would be roasted at their final destination.

I heard recently that coffee plantations are making a comeback in Vietnam, which is amazing given what happened next.

Within ninety to one hundred days of my meeting Felix Poilane, his coffee plantation looked like the craters of the moon, or a desert with gigantic pits a hundred feet across dug into the earth and later filled with monsoon rain. From the air in a helicopter, I could see those bombed-out craters filling with what looked like *alphabet soup*—or what was commonly referred to in Vietnam as, *people soup*. When a B-52 or other big artillery decimated a squad or platoon of North Vietnamese with a direct hit, some of them ended up floating in those craters: *people soup*.

I wondered what happened to the Poilanes and learned that the Marines evacuated the family in a helicopter to Hue, unfortunately just in time for it to be overrun by the North Vietnamese. They may have been killed there or possibly made it back to France. Felix survived, though I always believed he may have died with his family in Hue until 1988 when I read a book at the library that mentioned Felix Poilane and the classic ending to his life.

After the end of the seige of Khe Sanh, Felix wanted to go back to his plantation and see if there was anything left. He hopped aboard a C130 Hercules with a platoon of combat engineers who were tasked with tearing up airstrips and blowing up bunkers. As the plane landed, it was hit by artillery or mortar and crashed, collided into a water tower, and went up in flames. Most of the Marines onboard and Felix Poilane were incinerated, just like his coffee plantation.

This morning, as I reflect on *the French roast* and Felix Poilane, I think of that war. Now, there is this war and I'm going—back into the barrel. When I awoke today and walked outside to this June morning in Seattle, it was dark and gloomy with dead, stagnant air. The humidity was oppressive, just as it was in Khe Sanh before a monsoon, when a dense fog would move down the hills and settle into the valley. So today, the weather and the "French roast" made it easy for me to click that movie on, this first morning of the trial.

Yes, definitely choose the French roast. And maybe dedicate a moment of silence to the sweat and care that went into making sure one could count on their 'morning fix', prepared *oh so perfectly* at a Starbucks coffee shop on the ground floor of this monolith.

I look at the clock and it's now seven a.m. The time is fast approaching when I can count on Michael Pfau leading his troops through the door at any moment. Suddenly, I feel a pat on my shoulder and they appear from behind, then Michael Pfau's voice:

"Are we ready?"

Silently I say to myself, *it's a little late for that.*

Not that there is a choice. Once again, I reflect on the twelve-year-old. This time, I will not fail him. We may not achieve total victory, but at least this time his voice will finally be heard. I will tell his story.

As we depart for the four-block walk to the King County courthouse, I fall silent. I carry my gear, no different from my firearm in Vietnam, no different from my duty weapon as a police officer. I have my briefcase, and I have Michael Pfau at my side, every bit as formidable as the Marines who shared so much in common with me on every patrol, every ambush. This morning, Michael Pfau and I are taking on what is arguably the most powerful corporation in the world: the Catholic Church.

We approach the elevator that will carry us to the eighth floor of the courthouse.

Pfau asks, "Did you ever testify, or spend any time here, while you were a police officer?"

As the elevator doors close, I glance at the directory—and notice the buttons for the floors where the jail is located.

I look directly at the floors, indicating *KCJ*—King County Jail.

"Yeah, I spent time here all right, but not as a cop."

The morning speeds on, and before I know it, I hear the words, *All Rise!* announcing the entrance of the Honorable Judge Catherine Shaffer, presiding. I just start to eye the defense team when the jurors enter the courtroom. They are paraded by the witness table where I sit with Michael Pfau.

Since my days as a police officer, and to a certain extent, in Vietnam, I always felt I was able to *read* people pretty well, and pretty quickly. As each juror is seated, I begin my mental evaluation. I'm very impressed. They are all attentive, seem eager to hear the case, seem serious.

The only bad news is there are seven guys and five women. Arrogantly, I think, *I've got the chick vote, but the guys will hate me.* (I mistakenly thought a simple majority is all that is needed. I had no idea that it takes a 10-2 vote to win.) It isn't that the women have any particular preference for me at all, I know that. But I'm also aware from previous jury trials that I had testified in as a police officer that the women are usually more attentive, pay more attention to detail, and are much more objective. Most of all, I hope they have children. The men on the jury seem to be staring at me. The thought crosses my mind: *How many of the older males had found a way to make sure they never ended up in Vietnam? How many had been stopped by a police officer and been given a 'chickenshit' petty traffic ticket?* The women seem to be curious about me. How many of the women are life-long Catholics? At least one thing going for me is that one of the largest populations in the U.S. is made up of *ex-Catholics*.

I begin to panic inside. This is one of the times I need to get an accurate *read* and I'm left guessing. Any help at figuring out the jury is left to me, since Michael Pfau's observations and impressions are *not* going to reveal anything. I've been perplexed with him since day one. Trying to read Michael Pfau is like trying to read a sudden gust of wind and this morning is no different. A glance in his direction once again reveals nothing to me.

Frustrated with my thoughts, I turn to the defense team. Seated at the table are what I perceive to be four attorneys: three men and one women. One I recognize as Thomas Lemly, who had taken most of my depositions, and another two I identify as Boris Gavaria and Candace Keenan, both defense co-counsel. To my surprise, the fourth, who at first I think is an attorney, is no less than a rather old, pudgy Catholic priest in his black suit and Roman collar. His arrogance is bleeding from every pore; he gives me a look which I take to mean, *Sonny boy, you are in big trouble.* Probably just a remnant of my Catholic *guilt, shame, and confess* background. It takes me right back to the St. Benedict's rectory where Father Conrad had told me, *this is the first time you've been in trouble.*

What I learn next, however, is that not only is this man, Father Carrignan, *not* a lawyer, he is a former Provincial Superior for none other than the Oblates of Mary Immaculate. And, he is a witness scheduled to testify for the defense. My experience at criminal trials as a police officer led me to understand that future witnesses are not allowed into the courtroom prior to testifying. I think: *Why am I surprised he's getting special treatment? I surmise they're going to start trying to intimidate the witness from the first minute.* I'm left to wonder why there is no objection whatsoever from my attorney.

And so, after years of preparation and delays and uncertainty, let this trial begin. First, the opening arguments delivered by Pfau. No notes, the podium may as well not be in the room. Dead center before the judge and jury, he looks to me like he had been born and raised right there on the floor. Confident, but not arrogant, speaking in simple terms the jury can clearly understand, outlining my entire life story before the world. Not something for the faint of heart to experience.

Pfau begins to talk about Adamson. "The hundred anniversary is the trigger that began the process of Steve coming to see a lawyer, coming to explore what's going on, and triggered a number of problematic things he's had to deal with over the last nearly three years. And one of the key things he's going to tell you that happened at that reunion is he is going to tell you that he came to that reunion expecting it to be Adamson, Adamson, Adamson, Adamson, that omnipresent presence at Saint Benedict's Parish, the first male teacher, the first principal, someone that all his friends, family members knew. Someone his wife would ask him over the years, *was there something wrong with Adamson?; no,* Steve would say, *he was a wonderful guy.* And he got to that reunion, and there was nothing involving Adamson.

"And you'll hear from—see in the records that there's a reason for that. There had already been reports at that point that Dan Adamson was a pedophile who had abused boys, and they had wiped the slate clean, at least Steve's impression of it was, and something began, Doctor Conte will talk about this, began to creep into Steve's mind and unconscious is that *the secret is out.* Once they know that Dan Adamson is a pedophile, and everybody at the parish knows he's a pedophile, I am worried because there is this link that they are going to remember who Dan Adamson's special boy was, the boy who traveled across the state, the boy who Adamson paid tuition, the boy who did the projector room, the boy who built the AV system. Other things happened. He was confronted—not confronted, he was approached—by a kid he didn't know, and he said, *hey, you're Steve O'Connor, remember Dan Adamson?* This happened near the bathroom. The bathroom was a place where there was a particularly violent rape that occurred. And Steve began to struggle. He didn't understand why he was struggling. He began to struggle in the days after this. He began to struggle in the weeks after this, and he struggled mightily in the years after this." After further outlining the case in his opening statements, Mr. Pfau concluded.

It's now the opposition's turn at making their opening argument. The presenter for the defense is Mr. Tom Lemly. Our paths have crossed many times during the last few years. In the course of the discovery period, I was well aware that any mistake or misstatement during depositions could be used to discredit or impeach future testimony at trial. I was not defensive or disturbed by the questions generally presented at these depositions, but my perception of Mr. Lemly was that he thoroughly enjoyed any and all opportunities to inflict as much damage and re-victimization upon me, particularly on the subjects I felt had very little to do with the case: Vietnam most of all, and each and every unpleasant police action that I experienced. Not in my wildest thoughts did I know where, and how low, the Catholic Church and their attorneys would stoop to ensure they got their pound of flesh.

As Lemly begins, I distinctly see the jurors lean forward in their chairs, as if to say, *well, there must be two sides to this and the Catholic Church must have a very strong defense, so let's hear it.*

Personally, I've wondered if maybe they would be foolish enough to suggest that my accusations never happened. As this is not a circumstantial case, but a direct-evidence case, with corroborating testimony and credible documents, I'm guessing that would be unwise. No, I think they may even admit to, but trivialize, what happened, and then spend the entire trial trying to convince the jury of all the wonderful things that the Catholic Church does to address the problem once they discover a child molester in their midst. I would welcome this potential approach, as a person would have had to been in a coma for the last decade to *not* hear how the Catholic Church was handling, or mishandling, the accusations of crimes occurring against children. And so, tethered to the podium like it was a life jacket, with copious notes referred to frequently, we hear the defense.

"And as Mr. Pfau has indicated to you, there's no question about it, Mr. O'Connor will give very compelling and disturbing testimony about what his relationship with Dan Adamson was, and the abuse that he suffered there over the course of three, perhaps four years. No one can condone that kind of conduct. I'm not here to do that, and the Oblates are not either. Dan Adamson is dead. We will not hear any rebuttal from him. You'll not hear any rebuttal from me on that—on that testimony. There are only two people who know what happened between them, and Steve O'Connor is the only one who is still alive." *Not true,* I think, *there are lots of people who knew and are still alive.*

Then a laborious effort is made to blame the Archdiocese of Seattle, the Dominican nuns, parents, and not so subtly…me. I agree to a certain extent, up to the point when they eliminate any culpability at all on the defendant, the Oblates of Mary Immaculate—the order of priests that for over one hundred years ran St. Benedict's with an iron hand. Finally, he closes by reminding the jury to not, *leave your common sense at the door.*

As Lemly steps away from the podium, he shoots me a menacing look, and now that he's outside the earshot of the jury, he says something about a total lack of credibility that he was about to show, about a police officer who made up some story about a medal he never received.

This seems to be a funny thing to bring up now, at the end of the opening remarks, and as court is adjourning for the day. If he is referring to my Medal of Valor, then this was going to be amusing. The event that resulted in that award was captured on three separate local news channels, in addition to having been documented in several regional newspapers.

A few hours later, I'm just settling down to a cold beer when my cell phone rings. It's Pfau, and he *isn't* calling to see how I'm doing. It's mostly a one-way conversation, and it seems that there is more to the accusation than I first understood.

Apparently, in a last-ditch effort to find anything to discredit me, the defense has had some luck: The event had taken place in Spokane, where I was on vacation from my job with the Stanwood Police Department. I had traveled there to deliver birthday presents to my eldest daughter. The defense could not find me being a member of the Spokane Police Department, however. When they did find a tape of the event, they were unfortunate to have gotten the only footage that didn't show me with the victim, but showed Spokane fire fighters attending to the second victim, instead. In this tape, they interviewed one victim, along with several firefighters, and none mentioned a police officer at the bottom of the cliff. But that's because I was not on duty that day, and I was dressed as any civilian. To top it off, the Medal of Valor review process for the nomination of police officers had changed to a statewide agency since I had received the award. Therefore, a sloppy initial investigation did not turn up proof that I was a Medal of Valor recipient, conferred by the Rotary clubs of Snohomish County (north of Seattle). Lemly could have easily confirmed this by calling my former department chief. The photo of me receiving the award is hanging in the front lobby of the Stanwood Police Department.

I'm not surprised that my daughter Stephanie, the family historian, keeper of many objects, has that VHS news tape. The family jumps into action. Gail calls me late that night, telling me that she'll be on a five a.m. flight to Seattle with the Medal of Valor and certificate in tow, along with the news tape.

Day two of the trial would certainly be interesting.

CHAPTER 22

TO SILENCE THE CHILDREN: A TIME TO WEEP

June 5th, 6th, 7th, 2012

After the events of the previous evening, I am quite interested in how my attorney is going to go about confirming that I was a recipient of the Medal of Valor. A glance towards Michael Pfau, as usual, gives me no indication, however it seems to me that one of the law partners, Jason Amala, is certainly beaming. In arguments with the jury outside the courtroom, I hear bits and pieces, back and forth, comments and responses. Judge Shaffer is responding to a request by Lemly to address the fraudulent claim of some medal I never received. She responds to the defense and addresses co-counsel, Mr. Gavaria.

"We will address the heroic deeds of this police officer at the break. However, Mr. Gavaria, I do want to commend you on your *thorough, and excellent investigation* concerning this award."

Lemly shoots back, "It's a fraud, and he made it up!"

Pfau jumps in. "I have it in my office, the medal, your honor."

All of this back and forth clearly gives me the impression that the judge has seen the tape—the news channel that covered the rescue with my name scrolled at the bottom of the screen and an interview with me. Internally, I smile to myself. I am not quite sure how it ended, but the defense clearly saw the tape, and the subject was immediately over. Sometime later, a feeble excuse and apology are sent my way in passing by Tom Lemly.

My jubilance was short lived, however, as Judge Shaffer called the next witness to the stand. Prior to this moment, I assumed my story was the cornerstone of the case, but I now learn two victims of Adamson's, who Pfau contacted and interviewed in the past few years, will actually testify at trial. I am not familiar with the witnesses who take the stand today, nor do I recognize their names. With the first man on the stand, Darrell Cochran asks if he ever met me or recognizes my name. His answer mirrors my thoughts. *No he did not know me, nor had he ever talked to me before.*

Somehow I know. Somehow I sense it. What I always tried to block out is right before me now. My running away from the situation just created more victims. I replaced someone, and someone replaced me. From his stated date of birth, the witness had to have been right behind me. *Please don't go there. Please don't make me listen. Please tell me it stopped in the basement. I could deal with that. Please don't let me hear it go to the attic. Please let me hear he got away. Let me hear he told his parents and they did something.*

Who am I kidding? I already know what's coming. I already know the answers.

The testimony continues. Cochran stops when the witness starts to talk about Adamson pointing to the stairs. The witness can go no farther. Then, the crime descriptions end. I think to myself, *wow, all right, maybe when I get up there, Cochran won't make me go any farther.* I am not sure I could go up those stairs again.

The biggest shock comes next when he testifies—in detail— meeting with Fr. Conrad, where he speaks to him about Adamson. He shared that during his tutoring sessions at the teacher's home, Adamson showed him pictures of nude women and was in other ways inappropriate. Conrad reacted harshly, telling him that he was lying and to never speak to anyone ever again about this or he would *go to hell.*

He sounded as if he was reading directly from my deposition. Father Conrad gave him the same admonition. *You are a liar, you are going to hell, and you must never repeat these lies ever again, to anyone.* In that instant, there is an audible sigh and sounds of disgusted utterances, accompanied by jurors shaking their heads, one juror even slamming his notebook down. There were certainly not any smiles coming from the defense table.

I had waited fifty years for vindication, fifty years waiting for someone to listen, fifty years for someone to tell of the horrible events and horrible abuse perpetrated on children at St. Benedict's Parish. And at last, here it is. This was my therapy, finally hearing my life being validated, my suffering being exposed. And seeing the jurors, who without words, with only their troubled physical reactions, were screaming, *this is not right.*

I realize the defense will get their turn with this witness. *Do whatever they please, but do it to me. Spare this person. He has suffered enough. Has the Catholic Church no shame?* I stare at Father Carrignan sitting at the defense table. Not a single sign of remorse, pity, or compassion. How many others were there? The next witness. Same story, different in its descriptions, vague in the recall of events. But what was indelible in this victim's mind, *I told the priest.*

That evening I walk down Columbia Street to the waterfront, then back up to my hotel, then back down to the waterfront, then back to my hotel.

There is no peaceful sleep. There is intense guilt, instead. Guilt that I took money, tuition, and failed to stop it. Knowing the consequences. The consequences not only of my actions, but my inaction. Yet, here are two people who had nothing to gain, who came forward to relive their horrors, for a person they never met. I'm the very person who had participated in the events that contributed to Robb Kingsbury's victimization. It is not one of my best evenings.

As I lie on the hotel bed, sleepless, I decide to get up and pace around the room. A quick glance at the digital clock next to the bed reveals it is 1:30 a.m. Gazing out the window, my eyes scan the street below; it's deserted and quiet, a soft rain falling onto the pavement. Tomorrow, I will be back into the barrel once again. At this point, I feel for sure that there is no turning back. I owe it to the witnesses from today. Yet I feel utterly alone.

Then I look up to the fifth floor of the Columbia Tower, which is right across from my hotel room. Through the mist and drizzle, I can see the whole length of the law offices of Michael Pfau. The lights are not only on in his office, but on throughout *the entire floor.* People hurriedly going back and forth, papers being shuffled, coffee cups on desks. It seems the entire firm is a giant hornets' nest, all in formation, preparing for the upcoming battle at dawn. Alone? Not even. Right then I know we would hit the floor running in the morning, no matter what awaits us.

CHAPTER 23

PERMANENT DAMAGE:
A TIME TO BREAK DOWN

Reeling from yesterday's testimony by two other survivors of Dan Adamson's abuse, I was at least gratified that the attorneys did not push the witnesses beyond what they could withstand. I was also relieved to know that both victims were able to extricate themselves from Adamson's grip within a year. Even with the differences in time, I clearly recognized and understood the same permanent damage inflicted on both of them. Again I think, *how many others were there?* I grasp that the time for purpose has arrived, and that I would soon be the next one to testify.

My wife Gail is called to the stand to testify and I am not allowed in the courtroom. She is prepared and ready to go, though I don't think she is excited to be there. I think she'll be a good witness and the jury will like her. Michael Pfau directly examines her and Candace Keenan cross-examines her. She is on the stand for several hours, one whole afternoon, and then continues into the next morning. What could they possibly be asking her?

Mr. Pfau instructs us not to discuss our testimony with each other as there is a possibility that we may be re-called to the witness stand. So, we follow his directions and do not talk about the trial, her testimony, or mine, which will begin tomorrow.

I wonder if I'll have to diagram the inside of Adamson's house for the jury. I'm concerned because a few weeks earlier, I was in the conference room at the law firm, and Darrell Cochran, Pfau's partner, had brought in a large easel with a white drawing tablet, probably three feet by four feet, and asked me to draw the attic, basement, stairs, and bathroom of Adamson's *lair* in detail. I did fine and was almost finished with the drawings, until I started to draw the steps up to the attic; I froze in place and could go no farther. It was as if my hands had become paralyzed, and I began to feel a cold drop of sweat slowly edge itself down from my neck. I had a distinct feeling that, if asked to repeat this at trial, it would end with the same result.

A few weeks before the trial, Pfau informed me that he would not be leading my direct examination, but that it would be undertaken by Darrell Cochran, instead. It must not have sunk in at the time, but as he mentions it again today, I'm a little unsettled by this, since my contact with Cochran was limited to just a few previous meetings. At this late date, there wasn't any use in me confronting Pfau about making a change. Pfau explained to me that Cochran was well-suited and has the necessary demeanor to guide me through some of the difficult parts of my testimony.

As we leave Pfau's office at the Columbia tower the next day and head to the courthouse, we walk past a conference room to the elevator and I see my adult children, Christy and Ryan sitting there. They will wait all day to possibly testify at the trial. I am not allowed to talk with them. The next day during a break in the trial, I walk out of the courtroom and immediately see my kids, sitting on a bench outside the court, waiting. Again they are there all day. There are a number of challenges for them to get downtown to the King County Courthouse: hiring babysitters to watch their kids, notifying their workplace, taking days off work, and driving from Camano Island and Bellingham. It's a disruption in their lives and I feel bad they are being dragged into this trial. I think, *this is just another Oblate ploy to put pressure on me to quit, walk away, and have a mistrial called.*

My direct examination by Cochran begins.

Q: Mr. O'Connor, will you state your name for the record?

A: Stephen Joseph O'Connor.

Q: And where do you live?

A: (redacted)

Q: And who lives there with you?

A: My wife, Gail, and her dog, *Miss Vickie*, a dachshund.

There are generic questions and answers exchanged such as, *who were your parents? What did your father do for a living?* Then Cochran begins his direct examination about past events.

Q: Had you ever met either of the two witnesses who testified yesterday?

A: No.

Q: Can you tell me how it felt to hear their testimony?

A: Internally, it was very disturbing to me.

Q: What thoughts were going through your mind?

A: I knew where they were *going*.

Q: What do you mean?

A: When the first witness mentioned the word "attic," as opposed to "basement."

Q: And why was this so unsettling to you?

A: Because I was hoping that the witness had remained in the basement, as opposed to going up to the attic. If he went up to the attic, then I knew exactly what was going to happen to him. I did a lot of *hard time* in the attic.

Q: Is there anyone you wish was here today to hear your testimony?

A: Yes, my father. And Mr. Adamson. And even more importantly, Father Conrad.

Q: How about your wife, or your children?

A: Absolutely never.

Q: Why is that?

A: My whole life, I have always tried to protect them. To keep *dirt* off of them.

A: I would not have wanted them to ever hear this.

Q: How do you look at yourself?

A: A lot of guilt and shame about that period of time.

Q: Why is that?

A: Because I am looking back in time as a man who's now sixty-three and judging the inactions/actions of a twelve-year-old.

Q: Steve, let's go back to the time before the seventh grade. A happier time, in the summer of 1961.

Questions follow, and I describe a blissful time. A child who was dirt-poor but rich in spirit. A child who understood at an early age how wonderful a life it was to be growing up in Wallingford: the zoo, the park, Green Lake, all free for the taking.

I talk about moving from dismal rental to dismal rental, but still I was fortunate to stay within Wallingford, unlike my older brothers, who had attended several different grade schools in as many years.

Q: Did you find out that summer who your upcoming seventh-grade teacher would be?

A: No, but I had a pretty good idea it would be Mr. Adamson, by the way he kind of selected the boys by going into the sixth-grade class and tapping on their desks.

Q: Were any of the sixth-grade boys afraid about being sent to Adamson's class?

A: Well, some seemed to be looking forward to it, but most were very, very fearful. I mean, the Dominican Nuns were certainly a force to be reckoned with, but Mr. Adamson, well he was a whole different animal.

I am then asked to point out several of my classmates from a seventh-grade class photo. Then Cochran points to one in particular.

Q: Do you recognize the girl here with the blonde hair in ringlets?

A: Yes, she's my wife, Gail. We weren't married at the time.

This brings a resounding round of laughter from the jury, as well as from the defense table. By far, the most lighthearted moment.

The questioning quickly moves to the subject of baseball, such as pointing out team members from a class photo—players from our seventh-grade baseball team. I sit more rigid and erect as the questioning goes down the path I thought it wasn't going, to the descriptions of how I *took one for the team*.

It goes there. And it goes there in *spades*.

221

And it stays there, through the years of abuse, through the years of extortion, blackmail, threats, intimidation, through the years of irreparable damage. Hour by hour, it goes through the whole horror story. Thankfully, Cochran uses civil terms in his inquiries to the crimes, and likewise, I describe them without the sordid details, as much as is allowed. There is no confusion or doubt, however, with anyone in that courtroom as to the horror and sadistic nature of the events described.

Testimony resumes after the lunch break and I describe one crime after another, until the *bomb* drops. I noticed that, upon my return to the stand after the break, that someone had placed a large easel behind the witness stand. On the tray in front of the board is a large marking pen—just like the setup that had been used in the conference room at Pfau's office when I drew the schematic of Adamson's house. I have a sinking feeling as my apprehensions are immediately confirmed—*yes they are going to ask me to draw on that easel*—in front of the jury and the whole courtroom. Cochran then asks me to stand up and draw the confines of Adamson's house.

I stand and walk slowly to the right side of the easel. Looking at the blank sheet of paper, I will myself to think back to that place that is etched in my mind forever. I begin my 'architectural drawing' of the driveway, then the stairs, then the basement, kitchen, landing, and water closet that resided halfway up the stairs on the way to the attic. I use carefully chosen words, almost as if I am leading a tour group through a historical building. No problem, in control, voice clear and distinct. I pause after each description, pointing out the details of the layout.

Then, I lock up. While drawing the last flight of stairs that led to the attic, it happens. The cold, sweaty hand, shaking uncontrollably. I haven't been in this condition since Vietnam, or since the last terrible scene as a police officer. I'm locked. I can't move.

After what seems to be minutes passing, the silence in the courtroom is palpable. All I can hear is the distinct, clearly irregular throbbing of my heartbeat. *I have got to do this now. I must do this somehow.*

From deep down inside me comes a haunting voice. The silent voice of a twelve-year-old begging again to be heard. But I can't go up those stairs as that twelve-year-old.

Suddenly, my hand steadies, a normal rhythm returns to my heartbeat, and the veteran police officer reaches down and says, *Hey kid, I've got this for you.*

And he takes over. A staccato, deadpan, stoic, veteran police officer testifying as he had done many times before: *Bed is oriented east to west, dresser approximately forty-five to fifty inches from south-facing window, attic ceiling angled up to meet at a point at the top of the building, small tube-type television on dresser. The chest of drawers is approximately four feet high.*

At this point I forcefully take the marker out of my left hand with my right hand, loudly place it back on the tray, and sit back down—back straight, legs bent, feet carefully placed on floor, and nothing but a dead stare at Father Carrignan. Silence permeates the room, then the ever so slight whimper and sobbing by more than one juror.

Upon returning to the witness stand after a short recess, the questioning pivots to Catholicism.

Q. You were a cradle Catholic. You grew up in salt and pepper cords and a blue sweater uniform. Are you grappling with Catholicism now?

A. Most recently?

Q. Yes, what kind of struggles have you had recently with your faith?

A. I became a Catholic when someone put me in the uniform of St. Benedict Grade School and marched me up the stairs to the first-grade classroom. And for the past sixty years I have been a Catholic. Throughout my life I have tried to believe that there was some good in the Catholic Church. The night before I left for Vietnam, upon arriving at Gail Gibson's house for our prearranged dinner meeting, Gail came out to the car, then went back into her house to retrieve a small object. At the end of the evening, she presented me with that object. It was a St. Christopher medal. St. Christopher was believed by we Catholics to be the patron saint of travelers, of "lost souls." The significance was not lost on me. I suppose many people would say how silly this is. That a small medal represented my faith. But at this time, it did.

In Vietnam, you take your dog tags and tape them together so that they don't rattle when you are set up in an ambush. So I took that St. Christopher medal, and I placed it between my dog tags when I arrived in Vietnam. And those were my most cherished possessions in Vietnam. It was important because my dog tags said *Catholic* on them. And the rumor had been that should you end up at Graves and Registration (the morgue in Da Nang) and your dog tags said *Catholic*, the corpsmen would try to get all of your parts into the correct body bag. The correct leg with the correct torso, the correct hand with the correct arm, because we, you know, need all of our body parts to walk through the *pearly gates*.

Sounds silly, but that is how a lot of us felt and what we believed.

That St. Christopher medal went on every fire fight, every ambush, and every helicopter headed for some *Hot Landing Zone*. It was with me both times that I was wounded, with me when I contracted malaria, and was with me on the medical evacuation jet back to the "world."

When Gail and I got married, I felt it appropriate to thank her for its use, and returned it to her.

After many years of raising a family, and many moves from house to apartment to house, it never entered my mind that it was even around anymore.

Then, at my graduation ceremony at the Seattle Police Academy, as my police chief, Bob Kane completed the "pinning on" of my badge, Gail approached me with a small object clutched in her hand. She showed me what it was. And it was the same old, tarnished St. Christopher medal. And as she placed it in my hand, she said simply, "You're going to need this."

I glued that St. Christopher medal to the back of my badge with clear silicone caulking. That medal went on every bad 911 call with me. Every *head-on*, every shooting, every scene of man's inhumanity to man, and woman's inhumanity to woman.

And when I retired from the police department, I took that medal and placed it in my wallet where it remained for years, until last week. And I guess I can summarize my *turning in my badge of Catholicism* by describing it in the following manner. About a week ago, I took that same medal, and I walked out to the edge of the A dock at Everett Marina. I tossed that medal as far as I could fling it into the waters of Puget Sound."

As I end my description of turning in my badge of Catholicism, I conspicuously look Father Carrignan right in the eye again. At the beginning of my testimony, he had made it a point to move from the defense table and take up a position directly in my line of sight, at the very front row of the courtroom, in what I perceived to be a ploy to intimidate and shame me.

Cochran concludes his direct examination by reassuring me that he's not going to inquire about Vietnam.

"No one in this room who has learned about the terrible events that happened to you in Vietnam would argue that it was very traumatic for you, and I want to assure you that we are not going to make you relive those events here today."

With that, the day ends and jurors are excused. I would have another fitful, sleepless night to prepare for tomorrow's cross-examination by Tom Lemly, for the defense.

The next morning, *All Rise!* is announced once more. As I take the stand, I am reminded by Judge Shaffer that I am still under oath. The cross-examination begins, directed by the lead attorney for the Oblates of Mary Immaculate, Tom Lemly with the greeting, *Good Morning Mr. Adamson,* as he hands me a copy of my deposition to review. I hear a gasp in the courtroom, then a whisper, *did he just call him Mr. Adamson?*

Shortly into the questioning, it becomes clear to me that, contrary to my attorney announcing that I was not going to be asked about the events that occurred during the two years in Vietnam, that the Catholic Church was going exactly where I said they would go almost three years before: *Mr. Pfau, they are going to Vietnam in spades.*

Q. You did not talk at all about your service in Vietnam, although I think it is important for the jury to get a sense of your service in Vietnam. And the doctors at the VA recorded approximately twenty major traumatic events that were investigated there, right?

A. Yes.

Q. And this department at the VA was called the *Excess Trauma Unit* wasn't it?

A. Something similar to that.

Q. We would like to begin by having you describe a particular instance where a fellow Marine was gravely wounded and took a particularly long time to die, is that correct?

A. Yes.

Q. And we would like you to describe that instance.

A. In detail?

Q. In the exact detail you related to the team at the VA.

A. When I first arrived in Vietnam, I was a member of a Marine rifle platoon. In its "stateside" strength, it consists of approximately fifty to sixty Marines, led by a second lieutenant. However, due to casualties, several rifle platoons in combat were down to maybe twenty to thirty Marines, and it was not uncommon for a sergeant to be the highest-ranking member still alive. Our platoon had combined with what was left of two other platoons during this particular event, thus, there were several Marines in this group who I didn't know by name. One was a platoon leader who was with a radio operator near the end of a clearing. We were attacked by a large force of North Vietnamese and quickly were driven back to the edge of a river bank. We began taking many casualties, and shortly, we were down to maybe ten or twelve Marines.

Next, the radio operator near the platoon leader was shot. I crawled over to him, removed the radio, and brought it to the platoon leader, who then began to call in artillery strikes to our position. While he was still on the radio, he was hit by either a B-40 rocket or a rocket-propelled grenade. It not only blew his arm off, but also blew apart the side of his skull. At this time, I didn't think any of us would be alive very long as I observed several enemy advancing across the rice paddy dike to our front. The Marine was having what appeared to be seizures, or convulsions, and was unable to respond physically. I saw him attempt to remove his .45 pistol from its holster, but he was unable to. Soon, we were down to three or four of us huddled kind of in a circle. I thought I heard him mumble something like, *Shoot me, shoot me.*

Do I need to keep going?

Q. Yes. I think it is important for the jury to hear this.

A. At this time, someone "popped" a white phosphorous grenade and placed it on the radio. This is what you do when you are about to be overrun. So the enemy won't get your frequencies or call sign. I never thought we had a chance, but someone must have gotten through on the radio and Huey gunships arrived and started firing rockets and machine-gun fire to keep the enemy at bay. The Marine kept flopping around, and I tried to help him but there was nothing I could do. I tried, I tried, and it just wasn't good enough. He died a particularly horrendous, agonizing, painful death. I was a senior in high school, I was eighteen years old. I just wasn't good enough. Didn't do enough.

I describe event after event for Lemly, and he just keeps going. Finally I ask, *Are we going to keep going? Because they are all the same, they just keep getting worse.*

But it continues to the lunch break.

During any break in the proceedings, we hold a "get together" with Pfau, Cochran, Jason Amala, sometimes Jack Kennedy, and myself. This usually takes place in a bathroom down the hall from the courtroom. As we walk toward the bathroom I'm sure that there is concern about my ability to continue. For me, I have no doubt in my mind. I don't have a choice. I will continue, no matter the cost to me.

As the bathroom stalls are searched, and they determine that no one is present besides our little group, Pfau looks at me and says, "I can stop this at any time?"

I look at him and there is silence.

After a long pause I laugh to myself. He already knows the answer. He doesn't ask any question unless he already knows the answer. This question is no different.

Looking for something to hang on to, any object, vision, feeling, or sense that will help me through this day, I walk over to the sink and proceed to perform a 'ritual' that Chief Kane had directed me to do after a particularly bad event we were both involved in. I begin running water in the sink and place my hands under the faucet, methodically washing, washing, washing, again and again, washing my hands.

I turn off the faucet, pivot to face my attorneys, and answer, "It don't mean nothin."

It does not seem to be lost on Michael Pfau.-

After the direction the morning cross-examination had gone, I am pretty sure what was coming next as I walk back into the courtroom. And I am not disappointed.

Q. Mr. O'Connor, I know these are hard for all -- Let me try to summarize one other incident, because I think it was quite remarkable. And let me see if I can cover the main details of it, and you let me know if it's accurate; is that all right, sir?

A. I'd rather describe it.

Q. All right. You told us about the time that you were out on a combined action platoon in a very remote area. Could you tell the jury what happened on that occasion?

A. From start to finish? A combined action platoon is a group of—starts out with a group of fifteen Marines and Navy corpsmen in very remote areas. The program started in 1967 with compounds near hostile villages. Compounds had a tower. In the top of the tower there was a .50-caliber machine gun usually, and the Marines were in bunkers around the area. The practice was abandoned in late 1968 because the combined action platoons were being overrun by overwhelming forces, and all the weapons and everything were being stripped. So no matter how many "John Waynes" there were, you know, it was not uncommon to be hit by a hundred, two hundred North Vietnamese. So the CAP unit became mobile, but in this period of time, they were in a compound. There were Sierra CAPS, Delta CAPS, Tango CAPS, and Bravo CAPS. That was the designation for the combined action platoons.

I was not a member of this particular combined action platoon. It was near a village, near a village called Hoi An. It was a very dangerous place in those days. I was back in Da Nang attending a Vietnamese language class with the rest of my group, and I was called out to this CAP unit because I had once again been to tank school, and I knew how to set the "headspace" (distance between firing pin) and change barrels on a .50-caliber machine gun. That was not a weapon that was used with grunts with infantry; it was used on helicopters, tanks. But it was used in these towers.

So I was sent out to this combined action platoon for a temporary, week-long training. And in a rather unlucky sequence of events, the CAP unit had been receiving a lot of probing by the North Vietnamese. And while I was there, I might have been there like five days, but I'm not sure, they were—they were engaged by at least a company, maybe more of North Vietnamese who were determined to overrun the unit. Although a valiant effort was put up, the North Vietnamese—it happened in the middle of the night—started breaching the wire, getting to the bunkers, blowing up the bunkers. A lot of dead Marines, everyone out in the open, didn't look to me like there were very many left. The one Marine I was with was in a bunker with an M-60 machine gun, and we had a lot of hand grenades and stuff.

The bunker was sandbags on the top. They're dug into the ground. They're probably the size of eight feet by six feet, close, close proximities. At some point in time, toward the really bad part of the evening, the North Vietnamese were close. We could hear them outside, and were taking a lot of fire.

And what happened is, I don't know what hit it, but something big hit the bunker and the bunker collapsed.Maybe a rocket, maybe a mortar. The bunker collapsed, and it was one of the last bunkers that wasn't either on fire, or as I could tell by the firing withering away, breached.

So this Marine and I were in this bunker, and it collapsed, and with lots of sandbag weight, entrance collapsed, a lot of smoke, a lot of heat and a lot of—and, as it collapsed, it was like mangled metal, a lot of weight, almost like if you'd been in a car wreck, but with a lot of weight of the sandbags on it. And so I—I felt it, I was, well, I knew I was going to be dead real soon, but the other Marine was in worse shape. He was crushed by the weight of it. And I was unable to move like—like an earthquake, but my leg and foot were—were back somewhere. My other leg was stumbling. I had a couple breathing problems from the left side, felt like broken ribs maybe, or maybe my lung wasn't working, but one leg couldn't move. It was like this (demonstrating), let's say, one leg out.

But in this chaos, the other Marine had—he was in close proximity to me, and the firing— the firing subsided. I could hear a lot of North Vietnamese talking. I knew enough Vietnamese to understand some of what they were saying, and I could tell they were pulling the gear. They were pulling the flak jackets.

They mentioned *dieu khien*, which is Vietnamese for the commander. And *boc si*, I heard him say, *boc si, cuoc du* which, to me, meant the corpsman was dead. And I could hear him dragging equipment and ammo belts and things like that.

The tower had collapsed. And daylight came, and the Vietnamese were still rummaging around, and I heard a group of them come close to the bunker, I remember that, close proximity, but I'm down like that. And they kind of were looking around. They couldn't see in the bunker, I know that much, but I couldn't see what they were doing, but I could hear voices starting to go away. As the—I knew it was hot. I knew it was real hot and the sun was up. There was light, and the other Marine was in very bad shape, was crushed, and so his breathing was very labored, as was mine, but there was no water or anything. And except for an occasional noise, I think the North Vietnamese had gone or moved on, but I know there was something that was pulling at my leg. I felt that sensation, someone pulling, pulling part of me, but I want to say maybe, I don't know how long, enough for it to get dark, then light, whatever the time that would be, a day, nighttime.

And then, during that period of time, the Marine who was mangled in close proximity, was kind of bent down dead. And I was still alive, and I started to hear American voices—*what was that?*, and it was American voices. And I heard a couple times something about *they're all dead, they're all dead.* And I was trying to yell or do whatever I could, and it was a reactionary force of Marines who had been sent out. And took them quite a while. They dug out—both of us out 'cause we were—even though he was dead, he was tangled with me, rigor mortis had set in. So to pull me out, he had to—he was part of—his hand was underneath. You couldn't separate the two of us. And so I was pulled out and med-evac'd back to—it's a hospital ship called the *Sanctuary*. I had minor wounds. I had minor wounds like maybe broken ribs.

Q. And the tugging on your foot as the Vietnamese were coming through, they took off your jungle boot that was coming up out of the ground, didn't they?

A. So I was—when I was rescued, I had no— no shoe, no sock, no jungle boot on my—that's what they were tugging on. They were trying to get—they've got my jungle boot. But I wasn't breathing very well, so I was kind of in and out of....

That was the end of this incident, I could not finish or go on.

I feel I portrayed what it was like in Vietnam for me and my fellow Marines, describing each incident Lemly asked me, in detail, my way. I did not want to hear him reading the Vietnam incident reports. I wanted to tell it my way.

As I wait for the next question, Lemly is pausing, looking at his documents lined up on the lectern. Maybe he's had enough of Vietnam.

He then turns to questions about police reports and events chronicled in the archives and in the news reports pertaining to several incidents that I had been involved in while a police officer. I am required to go over, in detail, event after event: the drowning of an eighteen-month-old child I had attempted to revive by administering CPR; two separate shootings I was involved in; many fatal auto accidents; child abuse; child neglect. You name it, he's going there.

At last, the cross-examination comes to a close and he says, "*Thank you Mr. Adamson*— I mean, Mr. O'Connor. I apologize."

Lemly, possibly still believing he will get a reaction or some kind of outburst from me, quickly acts as if it was a slip up.

"Excuse me, I mean...Mr. O'Connor."

My attorney does not object, therefore the judge says nothing and moves on to the next witness.

As was our usual routine at the end of the day, my attorneys and I walk the four blocks back to the Columbia Tower to recap the day's events. It marks the only time I start to sense something with Pfau. I'm not sure exactly what it is, but I'm feeling that, somehow, I had *spilled* some Vietnam on him. Sort of like spilling coffee onto his shirt. I could only hope it would wash off

CHAPTER 24

CAN'T SEPARATE THE TRAUMAS: A TIME TO TEAR DOWN

Today and each day that Dr. Jon Conte, expert witness for the plaintiff, and Dr. McGovern, witness for the defense, testified or answered questions from the jury, I was sequestered in Mr. Pfau's office at the Columbia Tower. I only learned about these few days of testimony by reading the trial transcripts, the following year.

I had met Dr. Conte prior to the trial and we had several discussions; he interviewed me and I provided responses to written tests.

Dr. Conte holds a masters degree in social work, a PhD in social welfare, and is a professor at the University of Washington School of Social Work. He is also the founding president of the American Professional Society on the Abuse of Children, the founding editor of the *Journal of Interpersonal Violence*, which publishes research on child sexual abuse and other types of violence and the founding editor of *Trauma, Violence, and Abuse*, a journal that publishes reviews of research.

What follows are excerpts and highlights from Darrell Cochran's examination of Dr. Conte:

Mr. Cochran: Have you developed opinions about Steve O'Connor's condition and the impact that child sexual abuse has had on him, and have you developed those opinions to a reasonable degree of medical certainty?

233

Dr. Jon Conte: I have.

Q: Ok. Can you give us—

A: *Professional* certainty was the word I would use.

Q: All right. And can you give us a brief summary at this point of what those opinions are about the impact of the child sexual abuse which we've heard about in this courtroom on Steve O'Connor.

A: Sure. I think there are a group of symptoms. There's some symptoms that I would call post-traumatic responses, including PTSD. There are other associated emotional problems like depression and anxiety, and I think most significantly it's had a profound impact on the course of his life and on the quality of his life today.

Q: And have you come up with diagnoses that explain what impact the child sexual abuse has had on him?

A: Well, I don't typically diagnose in a forensic matter unless the diagnosis has implications for treatment. Now, in this particular case he does have PTSD, and there are evidence-based treatments for PTSD, so in that one diagnosis, yes, I have.

Q: And so post-traumatic stress disorder is the diagnosis that you've arrived at for that?

A: It's one of the effects of sexual abuse, yes.

Q: And you mentioned that you've been researching and studying on the issue of child sexual abuse back into the 1980s. How did you get started doing that?

A: That's an interesting question. When I was still here in Washington, I had a friend who is now the director of the Sexual Assault Center, and she had an early project—

Q: Director of the Sexual Assault Center where?

A: At Harborview, Lucy Berliner, and she had a project to train law enforcement officers to interview children, and she needed an evaluator, so I helped evaluate that program and then just slowly over time got more and more interested in child sexual abuse, and back then we sort of separated types of violence, and over the course of my career, we now regard the field as trauma with different types of traumatic experiences in that larger knowledge area.

Q: Like what types of sub issues?

A: Well, war trauma, rape, natural disasters. We've learned that there's quite an overlap, with domestic violence. We used to think they were very separate, but we now realize there's an overlap that, for example, one of the effects of childhood sexual abuse is to be at increased risk to be victimized again. We used to study the effects of witnessing domestic violence on children, and then we discovered that some of those children who witnessed domestic violence are also physically abused themselves. So these parameters that we put around the different types of experience when we did research and talked to victims about their experience, the barriers began to erode, and we generally call the field of study trauma now.

Q: What about self-criticism?

A: Same thing. People tend to blame themselves. Part of that is attribution of responsibility. I should have done this; I should have told somebody; I should have fought more. You develop ideas that reduce the anxiety, that make you believe there's something I could have done to prevent that bad thing, which means I can keep other bad things from happening. And then preoccupation with danger again is this idea that you never know when something bad is going to happen. It's also a post-traumatic effect in that people who are traumatized are often alert. They're checking out the perimeter. They want to see where danger is.

Q: Do you ever see something like people just checking out completely because of the severity of abuse?

A: I call that dissociation. Dissociation is a—it's a psychological process most of us have the capacity for. If you've ever had the experience of driving along and suddenly realizing you haven't been paying attention to where you are, that's dissociation. Dissociation is splitting off some part of consciousness. Some people who dissociate will go to a black place and they don't know where they are. You may look at them and they don't look like they're present. Other people who dissociate may create a fantasy place in their head where while they're being hurt, they go and imagine being in that place It's—again it's a defense mechanism. It's a way of surviving a bad experience.

Q: So let's talk about the impacts then that you see from child sexual abuse and other traumas.

A: Well, again, human beings are meaning makers, and so when you're in a situation, you're trying to make sense of it. Children have less ability than adults. Everybody tries to make sense of it, and because it happens to you, you often feel it's only happening to you; you often feel like you can't tell anybody. It can impact the self. You blame yourself. So impaired self-reference is kind of ideas about yourself. I'm being punished for this or it's happening to me because I'm bad.

Q: And what does the research show about the effectiveness of grooming tools like Adamson used on a boy who's prepubescent probably at this point, right?

A: Probably. Well, in terms of what you mean by effects. There are only, I don't know, five or six studies of grooming, two of which are mine. One based on victims and one based on offenders. So I guess what the research first teaches you is that it's an effective way of maintaining a child's cooperation with abuse. Now, in terms of damage or harm, it does several things. First of all, because a child doesn't tell the first time, they feel they're duplicitous, that they somehow have complied. Feeling that you're duplicitous or that you've complied to the abuse reduces the likelihood that you're going to talk about subsequent abuse. When you feel that you're duplicitous because you didn't tell after the first time or you didn't tell after the nth time, then that increases your sense of self-blame, I'm responsible for this, and again self-blame is a risk factor for a more negative effect of the sexual abuse.

Q: I might be putting the cart before the horse a little bit, because I want you to explain to us how you've evaluated this, but some of us have got the question in the mind, I know it happened over a three-year span of time and we know that Steve described the first event or two in a violent context. For example, when he's told to go upstairs and he is held down and choked by the back of the neck. And yet we also know that he kept encountering Adamson over a three-year span of time, and some of us probably have the question, you weren't being beaten all of the time to come there. You weren't being held kidnapped. So how does Adamson succeed in getting a boy like this to keep coming back, based on your review of the situation?

A: Well, there are a lot of things. You're raised in a family where you're taught to obey authority. You're abused by an important person, who has some status in the environment where you are. The whole point of the grooming is to condition you not to tell. There are positive aspects of the relationship, whether it's the money or playing with the train. You know, my field early on used to call this *victim blaming,* that we couldn't understand how a victim would participate or go along with something so horrible. And what we realize is that's the way adults think about it, and we have to put our mindset into what it's like to be a boy this age, embarrassed about what's happened, afraid of what's happened, hoping it's not going to happen again, being taught that you are to obey authority, having things that you want and need, whether it's money or the train or what have you. And in many victims, there's this kind of belief that well, it won't happen again. And so by believing it won't happen again, you set yourself up for it to happen again. Again, it's complex, but 70 percent of abuse goes on more than one time, often over many years.

Q: We heard about how it ended, or we heard about the one traumatic event that ends this with this injury to the right testicle. How does that play into your analysis?

A: Well, it's a very rare event. Most victims, they may have minor injuries, but nothing as serious as Mr. O'Connor describes. It was an opportunity for the system to respond, but apparently it didn't. It created a lifelong reminder.

Q: All right. Help us make sense of the abuse of Steve O'Connor. We know that he achieved a lot in his middle school years; for example, he was the eighth grade president. He went on and had success in track and cross-country at Lincoln High School. Help us understand that.

A: Well, I would describe Mr. O'Connor as a resilient individual. He had a lot of factors in his life, including at that time, not any longer, but faith. He was athletic. He used the term, pretending that I should know it, called *vain poser*. He said in high school, he started to dress well and he had a car and he had a job. Having a job and getting a car, that's all a resiliency factor. He was an athlete. He was very popular. He spent more and more time away from home where home was not as happy. And so he was able to build successes, get status. He denied ever worrying that he was gay, but he did say that by being a good dresser and always being interested in slow dancing at the church dances with girls, it would be a good cover if it ever came out. And so he developed—and well, he developed this facade of being adequate. It's not a false facade, because there are true aspects of his successes. He apparently was an athlete. He was very interested in architecture, and apparently was a very good architectural drawer-. So he had real successes, but part of the successes are because of his natural talents and part I believe to create this facade so nobody would know what was taking place.

Q: And this avoidance—by the way, does the fact that he is building the membrane and seeking to avoid the distaste of what's happening, is that a conscious process with kids this age or is that a—just a reaction?

A: That's a really good question. It's both, conscious and unconscious. Psychological defenses are mechanisms that work within our mind. They—many of them are not under conscious control. Dissociation, for example, may not be under conscious control. Actively suppressing it, trying to think about something else, and going to your job, thinking about the slow dance you're going to have at the dance on Saturday night that would be a conscious way of not thinking about what Adamson did. So we do both conscious and unconscious defending against the experience, and the whole point of it is to survive.

Q: You obviously have to view it from his eyes, because we don't know what his dad did or didn't do, but tell us about the fact that he went into the Marines. How does this play in or relate to the abuse by Adamson, from your perspective?

A: Well, my perspective is based on his report to me, but he talks about it in several ways. He talks about it as, he didn't use this word, but I would call it *a cry for help*. It's, *somebody pay attention to me; I'm doing this really outlandish thing*. It's a way of trying to get some response, and it's also a way of fleeing the abusive situation. It's also I think in a way a retaliatory action against his parents. You tell a parent and they don't do anything, and you're angry about it. And so you do something in the hope that the parent will then respond. And this is a whole complicated issue, but in child sexual abuse, the emotional loss of a parent happens most of the time, because there's something you can't tell them. And then when you do tell them, and they don't do anything about it, it's even a further loss. So it's partly cry for help, it's partly escape, and it's probably partly anger.

Q: Was it clear to you from a practice standpoint that the precipitating cause was Adamson and the abuse?

A: Yes.

Q: So then let's—you mentioned that you have done some research and there's some studies specifically on the interrelationship of child sexual abuse and war trauma. We heard grisly stories about what he went through in Vietnam. Talk to us about the interrelationship of the terrible child sexual abuse he suffered and the terrible war trauma he suffered, from your standpoint.

A: Okay. First of all, you have to remember that rarely when a traumatic event is going on or in the period when it's going on do you see trauma symptoms. But somehow the fact of being a victim of child sexual abuse and the risk and other resiliency factors that we've talked about can create a sensitivity or increase the risk that some of these horrible experiences at some point when you're out of the conflict will develop into PTSD. All we can say is that a prior traumatic event, and some highly stressful events, like having a mentally ill parent, will increase the risk that you'll develop more related trauma.

Q: Help us make sense of the interrelationship between the trauma he's suffering in the child sexual abuse arena and then in the war. How does it go on then and play out in Steve O'Connor's life?

A: Well, I think he's put a membrane, a wall, around the child sexual abuse. He says he thinks about it a little bit in Vietnam, but not a lot. He's got other things going on to occupy him, people shooting at him. He's had these, as you've described, bad appearances.

Q: Take us through then his adult life as it progresses and how you see the sexual abuse trauma interplaying in the rest of his life.

A: Well, I think he largely keeps it at bay. He remains in the military for a while, has I think several kids. He's thinking of becoming an officer; he's scheduled to go back to Vietnam, has kind of had enough, gets out. I don't completely understand the businesses that he was in. But he was apparently quite successful in business for years, was devoutly religious, raised his children in the church, used to, without any awareness of what he was doing, used to go with his kids to youth events, and he would walk perimeter outside, kind of on guard protecting his kids without any kind of realization that he was doing it, periodic thoughts about Adamson but never -- kind of never having it coming back, doesn't think about Vietnam very much. He told me that it was a very easy time not to think about it, because there was such antiwar feeling, and at one point he moves to Seattle and he said nobody wanted to talk about the war when he came to Seattle, and, you know, living myself in that age, it was. We wanted to kind of put it away. It was not -- we didn't have the attitude then we do now about people that defend the country. And so he goes on with life, has children, is relatively successful in business, by his report. I don't know.

Q: Then he gets into law enforcement?

A: Correct.

Q: What do you make of that?

A: He said he always wanted to do it. He sometimes talked about it as kind of a death wish. He apparently was a risky guy. He was very active as a cop. He'd tend to look for things to deal with, apparently by his report, fairly well, was involved in a number of traumatic accidents, horrible experience with a baby that died, I think in a hot tub. He had a number of traumatic experiences.

And periodically, while he was in law enforcement, the war trauma began to surface. The smell of the propellant from bullets would remind him or when he would take off his bulletproof vest, it would remind him; he'd smell the sweat. It would remind him of his flak jacket. And so the Vietnam experience began to kind of intrude into his law enforcement life.

Q: The shrapnel was literally emerging from his body, right?

A: Correct.

Q: We saw and we've seen the videotape of a reunion in late 2008 at Saint Benedict's Parish school a number of times. What do you understand about the significance of the reunion in terms of Steve's starting to disclose for the first time, in recent times, the abuse?

A: Well, he said—I mean he said a lot of things. He said he went back reluctantly. His wife wanted to go. They had met there, and it talks about it on the videotape. He was shocked to see that there were no pictures of Adamson because his perception as a young person was that this was a very important figure in the life of the school, and then he went to the restroom where he was assaulted, and the memories start coming back. That in a sense that experience of going back sort of broke the membrane or began to break the membrane.

Q: I remember when I saw the videotape for the first time, it ends with him blurting out, *it's been a wonderful life*. From a clinical standpoint, has it been a wonderful life?

A: You know, it's very hard to judge suffering. There are many things about his life that are admirable. He was a Marine, defended the country, successful businessman, a person of faith, and raised children, some ups and downs maybe in his marriage, like any marriage. So yeah, in many ways he's lived a good life. He is my age. I hope he and I both have a long life ahead, but the problem is that his life has now been changed, and by his report, he would have gone a different direction. He would have been an architect. So by dealing with the abuse, he made a life correction. Now, because of the resiliency factors, he's done well in many ways. But what his life is going to be like from now until whenever the end of his life is, is a different

241

story. I have no capacity to weigh suffering. Other people have to judge suffering.

Q: But you can weigh severity of the symptomatology that you see, compare that to other trauma victims, right?

A: Yeah. I would say at present, he has a high level of symptomatology.

Q: So is the depression then a combination of the child sexual abuse trauma and the war trauma, maybe even the police trauma all together?

A: Yeah, and other experiences in his life. He's at a point at his life where all of the bad things that have happened to him have now come back into his life, and anxiety and depression are one of the responses to that.

Q: And is there any way to divide out the sexual abuse trauma component of depression versus the war trauma, versus—

A: There's no reliable methodology for doing that.

Q: Have you found to a reasonable degree of professional certainty that Steve is suffering from anxiety in part because of the child sexual abuse trauma?

A: Yes.

Q: In terms of post-traumatic stress disorder, the depression and anxiety, from your review, particularly of Steve's kind of psychological insight to himself, was Steve able to understand that the child sexual abuse was causing those conditions over the last forty years of his life, fifty years of his life?

A: Oh, no, I don't think he was thinking about the child sexual abuse until after the reunion, and I don't know that he had anger until he started thinking about it. He may have had some depression and anxiety over time, and certainly after he goes to the VA or he goes to the VA because he has depression and anxiety, but no, I don't think he had a clear understanding of the various factors that had contributed to those symptoms.

Q: So I want to make sure that we understand the most important component parts of your opinion about what Steve's experienced and what he's currently experiencing. Maybe you can summarize for us the condition that he's in and the impact that the child sexual abuse has had.

A: Well, I think he has a range of symptoms that are associated in part with child sexual abuse, and the child sexual abuse led to an increased negative reaction to war trauma and police trauma. He has many resiliency factors. He has some symptoms that are not grouped under post-traumatic stress disorder, things like cognitive distortions, this great distress and anger, the shame and stigma. Post-traumatic growth would be reaching a point where he says, I'm not responsible for what happened; I finally spoke out; I've lived a good life; I served my country, and I've raised good kids. That would be growth and healing. It's not-- I'm not completely sure that he'll be able to do that.

Q: Just as to the PTSD, the depression, the anxiety, and to the extent that they are interrelated in terms of the war, and the police work and the other factors of the child sexual abuse, is there any way to divide out how they affect him?

A: No.

Q: You mentioned in your report at the very end that there's a sad irony that after all he's done for his community, that he's experiencing this. Tell us about that.

A: Well, as we go through life, we reach a point, I'm sixty-four, he's about the same age, you try to look at what you've done, and as you grow older you try to look at the positive things that you've done. He's done many admirable things, as I've said multiple times, and as my professional belief we now recognize that people who risk their lives to serve the country do a good thing. He has a negative view of it. He sees it as a reaction to child sexual abuse instead of service. He now feels guilty that he led men to their deaths. The sad thing I think is that he looks negatively on the positive things about his life.

MR. Cochran: No further questions, your Honor.

Questions from the jury for Dr. Jon Conte.

The Court: First question. How does rigid power and authority, such as Oblate school and structure, factor into grooming,

243

recruiting, and the ongoing degrading nature of the abuse? And then they also asked about what the impacts are over time.

The Witness: Well, it's a complicated question. First of all, in general, structures that have power over children, regardless of what they are, tend to use that power from time to time to select and groom and keep a child from disclosing what is going on. If the family has raised the child to respect adults or respect institutions, or if it's a family of faith, and they've taught the child to respect faith, and that also interacts with how the family has raised the child, then that can increase the power of the institution, or someone who wants to use the guise of the institution to abuse the child. So in terms of impact, one of the trauma-causing elements of abuse is betrayal, so when the institution is an educational one, or religious, or an institution that is supposed to protect, care, and nurture for children doesn't do that, or when a perpetrator uses the guise of being associated with the institution to abuse the child, then that can increase the level of betrayal that the child feels.

The Court: Dr. Conte, why would a sexually abused man take his own children back to the same church where all the abuse occurred?

The Witness: Yeah, that's a common question. Again, if you have this experience or experiences, and you build a membrane around it, then you act as if -- you create a narrative, and that narrative may be that you're religious, and indeed in this case Mr. O'Connor was very religious, conservatively religious, for many years—and so it's part of the denial or avoidance that goes into managing the trauma.

The Court: With lots of therapy, do you think Steve can recover the quality of his life?

The Witness: Well, again I believe in therapy. I'm a therapist. I've seen people make significant changes over their life. This is a very complicated matter. The short answer is yes, but I think it will be very difficult, partly because of distrust and the difficulty in forming a relationship, and all therapy for trauma at the end of the day requires the victim to go over in excruciating detail and to re-feel, and you don't just do it once but you do it several times, that's called exposure, and over time that process, which is very painful and often causes symptomatology, like more depression, more suicidality, what have you, overtime, then the memory no longer causes anxiety. Yes, but it's going to be difficult and take some time.

The Court: Why do you think the 2008 reunion led to this lawsuit when we know he had never forgotten the abuse?

The Witness: Because I think knowing that it happened and periodically thinking about it is not the same thing as understanding that it's really harmed you. I think when you go and you know you had this history and you go and you find that the person that hurt you has been kind of wiped off the map, isn't there anymore, and then as an adult when you go back to an actual environment where you were severely hurt, then it brings back the traumatic memories. And so and some of it may also have been that because the war trauma had started to come out and he had started to deal with that, and there were some symptoms around that, his same capacity to avoid and block may not have been the same. And so one of the things we do, and not just with Mr. O'Connor, but that a reminder, for example, seeing a photograph of the person that abused you in the newspaper, even though the abuse was years ago, that reminder can suddenly challenge the avoidance and the blocking.

Follow up questions from Michael Pfau:

Q: Dr. Conte, I'm going to not follow up on every question, but I'm going to go in reverse order, just because it's easier for me to remember. There was a question, the last -- one of the last questions about why did the lawsuit or why did the reunion lead to a series of events that led to a lawsuit. Would you describe the reunion as a triggering event?

A: Yes.

Q: Is that a word that you'd use in your – what do you mean by a triggering event?

A: It's a reminder.

Q: I'm providing two jury questions here. The other juror asked if the children were at Saint Benedict's, even for a very brief time, why would one reminder lead to depression, invasive memories, and then finally doing something after forty years, where other memories, like his wife talking about Adamson or having kids in the school, not lead to the same sort of awakening of memories and depression and that sort of thing?

A: I think the thing about the reunion you have to remember is that it hadn't happened before. It was a really big deal. He didn't particularly want to go. He did in fact go. He participated somewhat reluctantly, and so it's a potential trigger of a different order.

Q: And let me first ask the question this way. In *voir dire,* the preliminary examination of a witness or a juror by a judge or counsel, there was another vet and he was asked questions about Vietnam and PTSD, and he said that, and I'm paraphrasing: the symptoms kind of come and go and there's no rhyme or reason or no predicting it. Has that been your experience with PTSD and memories, that it's difficult to predict when an invasive memory may occur or when someone may get depressed?

A: For some people. And part of that is that there may actually be triggers, but the veteran is not aware of them. And some of those triggers may be internal. And some of it may be that when you're overloaded with stress or other things are going on, then your ability to keep the intrusive images at bay is not the same. So I don't know that they're truly random, but I think they feel random to the person because they can't identify a clear trigger.

Q: The final question on this. What about age and station of life for a person? Is that something that can play into when this trigger occurs and when this process of self-awareness may begin?

A: Certainly. For some people, as you age—let me put it a different way. In each developmental phase there's tasks, and in the early developmental phases there's getting educated, there's raising a family, supporting your family, doing the right thing, being a partner, amassing some resources so you can live, and so that takes a lot of psychic energy. As we enter into the last phases of our life, physically and work-wise, we tend to slow down, and as part of the slowing down for some people, there can be a life review, when you begin to think about the positive and negative things about your life. Some people say, I want to make a course correction, I want to live in a different way.

Q: The final follow-up. Is there any evidence in the record or in your interview that Mr. O'Connor sought to deal with the effects of his abuse before 2009?

A: Absolutely not.

Q: Is there any evidence in the record that as he began to get more symptomatic after the VA, and the hospitalization, in that sort of ten-year period between '99 and 2009, that he was aware that any of his symptoms were related to the childhood sexual abuse?

A: No.

Mr. Pfau: Nothing further.

The Court: Thank you.

The following week, the jury hears from Dr. McGovern, Dr. Conte's counterpart and expert witness for the defense:

Dr. McGovern's assessment and evaluation of Steve

Q. So did you make—in this case, after you received a request to do an assessment and an examination—did you make an assessment about Mr. Steve O'Connor?

A. Yes, I did.

Q. And what did you base your assessment on in this particular case?

A. In this case, when I first became, if I may say *involved* with it, I was asked to review medical records, primarily the records that had been compiled about his brief hospitalization, to look at how he was dealt with then when he was suicidal, walking perimeter, et cetera, having some very serious and significant psychological problems. I also was provided with a brief summary of his medical history, the awards that he had won, Purple Heart, et cetera, different citations from Vietnam, and from that information, I began to develop some hypotheses about the etiology of his post-traumatic stress.

Summary of Steve's life as a police officer and in retirement

Q: (by Mr. Lemly) How would you summarize your conclusions about Mr. O'Connor's level of adaptive functioning and his need for psychological treatment?

A: In studying Mr. O'Connor, he's led a very complicated but heroic life. He's one of the bravest men I've ever met. When we look at his life, the traumas that he has faced and overcome, it's amazing what he's done. We have the abuse as an adolescent, his ability to overcome and resist, to being in service, to face excessive war combat, which eventually led to a 100 percent disability. When he leaves the service, he becomes involved in manufacturing and chemical analysis, working for his family, providing support, moving back to the Northwest, and decides to become a police officer in Stanwood, to be a D.A.R.E. officer, to help children become better educated about alcohol, drugs, et cetera. From there he's awarded many citations. He's awarded a valor award for a very brave thing he did on the way to Spokane to visit his daughter. He then becomes an undercover narcotics agent, which takes more courage, for a period of time, faced greater adversity. Unfortunately, when he went to save people, from what I understand, in a ravine near Spokane, he became physically impaired, hurt his back, and suffered yet one more physical trauma. But what's fascinating is when you study his life, he is a resilient individual. He is a resourceful individual. He seems to grow and take on new challenges.

Retirement

A: (by Dr. McGovern) In the year 1997, it appears he decides to retire, due to medical difficulties, et cetera. Some shrapnel I believe is still coming through his flesh and hitting his gun belt, whatever it is, and he goes into a period of retirement, which probably most people would think is joyous. However, in his life, there probably wasn't much adventure there. There wasn't much risk there. I mean if you contrast, as he told me, about being under a house with a gun, some criminal was going to shoot at him, versus hitting a golf ball and shanking it, there's quite a difference. So I think what happened in the next few years, he lost contact with his fellow police officers; I believe one of them, Mr.(redacted), killed himself. He became more depressed over time. He didn't have as many pleasant activities in his life. He didn't have to make as much money for his kids. His last son, Ryan, went to college. He didn't have as much to do. And one of the things that Mr. O'Connor made clear to me, and I believe in his testimony, is he had to stay focused; he had to have tunnel vision; he had to stay active so he would not have recollections of his previous traumas, as a child, in Vietnam, or as a police officer.

And he developed a coping skill, a blocking skill that he utilized. However, when you have a lot of free time on your hands, as I learned with other retirees, you have too much time to think. You don't have as many activities that you engage in, and he started to ruminate about the past; he became more depressed; he became suicidal. He was thinking of walking in front of a train and fortunately went to the VA for a brief period of time here in Seattle and was able to, in a short period of time, successfully, with resilience, overcome those demons in his life to a degree where he could function.

St. Benedict's anniversary and decision to take action
A: He seems, at least on the surface, to be doing relatively well until he and his wife were invited, or decide to go, to the reunion at Saint Benedict's. He did not want to go. He had negative thoughts about going. However, he decided to drive across the mountain because of his wife's driving skills, or lack thereof, the snow, et cetera, got to the reunion, and a number of events happened that you've heard about, a speaker who gave a talk, him going into the bathroom, no pictures of Mr. Adamson, other memories coming back, talking to a man who reminded him of what happened to him when he was there, and all of that reactivated a lot of the residual emotional feelings that he was having, made him angry, and he pursued other options in his life. And since about 2009, I believe, he's been involved in what he calls his project, and his project is dealing with what happened to him, getting involved in litigation, which is extremely stressful on defendants and plaintiffs.

249

It's very hard on people, having to reveal things about his life that perhaps he never wanted to reveal. He did not want to tell his children, from what I've read, about what happened to him when he was at Saint Benedict's. He didn't want to talk about that trauma in his life, but through this whole process of discovery, of litigation and depositions and whatever, he's been in a very painful situation. It's understandable. He doesn't spend as much time with his family. He spends a lot of time with *Affliction*; *Affliction* is his boat, his 45-foot boat. He's withdrawn from his family. He's feeling ashamed and embarrassed, and he uses the phrase, *I don't want to throw mud on my kids and my family.* So he is embarrassed, he's alienated, he has things in his past he's not proud of, and all of this has come together during this process.

Steve's physical health, the need for therapy, and his prognosis
A: If you've seen the movie, *The Perfect Storm*, it's like all of these things have been weighing upon him over the years, and it's now come to a head. That's the bad news. The good news, is in my opinion, he should be in therapy. He should be in what's called *victim-focused behavioral therapy* that will help him deal with these traumas in his life. He mentioned it to me during the evaluation that between day one and day two that he had an accelerated heartbeat, and he had to get up in the middle of the night and deal with it. So it is a big preoccupation to him, his health, how he's going to deal with it. So he needs to get medical therapy; he needs medical help and assistance, psychotropic medications, and I also think it would be wise from my point of view for him to have some family therapy, so he can talk to his kids, who he loves dearly, from what he told me. He feels he's been a very good parent. He gave his parents a rating of D, and D. He gave himself a rating of A. He wasn't glossing over it, but he said, I've been a good father and my kids are really good kids. He thinks his youngest son is a little arrogant, but whatever, a good baseball player. So he needs to be in therapy ASAP.

Q: (by Mr. Lemly) You have talked with us about the stressors or traumas that Mr. O'Connor has experienced throughout his life. Can you determine to a reasonable degree of professional certainty how much each one of these causes has contributed to Mr. O'Connor's current impression of PTSD and anxiety?

A: No, I cannot.

Q: Is there any way to separate those various cause and effect relationships out?

A: No, because of the complexities of his trauma at different developmental stages in his life, I don't know of any, and I've looked for years for a formula. I don't know of any scientific formula that would answer that question for us. He has what's called *complex trauma.*

Q: And that complex trauma results in the current depression and PTSD and anxiety?

A: It contributes to it, yes.

Q: So Mr. O'Connor has talked about one of the problems of stress or symptoms that he's experiencing in his life now is his sense of isolation from his family. Do you recall discussing that and seeing that information in his interviews and deposition testimony?

A: Yes. He said that he is staying away from his family. He doesn't have as much contact. He spends less time in Spokane. When I interviewed him, I believe he was at a hotel here. Or he would spend some time on his boat. That's correct.

Q: Dr. McGovern, Dr. Conte expressed to the jury considerable concern as to whether Mr. O'Connor could recover from the current psychological distress that he is suffering. Do you share that level of concern and pessimism?

A: No.

Q: Based on your professional training and treatment of individuals, why is that?

A: As I said earlier today, Mr. O'Connor is a very brave person. He's overcome many travesties in his life. He has the ability to change and to make these transitions with the help again of some good therapeutic assistance.

End of Mr. Lemly examination of Dr. McGovern

Cross-Examination of Dr. Kevin McGovern by Michael Pfau.

The Court: Go right ahead, Mr. Pfau.

Mr. Pfau: Thank you, your Honor

Q: Good morning, Doctor.

A: Good morning.

Q: Doctor, I also want to talk about some of your testimony yesterday, and I wrote it down and then typed it up, but you were talking about Steve, and you said, Steve O'Connor shows signs of anxiety and depression, correct?

A: Yes.

Q: And that's consistent with the way he was describing his life, correct?

A: Yes.

Q: In other words, the signs you saw and the test results you found were consistent with Steve's description of his life and what he's gone through, correct?

A: Oh, yes, correct, yes.

Q: I think you also, I don't think, I wrote it down, you said that Steve presently shows signs of social isolation, withdrawal, and anger, correct?

A: Yes.

Q: And at times explosive anger, right?

A: I'm not aware of him being involved in explosive activities. I know he gets argumentative. He didn't give me any examples of being out of control, being explosive. It could be.

Q: And child abuse can cause anxiety for adults years later after the child abuse, correct?

A: When they review it and think about it, yes.

Q: And child abuse can cause depression years after the abuse, correct?

A: That can happen, yes. Obviously, yes.

Q: And with victims of childhood sexual abuse, we see evidence of social isolation, correct?

A: In some cases, yes.

Q: And you see that with Steve, correct?

A: Yes.

Q: And with victims of child abuse, you often see withdrawal, correct?

A: That can happen.

Q: And with victims of child abuse, we often see anger, don't we?

A: In males especially, yes.

Q: And we see that in Steve, correct?

A: He's angry.

Q: With victims of child abuse, we often see feelings of worthlessness, correct?

A: Yes, because they didn't take affirmative action, they didn't stop the abuse, yes.

Q: Right. And with victims of males sometimes they years later say to themselves, *why didn't I do more to stop this*, correct?

A: It's a common response.

Q: It's a common response as an adult looking back saying, *oh, my God, how did that happen to me*, and they think about it as an adult and they say, why couldn't I stop the abuse, correct? That's one of the questions?

A: It's one of the questions.

A: But I think eventually he did stop it, which was—

Q: After what, three years of being sexually abused he stopped it?

A: Yes, fortunately, yes.

Q: Let's talk about Steve's abuse. And on that continuum or that spectrum of abuse, Steve's abuse is real bad, isn't it?

A: From the way he described it, it was severe, yes.

A: I did not go into detail with him because I read about it in his deposition, and he had also told me that morning that he had one of his other anxiety attacks the night before. I didn't want to take the risk of him having another anxiety attack with his heart concerns.

Q: Right. And you were concerned that talking about the child sexual abuse with Steve, in the context of your forensic review, might cause a panic attack, correct?

A: Yes.

Q: 'Cuz he had told you he had panic attacks when he talks and thinks about the sexual abuse, right?

A: Right. He said the night before he had one of his heart acceleration episodes.

Q: And did you deduce that he was nervous about coming in to see you?

A: Absolutely, sure.

Q: And talk a little bit more about this later, but Steve, it was hard for him to talk about the issues you talked to him about, correct?

A: My understanding was he didn't want to talk about that. He didn't want to talk about Vietnam. He didn't want to talk about the police shootings, because when I started to probe into those areas also he, I don't know if the word *agitated* is a good word, but he, you know, basically, *did you read this stuff; do you know what's going on; I don't want to review it.* That's common. That's a very common response.

Q: And Steve wasn't hiding anything from you, he just didn't want to talk about the abuse, correct, and you made a clinical decision—

A: I did not expect him to go through it again. He had already gone through it in his deposition, and I didn't feel—when I do my relations, I don't again regurgitate that information, because the information's already been talked about, and it probably is only going to agitate the individual.

Family life and Steve as a vulnerable kid

Q: And this kid, Steve O'Connor, he had a relationship with his parents that wasn't optimal, correct?

A: From what I know, what he told me, yes. He gave them, I think I said yesterday, Ds for their grades as parents, right, Ds.

Q: But you used the term *double D.*

A: It was a double D. I'm sorry. I meant a D for mom, and a D for dad. That's what I meant by double D.

Q: His dad may not have been as involved as he should have been or his dad may not be as involved as dads today are, but his dad was not abusive to Steve, was he?

A: Not that I'm aware of.

Q: I guess what I'm getting at is there's no indication that Steve, prior to being abused by Adamson, was either sexually or physically abused by his parents, correct?

A: No indications, no.

Q: And there's no indication that Steve, prior to being abused by Adamson, was neglected in a clinical sense from his dad; his dad was just not here for him in his mind, right?

A: In Steve's mind, his dad was a hard-working individual who provided for the family as best as he could, but there wasn't a lot of ongoing activities. So you would not describe that as --maybe aloof, but not being abusive.

Q: But this much we do know, Doctor. We know that a kid like Steve would have been vulnerable to a sophisticated child molester because his parents were not that involved in his life, correct?

A: He would be more vulnerable, that's correct, yes.

Q: And vulnerable kids tend to get abused more than non-vulnerable kids, right?

A: Offenders look for vulnerable kids.

Q: I mean—

A: That's what they seek out. They're looking for kids who are vulnerable, who will be compliant, who will be obedient, who will go with them, yes.

Manipulation and extortion
Q: Steve was also—in addition to being threatened and physically and sexually abused at the same time—there was a level at some point of extortion with Adamson, right?

A: That's my understanding.

255

Q: And what I mean by that is at some point there was a *quid pro quo* or an agreement that I will give you money in the form of a job or tuition in exchange for sex?

A: That's what Steve described, that there would be an exchange for sex for tuition to Seattle Prep, yes.

Q: And whether that was spoken or unspoken, Doctor, that's something you see all the time in your work is abusers use things as simple as an ice cream cone or *hey, I've got some candy, little girl, come into my car,* that's how a lot of these guys lure these kids in, right?

A: They have a technique. They have a strategy that they utilize, yes.

Q: And then once a kid is in the vortex, they can use sophisticated measures to keep them, I mean the classic example is that woman in California who lived with her abuser for what, twenty-eight years or something, and thought she was part of the family, correct?

A: That's correct, yes.

Q: And that level of extortion adds another level of damage and complication to even just the physical actions, doesn't it?

A: Certainly, because it's another level of manipulation that you have to look at and somehow try to deal with or resolve and will affect your—some abilities to trust people, certainly.

Q: Messes with your mind, right?

A: Certainly.

Q: And from 1961 to 1965, during the abuse, Steve was living in a very, very dysfunctional world, wasn't he?

A: Yes, if you look at the abusive pattern, how he responded to it, et cetera. I think even after the sexual abuse stopped for a period of time, between his freshman and sophomore year, he still had contact with this man at school, teen club. Obviousl,y if I may say, the final blow, the major blow, was when they had the altercation, but there would be some anxieties about him, *am I going to run into this person, am I going to see this person, is he going to again encourage some type of physical or sexual abuse,* certainly, and you want to avoid people like that.

Q: Right.

A: They're like bullies, you want to avoid them.

Q: Right. And there is a level of extortion beyond the money at a certain point, even after. Steve began to physically resist three years after the abuse began, then Adamson started really to engage in kind of a mental extortion and he'd say, *if, you know, you don't do this or you don't come over, I'm going to tell your girlfriend* or *I'm going to tell people or I'm going to let people know, through whatever channel, what's going on,* correct?

A: There was the implication, I'm going to tell people you're gay.

Q: And our society in the 1960's sadly was not as open as we are today about those issues, right?

A: Very true, yes.

Q: And so for Steve—and there's no evidence that Steve is antigay or homophobic or anything, right, as part—

A: Not that I know.

Q: But as a teenager, he was deathly afraid of being outed; that's one of the major themes we see in your interview with him and your interview with Dr. Conte, right?

A: Well, of course a teenager in high school does not want to be described as being gay or homosexual for various reasons, especially at that time in his life; your adolescence is emerging, your sexuality is emerging, and back in—if I might say, back in those days, Mr. O'Connor and I are relatively close in age, you did not want to be characterized as gay.

Q: And while he wasn't abused by a family member, he was abused by a person that he knew in a position of authority, correct?

A: Yes.

Q: He was abused by someone who had been over to dinner at his house at one point, right?

A: That's my understanding, yes.

Q: And he was abused by someone who at least he perceived as having a place of great stature in his community?

A: Yes. It was prestigious to be with this man. I think he defined himself as *Adamson's boy*. So this person did have prestige in the community. And when we think of all of those things, this is a very sad case.

Q: In fact, it is a very sad case, and it's a very complex case, correct?

A: Complicated, yes.

Q: And it's complicated because, as you said yesterday, there are—well, this kid was horribly abused—well, it doesn't even stop there. At a point when he tried to resist, the abuser kicked him in the testicles and he ended up having to go in for surgery, right?

A: Which is very uncommon, yes. Yes, he did have to go into surgery, yes.

Q: And I think the words you used in your interview, *he left for Vietnam distraught, confused, and bewildered.* Do you remember using those words?

A: Yes, I used those words.

Q: That was his state of mind as he was leaving for Vietnam, right?

A: And in pain.

Q: And in pain.

A: Testicular pain.

Q: Testicular pain. And then he tells his dad, and his dad in his perception doesn't do anything, and then his dad drops dead a month later. I mean it's incredible, isn't it?

A: It's very sad, yes.

Q: And then, Doctor, he goes on -- well, interesting, something he told you in the
interview, he said he thought his dad might have done something but he dropped dead before he could have; do you remember him telling you that?

A: Oh, absolutely because I explored that with him, and he said his dad may have taken action if he had not died, yes. There was a possibility there. He did not know.

Q: Right. He then goes on to Vietnam, and the jury's heard this, so I won't repeat this, but what makes it complicated is you have trauma upon trauma, correct?

A: Yes.

Q: And one of the real complicating factors in this case is that you have, within a short period of time, two really incredible traumas in terms of the sexual abuse and Vietnam?

A: You also have the death of his father.

Q: Right. I mean—

A: So things that happened. Well, you have several problems. You have the abuse; you have the disclosure; you have the lack of action; you have some decisions to try to get some type of awareness from his folks by saying, hey, mom and dad, I'm going to become a Marine and go to Vietnam, followed by what he saw as no action, followed by his father's death, followed by being in Vietnam I think four months later. So there was an awful lot going on in his life in a very condensed, brief period of time, yes.

Q: But-absolutely, I agree. But we also have on one end of it, we have horrible, horrible sexual abuse by anybody's standards, right?

A: Yes.

Q: And containing all or most of the risk factors for poor outcome followed by combat trauma?

A: Seven hundred days of being in the jungle, and trauma, and being wounded and being hospitalized, yes, sure.

Q: You know, and another topic I want to cover with you, you went to great lengths to describe Steve's resiliency, and being resilient doesn't mean that you're not in pain, correct?

A: That is very true, yes.

Q: And being resilient doesn't mean that you don't suffer from DSM-IV mental diagnoses, correct?

A: Correct.

Q: And at a certain point, certainly in Vietnam, it was a question of survival, wasn't it?

A: Under the circumstances he described?

Q: Yeah.

A: I would say it was a question of survival, sure.

Q: And when he was being physically and sexually abused by Adamson, it was a question of survival, wasn't it, different type of survival, but survival?

A: Sure.

VA visits in 1997 and 2000

Q: In 1997 you're aware, because you've read his deposition that he went into the VA with no intention of talking about Vietnam; you're aware of that, aren't you?

A: My understanding is they brought it up.

Q: Right. He went in because his gun belt, Doctor, was rubbing against an old war injury, right?

A: A war injury from shrapnel, yes, and I think that that was caused, yes. The answer is yes.

Q: And they started asking him questions, stuff he hadn't talked about, and you saw then, like we see after the reunion, a flood of anxiety and emotions, et cetera, correct?

A: Yes, that is true. My understanding is that he—they continued to ask him about his Vietnam experiences. My understanding is he described at least twenty combat-related experiences. I think he said they had morbid curiosity. They continued to *ask and ask and ask and ask,* and decided then that he had been exposed to excessive war combat exposure, and at that point somewhere he received a 100 percent disability, yes. But it was not -- to go along with what you were saying, okay, and to help you with my discussion, it's my understanding he went in there. He didn't plan on talking about that, yes.

Q: He went in there a cop—

A: A cop.

Q: —wanting some relief from his gun belt, and he came out disabled and never worked again, correct, or it led to his retirement?

A: Led to his retirement, yes.

Q: And you talked about the episode in 2000, Doctor, really,

really scary stuff, right, walking the perimeter, I mean you made a very big deal about it in your opinion, suicide, talking about suicide, from a clinician's point a really scary event, correct?

A: He had—it was scarier because he had developed alternate plans for suicide, two different plans that he could utilize to kill himself, which increases the risk factor of him finalizing his life.

Q: And that was a really, really scary event for Steve, wasn't it? Did you explore that with him? Did you ask him how he felt?

A: Scary? I don't know if I asked him how he felt, but obviously from the records it was a difficult time because Steve has a tendency, from what I understand about him, not to go for help, but for some reason he realized somehow this was very, very serious. I don't know if he talked to Gail his wife about it, but somehow he got to the VA Hospital, yes.

Q: You've described him as one of the bravest men you've seen, correct?

A: Absolutely.

Q: And would you describe him as a proud man?

A: Steve?

Q: Yeah.

A: Absolutely.

Q: And would you describe him as someone that does his best to keep up a certain appearance?

A: Proud people would keep up an appearance. He was also a police officer at that time, and cops, if you study the psychology of cops, if I may use that term, they like to be tough, stoic individuals, and they don't like talking about their personal problems and anxieties.

Q: So in your interview, you didn't talk with Steve, did you, about how he felt when he was hospitalized, forced to explore these issues in 2000, and when he was suicidal; it was a very embarrassing thing for Steve, wasn't it?

A: Well, I don't know. He decided to go to the hospital, so I don't know if he was forced to talk about those things.

High school performance and Dr. McGovern's assessment

Q: Doctor, let's talk about some other things that were occurring in high school. He dropped out of high school, correct?

A: He left high school, yes.

Q: He never went back for his senior year. He also, Doctor, he stole a car, didn't he?

A: Did he steal a car? He stole a car after he went into the Marines, yes.

Q: And he was seventeen years old, so he was high-school age when he stole that car, wasn't he?

A: I'm not sure if he was seventeen or eighteen, but he stole a car around that time, yes.

Q: And he ended up in jail, correct?

A: Ninety days in the King County Jail, yes.

Q: And not only ninety days in King County Jail, but he was worried about getting court-martialed right after he went into Vietnam.

A: Yes.

Q: So he almost got bounced out of the Marines for stealing a car, and this is a kid, you will agree with me that had no criminal history prior to stealing that car, correct?

A: Correct.

Q: Doctor, we were talking about Steve's grades, and I think you agreed that they were not very good in high school, correct?

A: Correct.

Q: Then I asked you about his stealing a car, he was out of high school but he was high school age. He told you something else in the interview, which you didn't mention yesterday, I don't think, and that's he told you that he wanted to kill Adamson, correct?

A: That was a thought, yes.

Q: And so when he was seventeen, he wanted to kill Adamson, right, he wanted to?

A: That was a thought he had about why he had the vehicle was to run over Mr. Adamson, who was playing the organ at his father's funeral.

Q: His dad's dropped dead, he comes back, and Adamson's playing the organ; there's nothing he can do about it, right?

A: He was angry. He was angry, yes.

Q: And you would agree with me that that must have been a really, really painful thing to lose your father, come back after trying to get out of town, and seeing the rapist playing the organ?

A: Yes.

Q Would you agree with me that even before—well, I think you said given your testimony—it's a prerequisite to therapy that someone needs to begin to open up about these things before they can effectively heal?

A: Well, you have to be able to discuss them before you can heal, unless you heal through your own resources, yes.

Q And Steve, rightly or wrongly, has a history in life of—look at Vietnam, for example—of at least partially healing though his own resources, correct?

A That's my understanding, yes.

Q You and I may disagree—and I think we both agree—that Steve could benefit from counseling, but if you look at it from Steve's perspective, he has a history of working out problems himself, correct?

A: Yes

CHAPTER 25

LIGHTING THE DARKNESS: A TIME TO HATE

After the testimony of Dr. McGovern during week four, several witnesses are called. Among them is Father Carrignan, the representative of the Oblates sitting at the defense attorneys' table throughout the trial. He is being recalled to the stand for additional cross-examination by Michael Pfau. He has now testified four times, starting the second week of the trial. In an odd sense, I feel pity for the priest. Not much, and quite fleeting in its duration. After all, once with Michael Pfau is quite enough. I would not have wished another day on the stand under his questioning for anyone.

I admit, I am puzzled by the recall of this witness. Thinking about my earlier observations of the numerous sidebars of the attorneys huddled around the judge's desk, out of earshot of the jurors, led me to believe that maybe this was the reason for the additional examination. There had been several lively and heated discussions about some "documents" that had apparently been asked for several times during the discovery process, and the defense denied they existed.

Michael Pfau had actually obtained them (30B-6) at this late date. It also appeared that they were not only very damaging to the defense, but clearly contradicted Father Carrignan's testimony about how, exactly, the heads of the Oblate order of priests, in addition to how the Vatican, itself, handled reports of sexual abuse of children. Ironically, these documents covered events that took place during the exact period of time that the abuse was taking place at St. Benedict's. These documents were explosive in that they impeached Carrignan's previous testimony and exposed how the Oblate order moved around and covered up for "problem" priests, child-abusing priests. There was no mention of the victims; it was all about "avoiding scandal."

This is going to be good.

Cross-examination of Father Carrignan by Michael Pfau

Q: While you've testified that you didn't know or claimed not to have known about Oblate Priest B[†] and the child being abused, you will agree with me that the provincial, or someone at the Western Province, knew about that priest, knew about that priest's problems, and knew about that victim, correct?

A: The documents that we reviewed today would indicate that, yes.

Q: And the documents we reviewed today indicate that there was knowledge at the highest levels of the Western Province, and there was knowledge at the highest levels of the worldwide order, about Oblate Priest B, correct?

A: Yes.

Q: Yet your corporation designated you to be the person to provide the information to the plaintiffs, and you knew nothing, according to you, about this, correct?

A: That's a fact.

Q: You would agree with me that the documents we looked at earlier were Oblate documents that came from Oblate files?

A: Yes.

Q: And were stored by Oblate personnel?

A: Yes.

Q: In Washington D.C. or Oakland before the provinces merged, correct?

---

† Oblate Priest B sexually abused children from 1961-1965. He was assigned to the Philippines, then to the Western Province in another parish with a school. Confidential letters were written to the highest Oblates in Rome by Fr. McDonald, Western Province Provincial. who covered up the crimes and failed to act.

A: Yes.

Q: So at the time in April, when Steve O'Connor asked your—your province, your corporation for that information, that information existed within the files and knowledge of the Western Province, correct?

A: Yes.

Q: Do you know why it wasn't turned over?

A: I really don't know.

Q: Would you agree with me, Father, that those documents, at least the eight that you've looked at, talk about the provincial hierarchy in the Oblate province?

A: Yes, Father McDonald was provincial.

Q: And you would agree that those documents talk about the provincial and how he reacted to issues of child abuse during the same time period that Steve O'Connor was being abused?

A: To what was being asserted in those documents, yes.

Q: And you would agree with me that those documents demonstrate evidence about how that provincial in the Western Province was responding to complaints of child abuse between 1961 and 1965, correct?

A: For those—for that particular situation, yes.

Q: And in fact, and this appears to be a coincidence, but the documents detail problems with the priest from 1961 to 1965, the very years that Steve O'Connor was being abused, correct?

A: Yes.

Q: And the very years that Father McDonald was making decisions about placements of superiors and pastors, correct?

A: Yes.

Q: Were you asked to give a second deposition in this case?

A: I believe I was this last week, or two weeks ago.

Q: Did you give a deposition during this case on June 15th?

A: Yes.

Q: Father, you were asked questions during your second deposition about any complaints or allegations of abuse, correct?

A: Yes.

Q: And you were asked to give a second deposition because between the time of the first deposition and the time the trial started plaintiffs learned that there were, or at least there was an abusive priest identified during the time period in question, correct—

A: Yes.

Q: —Father, between the time you gave your first deposition, well, and your second

deposition, which took place at night or a weekend during this trial; do you recall that?

A: Yes, I do.

Q: And the reason you were deposed again is because Steve O'Connor learned for the first time during this trial that there was an Oblate priest who had abused children, correct?

A: Yes.

Q: Will you turn, Father, to page 6 in your deposition.

Q: And you were asked about that document which identified Priest B, correct, line 22? Was that the answer you gave?

A: Yes.

Q: And that was referring to how the information was provided to us?

A: How it was found, yes.

Q: Just prior to June 15th?

A: Right.

Q: And then you were asked, Father, on page 12—let me ask you, Father—find the page and then I'll ask you another question. Father, on June15th, you were also the designee or the person designated by the Western Province to answer questions about the information we had just received during this trial, correct?

A: Yes. I was asked to come here.

Q: And would you turn to line 10, Father, of your deposition, your June deposition.

A: Yes.

Q: And on line 10, Father, you were asked this question, correct: *Is this the same Oblate priest, Oblate Priest B, who is alleged to have abused children in the early 1960's,* correct?

A: Yes.

Q: And your answer?

A: Yes.

Q: And is it your testimony, Father, that you had no notion that Oblate Priest B was moved around after complaints of abuse?

A: I had no knowledge of that, no.

Q: Will you turn to page 14, please, line 19, Father. And you were asked this question, but did the Oblates do anything to investigate and find out if this priest molested any other children beyond these three? And your answer was?

A: Which line are we on again here?

Q: Page 14, line 22, Father.

A: Ok. That's when they found out in the year 2000. I don't know. I can just presume, yes. I had no direct knowledge. I was not there. I was not part of the activity.

Q: As the corporate representative in this case, you told Steve O'Connor's lawyers that they found out about Oblate Priest B in 2000, correct, first found out in 2000, correct?

A: That's what I read in the exhibit, yes.

Q: And then on page 15, Father, I asked you the question, or you were asked the question, so do you know if the Oblates did anything to remove this priest from ministry while they investigated these allegations of abuse?

A: I don't know.

Q: And that was not only your answer, but it was the answer on behalf of your client, correct?

A: You know, that's the way this is interpreted. However, I don't know what they did. That doesn't mean that they didn't do anything.

...

Q: Report on province. Would this document have gone to

Rome, along with the visitation reports, as part of the overall provincial report?

A: It was a letter to Father John Walsh, the Assistant General.

Q: It was written to Rome, but would this also have gone to the files as part of the annual report to Rome that you talked about when assessing visitation reports?

A: That's a note that's initialed by Jon Walsh telling him that your annual statistics report on the province is overdue, and he's asking him to send it in. I think that's independent from the content of that letter.

Q: It is indicating, however, that Rome is in contact with the Western Province, correct?

A: Yes.

Q: And Rome's in contact with the Western Province because there's a priest with a problem, right?

MS. KENNAN: Objection. Lack of foundation.

The Court: Sustained, unless you can answer that.

Q: (BY MR. PFAU) Can you answer that, father?

A: Tell me the question again.

Q: Sure. Is Rome in contact with the Western Province because there is a problem with the priest?

A: Rome's in contact with the Western Province on an ongoing basis.

Q: Are they in contact here because there's a problem with a priest?

A: The letter was on that occasion to Father Walsh, and then he noted that thing on the bottom telling him your annual statistic report is missing.

Q: (BY MR. PFAU) My question was a little different, Father. Here this document demonstrates that Rome, with the highest levels of the Oblate order, are in contact with the Western Province about a problem priest, correct?

A: Yes, that letter.

Q: And what is happening is Rome, or the highest levels of the

Oblate order, are sending a problem priest from the Philippines to the Western Province, correct?

A: As far as I remember, yes.

Q: And you will agree with me that these eight documents involve a problem priest being transferred from the Philippines to the Western Province, correct?

A: Yes.

Q: And Father McDonald, the provincial, accepts responsibility for that priest, correct?

A: Yes.

Q: Let's turn to 209, please. Father, one more question. 208, in that letter, Father Walsh tells the provincial that he's keeping this to the strictest confidence, correct?

A: Yes.

Q: In the 1960's, Father, did the Oblate priests keep problems like child sex abuse secret?

A: I would say in this case, there is a decision to keep that particular event confidential, yes.

Q: (BY MR. PFAU) And Father, my question is broader. In the 1960s, did the Oblate order keep the fact that priests were molesting children in the strictest confidence?

The Court: Sustained.

MS. KENNAN: You read my mind, your Honor.

The Court: I think I felt you rising.

MS. KENNAN: Thank you.

Q: (BY MR. PFAU) We'll turn to 209, Father.

In this, if you look at this letter, they're talking about assigning this priest, and they are concerned about assigning him to parish work that would involve a school, correct?

A: Yes.

Q: Let's turn to 210, please. This letter was from August 29th, and it is Joseph McDonald writing to Walsh, who is the Assistant General, correct?

A: Yes.

Q: And what he's telling him is it's a sad letter he has to write, correct?

A: Yes.

Q: And the situation that at least McDonald had prayed would not happen again had, and it's a recurrence of the problem for Oblate Priest B, correct?

A: Yes.

Q: Father, there were certain words that counsel asked you about that were repeated: *problem, trouble, situations, doings, conducts.* You recall those words, right?

A: Yes.

Q: There is no reference to sex abuse in these documents, other than the one, but you know this is a case of sex abuse, correct?

Q: Father, you now know that Oblate Priest B had problems with sexually abusing children, correct?

A: You know, I don't know directly. I was not there, but I would say yes, that would have been most likely the situation.

Q: And the words that are used are *trouble, problem,* et cetera. Father, was it the practice of the Oblates in the 1960's to write and speak in code about child sexual abuse?

A: I wouldn't know that.

Q: Father, look at the paragraph that starts, *there is nothing more for me to do now*; it's the third paragraph.

A: Yes.

Q: The provincial says he cannot trust this priest in any parish, correct, over a period of time?

A: Yes.

Q: Father, if you look at the next paragraph that reads, *I am still the only one here.*

A: Yes.

Q: Father McDonald is telling Rome that he is still the only one here who knows of the background, correct?

A: Yes.

Q: So they have placed him in ministry without telling anyone that he had problems in the Philippines, correct?

A: Yes.

Q: Then he says in the next paragraph, *such a situation in a new province, because the province is new, is indeed a drawback.* And he tells Rome that he is sitting on pins and needles each hour of the day wondering if he, Oblate Priest B, is repeating the past performances, correct?

A: He's saying that, yes.

Q: So he is telling Rome at the highest levels that he is really worried about this situation, correct?

A: Yes.

...

Q: (BY MR. PFAU) He says at the bottom of that paragraph, second to last paragraph, that I assume the risk knowingly and willingly in order to help out a brother Oblate priest, and if God intends this as my *cross fiat voluminous del,* which I think is Latin, correct?

A: Yes.

Q: He is indicating that he has assumed the risk of this priest molesting again in order to help out a fellow Oblate?

A: He's saying that, yes.

Q: Let's turn to the next page of this document. And Joseph McDonald, the Oblate provincial during the 1960's, when Steve O'Connor was abused, tells Father Walsh that every time he, Oblate Priest B, goes out I say a prayer that he will keep to the narrow path. So he was praying that this priest won't molest again, correct?

A: I would say that's his prayer. I'm not certain for everything, but I'd say that's what that seems to be.

Q: In fact, the next sentence says, *I have prayed rosaries ever since Romean days when I first learned of the case.* He says he's been praying the rosary ever since the discussion in Rome, correct?

A: Yes.

Q: Father, there is no indication in these first three letters that he is alerting anyone other than himself, to this problem, correct?

A: Not in the letter, no.

Q: Let's look at 211. And by the way, in 210, the situation happened within two weeks of this priest being placed in a parish, correct? Do you recall that, Father?

A: I'm not certain of the dates.

Q: The next document is November 12th, 1961, so about five months later. And if we look at the paragraph that says, *last year, when the trouble was being handled, he was provided with an opportunity of making a prolonged retreat and receiving professional help of a psychiatrist.* You have testified in this case that what the Oblates provincial would have done would have notified a bishop or notified the police, correct?

A: Yes.

Q: That wasn't done in this case, was it?

A: It was not.

Q: And in fact, this priest wasn't even ordered to go see a psychiatrist, he was just given the opportunity to go see a psychiatrist, right?

A: I don't know that for a fact.

Q: In the next paragraph, Father Walsh indicates that Father has become a sick man and a dangerously sick man. Those are strong words; you've been a provincial, correct?

A: Yes.

Q: Would you agree that this is someone who needs to be out of the ministry?

A: I would agree.

Q: Let's turn to the next document, which is exhibit 212. It's now October, exhibit 212. Four years have passed, Father, and it's October 11th, 1965, and this priest is still in the Western Province, correct?

A: Yes.

Q: And we see here that there's been another complaint of abuse, correct?

A: Yes.

Q: Let's turn to page 213. So, Father, we now know that there have been multiple molestations after this priest was transferred from the Philippines, correct? The provincial is writing to Reverend Louis Sohler at Saint Alice's Catholic Church because there's been another complaint of abuse, correct?

A: See, I don't know for a fact.

Q: What we do know is Father McDonald tells this priest that he will take care of it and he is dealing with the matter with our authorities on a higher level, correct?

A: Yes.

Q: That means he's taking care of it in-house within the Oblate family, correct?

A: I would say that would be when he's saying our authorities on a higher level, he could be referring to the General.

Q: There's no indication that they called the police, correct?

A: Not in that letter.

Q: And there's no indication in any of these letters that the Oblate provincial alerted a bishop, is there?

A: Not in the letters that I read.

Q: And what he says in the third paragraph is how can I as provincial allow these things to happen and not take action? Well, he as provincial has allowed these things to happen over the last four years, hasn't he?

A: He didn't take action.

Q: So after numerous complaints and instances of problematic behavior, Father McDonald, the Oblate pastor in the 1960s, sent him to an unsuspecting diocesan parish, correct?

A: So the letter indicates, yes.

Q: And he abused again, correct?

A: To my knowledge, he really did not handle it right.

Q: And he handled the situation the opposite way that you've told this jury that the Oblates operated in the 1960s?

A: That is what my expectations were, yes.

Q: And here he's writing to Rome and he's saying, *one of these days it's going to be a police action in this case and California is really adamant on this sort of thing. They must register in the state once convicted of such conduct no matter where they go in the state.* So he's telling this priest that's serving in Rome near the Vatican City that as of 1965, in California, the State authorities don't mess around with this kind of thing, correct?

A: Yes.

Q: They send them to the police, correct?

A: Yes.

Q: And he's not saying, *I'm going to send him to the police,* is he?

A: No.

Q: He's not doing what you told this jury the Oblates did in the 1960s, is he?

A: What I would have expected a priest to do, yes.

Q: And in fact, what he's telling the authorities in Rome is, *if this keeps up, the police are going to find out and he is going to get arrested,* correct?

A: Yes.

Q: And if you look at the middle of the paragraph, something defense counsel didn't read with you, he says, *each day I live in this job, I feel that something is going to, in quotations, break and the scandal will increase for the Oblates.* He is not—not once have you seen any reference to the victims, have you?

A: Not that I have seen, no.

Q: And what he's worried about here, when writing Rome, is that the scandal is going to get worse for the Oblates who have placed this priest in a parish, correct?

A: Yes.

Q: And he says, *the province is too small, the Western Province in 1965 is too small to absorb him,* and he says, *we cannot afford to expand his scandalous conduct.* So he's not talking about putting him away or taking him out of the ministry at this point; he's just saying, *if he stays here, he is going to molest more kids,* but he doesn't reference kids, he just references scandal, correct?

A: Yes.

The Court: Let's stop here.

MR. PFAU: No further questions.

Along with the testimony of Fr. Carrignan, there are three other religious leaders who have testified at trial.

First, Father Dillon, the former Assistant Pastor at St. Benedict's in 1962 testifies in his direct cross-examination by Mr. Gavaria that he does not know about Adamson's train set and does not remember going to the house. Under cross-examination, Mr. Cochran asks:

Q: Let's talk about Dan Adamson's train set. You were asked about it in testimony during this deposition and we got the chance to ask you questions. At first, you said you didn't remember it, but then you said you did kind of remember it, right?

A: Yes, on second thought, yes.

Q: Okay. You remember Dan Adamson, the teacher, having a train set, and do you remember him inviting students to his house to see it?

A: I don't remember who he invited into there. I think I once myself that I was—saw his train set.

Q: And did you—so you were invited to his house. Do you remember talking with anyone besides Mr. Adamson while you were there?

A: No.

Q: And was he there at the time?

A: Yes.

Q: And do you remember the purpose for him showing you why he had a train set down in his basement of his house?

A: It was his hobby.

Q: And do you remember, was that early in the time that you were at Saint Benedict's?

A: I don't know exactly when I became aware of him having a train set.

Q: Okay. Do you remember talking to anyone else within the Oblate community about Dan Adamson and his train set?

A: No.

Q: Do you remember—and, specifically, do you remember talking to Father Brunet about the train set, about the fact that Dan Adamson was living with his parents at the age that he was?

A: I don't recall what -- If I did, I don't recall.

Q: In terms of Dan Adamson's activities as the C.Y.O. director or the choir director, those weren't school activities, those are parish activities, right?

A: Correct.

Q: And again, the importance of the activities for the children, whether it's the school or the teen club or the youth sports organizations, all of those are for the health of the parish that the Oblates are administering, right?

A: It's for the good of the students, yes.

Q: Right, and the good of the—the adult parishioners there, right?

A: Yes.

Q: Ultimately, good for the Oblates themselves, right, in terms of having a healthy parish, and having a nice cycle of kids into grown-ups that are in the parish for a long time, right?

A: Yeah, as a priest, try to have a good healthy parish, yes.

MR. COCHRAN: All right. That's all the questions I have at this time.

The Court: Thank you....

Another associate priest at St. Benedict's in 1962, Father Brunet, provided sworn testimony in a taped interview from his home in Alaska. In an excerpt from the transcripts, there is the following exchange between Father Brunet and Mr. Pfau.

Mr. Pfau asks Father Brunet about how he would address a report of child abuse that a child might confide in him.

Q: Is it your testimony that you're not sure whether you would tell that child to go to the police or his parents or another authority figure?

A: I don't know. I would probably talk a little more to the child.

Q: You would talk what?

A: Maybe—maybe something more to the child, but I would, you know, encourage them to see someone, yes, but that's all I could say.

Q: So—

A: But to go to the police, I wouldn't, no.

Q: Why wouldn't you?

A: Because there was nothing else -- you've got other people to see before that. There's other things. Well, he could go and talk to the police if he wants, that's up to him, but—

Q: Is there some reason you wouldn't encourage a child to go to the police?

A: This is a trick question.

Q: Well it's—it's not a trick question, Father. What I'm -- what I'm trying to establish is that even if a priest learns about the likelihood of child sexual abuse in the confessional there are things that a priest can do without violating the sanctity of the confessional that could still aid that child in ending the abuse. So it's not a trick question at all. It's a -- it's a—

A: Well I'd do what I could, but I'd have to -- you know, I don't know what the situation -- yeah.

Q: So would you agree with me there are things that a Catholic priest can do without violating the sanctity of the confessional—

A: Well yes, yes.

Q: —to assist a child?

A: I won't tell you, though. I won't tell you.

Q: You won't tell me?

A: No.

Q: You won't tell me what the child was confessing, right?

A: I wouldn't tell what the child is confessing. I won't tell anything.

Q: But—

A: I don't want to be touched on it. I don't even want to be—

Q: You don't want to be—

A: I don't want to be questioned on it, because -- it's something in confession, I'm not going to go into that.

And finally, the sworn testimony of Sister Nathan, Joann Unger, the former principal at St. Benedict's in the late 1960s, who was the teacher of the 7A class during the abuse. Her classroom was located directly across the hall from Dan Adamson's class.

From direct examination of Sister Nathan by Mr. Gavaria

Q: Okay. And when you taught seventh grade at St. Benedict's School, where was your classroom, if you can describe it?

A: The third floor.

Q: Okay. And was there another seventh grade teacher when you were teaching at St. Benedict's School in 1961?

A: Yes.

Q: '62? Who was that teacher?

A: That was Daniel Adamson.

Q: Okay. And where was Mr. Adamson's classroom in relation to your classroom?

A: Across the hall.

Q: Okay, and how would you describe Mr. Adamson?

A: At that time, I didn't know him very well, so he was very cordial, very polite. We worked on few of the projects together.

Q: Okay.

A: He was very easy to work with.

Q: And I -- In that first year you were teaching at St. Benedict's School, did you socialize outside of school with Mr. Adamson?

A: No.

Q: And you testified that your classroom was across from Mr. Adamson's classroom. Do you remember a student in Mr. Adamson's class called Steven O'Connor?

A: No, I don't.

Q: And when you were teaching at St. Benedict's school in 1961 to 1962, did you ever hear that Mr. Adamson would have students over to his house to play with train sets?

A: He told me then.

Q: And what did he tell you, if you remember?

A: Just that.

She denies knowing me— just four years earlier she came right up to me that night of the St. Benedict's 100-year anniversary, called my name out loud, and asked if I knew who *she* was.

Cross-Examination of Sister Nathan by Darrell Cochran

Q: I'm going to ask you now a few questions about your specific interactions with Dan Adamson when you were principal of the school. When you were serving as principal, was Dan Adamson still teaching at—

A: Yes.

Q: —St. Benedict's? Ok. And did you supervise Mr. Adamson?

A: Sometimes, yes.

Q: Ok. And did you ever counsel or coach Mr. Adamson about anything in any way?

A: I told him that he may not discipline children physically.

Q: And why did you tell him that?

A: Because he talked about it. I don't know how much he actually did, but he was sort of bragging about a paddle at his room once and I, you know, I said it's against the law.

Q: And did you talk to anyone else about that bragging by Mr. Adamson?

A: I'm sorry, what?

Q: Did you talk to anyone else other than to Mr. Adamson about his bragging about paddling?

A: No. I might have talked to the pastor about it, but that's --

Q: Do you remember a specific conversation you had with Father McHugh?

A: No.

Q: No?

A: No.

Q: And did you ever follow up with Mr. Adamson following that conversation?

A: Yes.

Q: Okay. And what happened in the follow-up?

A: I think, as far as I know, as far as that stopped.

Q: And did you ever—when you were serving as principal, did you ever have any conversations about—with Mr. Adamson— about his taking students to his house to play with trains?

A: He told me that one day, and I said asked him why he was doing this, and he said, *well, I have a train set. They really like to watch the trains,* and that's all he told me.

Q: And did you follow up with him in any way about that?

A: Not at the time, no.

Q: Okay. And did you know that Mr. Adamson, when you were principal, was employing students to tune and repair organs?

A: Yes, I knew that.

Q: And did you have any conversations with Mr. Adamson about his employing students to repair and tune organs?

A: I asked him about it, and he said that he really needed some help, and so the students were glad to do it. That was kind of his response.

Q: Okay. And did you ever have any conversations that you can—specific conversation at all with Pastor McHugh about Dan Adamson in any way?

A: I believe on one occasion I mentioned that, I asked Dan, excuse me, specifically not to physically discipline children.

Q: And do you recall when that occurred?

A: No, I don't.

Q: Okay. And do you recall whether -- where physically at the school or at the parish this occurred?

A: The parish.

Q: Okay. And do you recall what Father McHugh told you?

A: No, I don't, but it wasn't something that said *I'll be right over there.*

Questions from the Jury to Sister Nathan
The Court: When you asked Mr. Adamson why students would

go to his house, or why he used them to help fix organs, was it at all because you were suspicious of anything?

The Witness: Well, I was certainly curious. I'm not—I really trusted him. I—it did not occur to me at that time that there was anything beside what he said it was. A few years later, I probably would have thought about it differently. But at the time, I took him at his word.

The Court: Sister, what is the relationship between the Director of Schools and the Archdiocese, if you know?

The Witness: The school offices at the chancery, which is the center, the office of the Archdiocese, it's all one large group of people that run the Diocese. One part of that is the school.

The Court: Sister, who does the hiring of lay teachers at the schools at which the Dominican Sisters taught?

The Witness: That was a combination of the pastor and the principal.

The Court: Sister, with regard to Dan Adamson telling you about having children at his house, did you have any other thoughts besides the one you've already told us about?

The Witness: Any other thoughts?

The Court: Any other thoughts than the ones you already told us about?

The Witness: I'm sorry to say, no, I didn't. I trusted him. I didn't think there was any problem there at the time.

The Court: And what, if anything, did you do after you had this conversation with him?

The Witness: I just remember thinking about it, and I didn't really do anything.

As I return to my hotel room, I notice the off-and-on rain of the past few weeks has ceased, revealing a glimmering Puget Sound. From my twelfth-story window, I stare at the majestic Olympic mountain range to the west. It is now nine o'clock, yet the sun is still shining just above the horizon. It's twilight and fittingly, as well, it's the twilight of the trial. In the next few days, the closing arguments by both sides will be presented, final rebuttal by Michael Pfau, jury instructions, deliberation, and then the verdict. I am still upright, continuing to breathe in and out, and no matter what the outcome, I have finally confronted and ultimately found some sort of justice.

I reflect on Adamson's parents, particularly, his mother, standing in the kitchen as she always seemed to be: You boys want some lemonade before you go home? She enabled him, she and many others; the priests, nuns, parents enabled him and failed to protect children. Now, I have found *a time for purpose* and I can look at myself in the mirror, no matter what the outcome.

There certainly will always remain the permanent damage. But I can begin to form the scar tissue, to cover the damage. Just like the gunshot wounds to my leg, whenever sitting on the edge of a chair, I still feel sharp pain. Winter cold will always cause tightness and aching. All that I need to do is flex my leg muscle to get an instant reminder of a long-ago war for a long-forgotten cause.

But this war is different. It has a purpose, and tomorrow morning, it will begin to come to a clear and, hopefully, just end.

CHAPTER 26

A WONDERFUL LIFE:
A TIME TO MOURN

On the last day of week four, Michael Pfau had completed his examination of Fr. Carrignan for the fifth time, and after a break, he began his closing arguments. This occurred on Thursday, June 28th. Mr. Lemly started his closing that afternoon and was granted more time to finish the following Monday, June 2nd. Mr. Pfau follows Mr. Lemly's closing argument with his rebuttal later that same day, ending the trial, except for the jury's decision.

The topics of this trial—presented by both plantiff and defendant in the closing arguments, but with very different interpretations—include these main issues:

Both sides agree that the abuse occurred, but which party is responsible?

Does the Borrowed Servant Doctrine apply to the Oblates?

Does the Statute of Limitations trigger apply while Steve attends the 100th anniversary, where he recognizes the cause and injury of his abuse?

What is significance of the corroborating direct evidence of witnesses who testified?

What do the 'secret documents' reveal about how the Oblates dealt with the knowledge of sexual abuse by their priests, and their patterns of cover-up?

How will proximate and superseding causes be determined?

The abuse was committed by Dan Adamson, who was hired and supervised by the Oblates, and after being notified of the abuse, the Oblates did not take action to protect children; subsequently Steve sought to remove himself from the abuse and joined the Marine Corps as an infantryman in Vietnam. The two psychologists serving as expert witnesses at the trial (one for the plantiff, one for the defendant) agree that the traumas cannot be separated: the sexual abuse Steve experienced as a child, the Vietnam War combat trauma and PTSD, and Steve's work as a police officer.

Mr. Lemly does not deny that the abuse happened, and agrees it was horrendous. He argues, however, that the Archdiocese held the primary responsibility and authority of managing the parish. Mr. Pfau argues that the Oblates, who held a contract with the Archdiocese to oversee St. Benedict's Church and School for one hundred years, are the responsible party. They hired and supervised Dan Adamson as a seventh-grade teacher and allowed the abuse to occur, failing to stop the abuse after it was reported multiple times to the Oblate Pastor, Father Conrad.

Mr. Pfau begins his closing argument; his main points (some will arise again in his rebuttal):

Fr. Conrad, Oblate pastor of St. Benedict's hired Dan Adamson, had the ultimate authority at the school, and appointed Adamson as CYO Director, the teen club leader, the head of the youth group and the boys' choir. Fr. Conrad was told on three separate occasions that Adamson was sexually abusing boys and Conrad failed to follow up, report it, and call the Archbishop or the police—all to avoid scandal. The Oblates were negligent, they allowed the abuse to continue happening, and they are responsible.

The Borrowed Servant Doctrine does not apply. The Oblates did not lend an employee to the Archdiocese, which had exclusive control, and there is no doubt that Father Dillon, Father Conrad, and Father Brunet were the agents of the Oblates. The Oblates monitored them, were responsible for their well-being, paid their insurance, travel expenses, and ultimately, their funeral expenses. The Oblates were responsible for visitations to monitor their priestly ministry. The priests vow obedience to the Oblate Order.

In Pfau's own words, "The Statute of Limitations is a pretty simple concept—it basically gives people periods of time to file a lawsuit....Our legislature has enacted one of the broadest Statute of Limitations for childhood sexual abuse in the country." So within three years of the act alleged to have caused the injury or condition, within three years of the time the victim discovered or reasonably should have discovered that the injury or condition was caused by the said act, or, and this is the clause that applies to this case, within three years of the time the victim discovered that the act caused the injury for which the claim is brought." So for this case, "the focus is on when the victim of sexual abuse in fact discovers the causal link between the abuse and the injury or injuries for which the abuse, for which the suit is brought." In other words, Steve's triggering event for discovering the causal link of Adamson's abuse and his injuries happens when he attends the 100th anniversary.

Proximate Cause. "There are really two proximate causes of the injury; it's the failure to protect the kid, failure to keep him from being injured, and then there is also, the proximate cause of the teacher doing the injury.

Superseding Cause. Steve, who is harmed, decided to get out of the situation by joining the Marines—that is not a superseding cause. Says Pfau, "Dr. Conte and Dr. McGovern have both testified that you can't segregate the harm at a certain point between Vietnam and the child sexual abuse. It is not a superseding cause under the law."

Damages. Mr. Pfau presents four stages of Steve's life as a guideline in awarding damages:

1. Stage one: Lasting 1961-1965, entitled rape, sexual assault, manipulation and extortion of a child. $2-4 million.

2. Stage two: Vietnam, Steve served two voluntary tours; completely out of character for him to join the armed forces; the trauma he suffered in Vietnam would not have occurred but for the abuse of Adamson. $2-4 million.

3. Stage three: Cycles of depression, anger, and withdrawal for thirty years. $1-2 million.

4. Stage four: the anniversary to the present. Steve suffering severe depression, anxiety, social isolation, anger, guilt, shame, and intrusive thoughts related to PTSD after memories were triggered

at the reunion. Treatment will be difficult. Even though Steve is resilient, this does not mean he didn't suffer and it doesn't mean he didn't experience those things. $1-2 million.

Mr. Pfau thanks the jury to end his closing arguments.

After the jury takes a brief break, court resumes.

Judge Shaffer: "Ladies and gentlemen of the jury, please give your attention to Mr. Lemly on behalf of the defendant."

Mr. Lemly:

"In the opening, four weeks ago, (it seems like four years ago to some of us) I said, this is a difficult case. I said we had to look at the whole lifetime for this individual, Steve O'Connor, sixty-three years. The traumas he suffered, more than a lifetime's worth of trauma. No one would deny that. The abuse he suffered at the hands of Dan Adamson was terrible. No one would have to explain it, or accept it. The trauma in Vietnam, two combat tours of duty in Vietnam as a United States Marine.

"His personal heroism in Vietnam. He won a Bronze Star, several notches down from the highest honors we can give a military person, fought courageously, wounded, but very courageously. He had great success in civilian life. Moved up from entry-level positions, basically, into management positions, supervising a number of persons, and then working as a contract consultant for many years. And then he decided to join the police force. The initial thought was he would be a D.A.R.E. officer, not carry a weapon. So he didn't go into this for adventure, but found out he would have to carry a weapon, and it ended up with several shootouts and other trauma there. And then after he actually retired, the death by suicide of one of his closest friends and one of his brothers. So trauma there as well. But outstanding service during this period and many good years with his family, with friends, on his several boats, active in his church and his community, a variety of different good activities and healthy activities.

"It is also a difficult case because of the complexity of the relationships of the people and the organizations that were involved at St. Benedict's. We heard a good bit of evidence coming in yesterday about a Priest B and much talk by Mr. Pfau about a Worldwide Order, Rome, and so on. This is really, as I suspect you would see, background only. It's not the focus of this case. It is obvious that Father Carrignan was pained and disappointed to see what he saw in those documents and to see people dealing with an abusive priest in the '60s in a way that he felt was inappropriate and not the way that he would have handled that."

Mr. Lemly goes on to question the credibility of my testimony. Did he really tell Fr. Conrad? He claims he made a report to Father Conrad and then referenced this in confessional with Father Dillon—but, it's been fifty years ago. He goes on to cast doubts about Mr. Fish's testimony, calling them "dream like sequences." He summarizes Fish's testimony by casting any conversation the boy had with a priest or his own mother as vague, nothing specific about sexual abuse or anything.

"So I submit to you that you will find as you evaluate that testimony, there is very little to say that Father Conrad, or anyone else at St. Benedict's, could have known anything about difficulties with Adamson at that time. Everyone who has talked about him, his brothers, Sister Unger, the other folks who have testified, have said that he was held in high regard by the community. He had grown up in the parish. His parents still went to church there. He had grown up in the church and the school. It is clear now that he was a very bad guy. He should not have been teaching. And it is very unfortunate that he was in the role that he was in. But that conduct never came to light for forty years after the time that Steve O'Connor was there."

Lemly continues with how I did not run away directly after the altercation with Adamson when I was injured, and that I waited a year to tell my dad about Adamson's abuse and was disappointed and angry when my dad took no action. According to Lemly, I decided to take action by joining the Marines, in part to get their attention; they did not object to me going into the military, but they encouraged me to join the Air Force, instead. In the end, my parents signed the papers so I could join the Marine Corps.

"Again, millions were either joining or being drafted at that stage. He made that decision to go into the Marine Corps. Again, very difficult to say there is a clear cause-and-effect relationship between what was happening at that stage and going into the Marines. He had many different choices. It is a choice he made. He was a guy who liked to be active, macho, show his strength. This is a choice he made at that time."

Lemly proceeds to talk about the sudden death of my father, my life after Vietnam in California, now married and having children. He goes on to point out that I declined an offer to attend an officer candidate program for the Marines, due to another tour of duty in Vietnam. He covers our move back to Seattle and me taking classes at the community college, but not pursuing the GI bill to finish college and have the government pay for my education. Throughout his closing, Lemly repeats that I made choices about my career and service in the military all along. He states that life is good for the family, financially stable, that I am an active parent, and successful in a manufacturing job as manager.

"In 1989, he makes a decision to join the police force in Stanwood. Again, there can be no possible cause-and-effect relationship between joining the police force and anything that had happened at St. Benedict's. But though he joined the police force thinking that he would be a D.A.R.E. officer, be doing lectures on drug prevention, education in schools, and the like, he either shifts that goal or finds out that's what's involved in the Stanwood police force and does have shootouts and routine activity that subjects him to additional trauma in his police role."

Lemly explains that I completed ten years of service on the police force after which I go to the VA hospital to see about the shrapnel that is causing pain around my gun belt. The doctors engage me in talking about the extreme trauma that I experienced in Vietnam.

"But at any event, both the Veterans Administration and the Social Security did find in 1997 that he is 100 percent disabled due to PTSD and depression based on mainly the combat trauma in Vietnam, but also some of the police duty, and he retires at that stage.

"The family moves to Spokane, his youngest son leaves for college, and retirement is a very different life and pace for Steve from his career as a police officer. So in the fall of 2000, he goes into the VA Hospital and tells them that he is deeply depressed and he has got an executable plan for suicide. He spends six days in the psych unit at the VA Hospital. And you have seen the records there where he talks about his combat history."

Lemly posits that this is the first time that I sought opportunities for medical treatment for psychological issues.

"He receives treatment for this six or ten day period at the VA. He receives counseling, receives medications and recovers fairly quickly. He leaves saying he feels good, and from then on he begins to get regular generally annual psychological examinations at the VA Hospital."

Lemly describes the depression screenings I've received over the years and the variety of test responses. The point he wants to make is that I am capable of seeking and getting treatment and counseling as shown through the various exhibits—namely medical records from the VA.

"So after the reunion, Mr. O'Connor does not see a medical doctor, or a psychiatrist, or a psychologist to deal with the feelings that he is experiencing as a result of going over to St. Benedict's again. A year later, he consults and retains his lawyers. He was not diagnosed with any medical condition related to Adamson, or to any other aspect of his time at St. Benedict's, until he saw Dr. Conte, his testifying expert witness here, several months before trial. Not once since the reunion has he ever gone to a social worker, a psychiatrist, or a psychologist to get a diagnosis as to *why I am feeling this way?* and *what I can do about it?*

Lemly talks about the parties involved, the Oblates and the Archdiocese, and what their relationship was with St. Benedict's. He argues that the Archdiocese is the central Seattle area overseeing 175 parishes, one of which is St. Benedict's. He counters Mr. Pfau's portrayal of the relationship between the Archbishop and the Pastor, referring to witnesses from the Archdiocese (the Chancellor) and Oblates who testified by presenting examples of where the Archdiocese was at the top of the hierarchy in setting policy and procedure for the parish and school, and how they were involved in approving the overall operations. He states there is no question that the Archdiocese owns St. Benedict's church, the school, and oversees the operations.

Lemly shows how Father Conrad had to go to the Archbishop to gain approval for Mass schedules, renovations, school schedules, and financial campaigns. He points to the fact that the Archbishop was responsible for appointing the priest as pastor to the parish, and had authority to remove him. All of this to convince the jury that the Archdiocese, not the Oblates, bears the blame for failure to protect the children at St. Benedict's school.

He then implicates the Dominican Sisters, who he says were responsible as teachers and the principal at St. Benedict School. They were present each day at school, and the principal hires and evaluates teachers. He argues that no one knows if the Pastor, Fr. Conrad, was involved in hiring Adamson, along with the Principal, Sr. Marie. All involved are deceased, so it's impossible to know.

Yes, he spends the next two days showing exhibits of invoices for the repair of the roof at St. Benedict's in 1965, and who wrote the check. If that didn't seem to work, he blames the Archdiocese, the Dominican nuns, my parents, my brothers, and not so subtly, me in particular. Anyone but the priests who ran St. Benedict's exclusively for one hundred years. His attempts to deflect blame are not lost on me, nor the jury.

Next, Lemly addresses the *instructions to the jury*, a series of guidelines that address the decisions they must make regarding guilt, responsibility, and potential award for damages:

"Let's look at a couple of the key factors with regard to damages. The benchmark for this instruction: you must find reasonable and fair compensation for Mr. O'Connor. Again, balanced by the prior instructions, the decision must be fair with regard to the interests of all parties involved here, not based on sympathy, though we all feel sympathy for Mr. O'Connor for what he has suffered, but reasonable and fair compensation.

"Filing a lawsuit does not grant a plaintiff a lottery ticket for a huge windfall gain. Mr. Pfau's suggestions to you were broken into four phases so the total would not be so shocking, but they ranged up from six to twelve million dollars. He started with claims for the abuse itself, and then moved on to a second claim for damages related to Vietnam combat trauma. I suggest to you that you may find that this claim dishonors those who served in Vietnam, and received $200 or $400 a month in pay as privates and sergeants in Vietnam and no other compensation for experiencing similar trauma.

"You will have to determine in assessing this claim, among other issues, again, is he—was he in Vietnam because of something that Father Conrad or the Western Province did, or were there other factors that led to his being in Vietnam and, therefore, that should not be an issue that's attributed to the parties in this case. You'll have to determine if it's more likely than not that Steve O'Connor would have gone to Vietnam even if he had not enlisted in 1966. As Doctor Conte said, eight and a half million young men, mostly at that time, served in Vietnam.

"We talked throughout this case many times about the sort of Ozzie and Harriett aspect of that early years of Steve O'Connor in Seattle, the late 1950s, the early 1960s. There are a few of you on this jury who know from your personal recollections how traumatic the second half of the '60s in this country were. They were among the most tumultuous in American history, setting aside the great depression and the U.S. Civil War. We had the JFK assassination, Vietnam escalated, and there was violent and continuing political protests related to that. Military draft was reinstated in 1965. Riots, mainly race riots, in many large American cities. And the civil rights movement was going on, particularly in the south, but in many other cities across the country, to advance the rights of black people in this country. Martin Luther King and Bobby Kennedy were assassinated in this time frame.

"Many young men and women were caught up in this torment. As it happens, same summer that Mr. O'Connor joined the Marines, I flunked out of Duke and got my letter from the draft board. So this was an issue that concerned virtually every young man between the ages of eighteen and thirty. The chances of a school scholarship for someone getting mostly Ds is extremely low, and so the likelihood that he would have later enlisted in the military or being drafted, I submit to you, based on the evidence that you have before you, is quite high.

"And you see, particularly in the U. District, if you walk through there, the kids who are homeless in that area. The evidence in the newspapers from the providers, so many of those kids have been abused and had no place else to turn.

"The third phase of Mr. Pfau's claim for damages was that period after Vietnam, 1969 to the fall of 2008."

Mr. Lemly argues that during these years I served in the military in California, had an opportunity to go to officer training, but declined as I might have had to serve another tour in Vietnam. He summarizes my career in manufacturing, then the move back to Seattle, where I experienced the ups and downs of depression. Here, Lemly stops and asks *haven't we all suffered from depression at one time or another?* He talks about the strength of my family, my involvement as a parent and in the community, and my career as a police officer. And although he admits I experienced some trauma as a police officer, Lemly believes it is not related to my service in Vietnam, however.

Lemly considers the fourth measure of damages that Mr. Pfau suggested, for that period after the reunion in 2008. He argues that I did not seek a mental health provider for treatment or counseling, even though my claim is based on the fact I need to be treated for psychological illness. Instead, Lemly argues,I hired an attorney and filed a lawsuit against the "church."

Toward the end of the second day of his closing argument, Lemly keeps going back and forth, trying to explain what a successful life I had lived, what a war hero, what a great father, what a heroic police officer. I finally figured out where this is going.

"Mr. O'Connor was made of stronger steel than so many other victims, and it is very much to his credit, and it is a factor that you will need to consider as you consider the appropriate damages in this case.

"As Doctor McGovern said, in summarizing his testimony, the best single marker for evaluating the likelihood of successful treatment of an individual who is suffering major depression and PTSD is the lifetime history of dealing with stress, with trauma, the way that he adapted to this and grew through this over the years."

Oh, I get it, I shouldn't be awarded damages because I was resilient. I am forged from a different metal. At that moment, I reflect on what I said at the reunion three years ago. "Most of my life skills, I learned right here at St. Benedict's grade school." I learned to endure the unendurable. We learned to take care of each other, because it was made very clear to me that those entrusted with our care at that school were certainly never going to do it.

"Both Dr. Conti and Dr. McGovern agree that this is a good first step towards dealing with the traumas. So then, one year into the legal process, he suffers the onset of a heart attack. He spends several days in the hospital and is treated. Mr. O'Connor tells his heart doctor that he is 90 percent sure he is going to drop dead, as the same condition, including the onset of extreme irregular heartbeat, is what his father had been experiencing shortly before he died."

As I listen to his closing he suddenly shifts the narrative from "if" some entity, or person was responsible in this case, to *who* was responsible. As with his opening argument, this seems as if it was headed for not a denial of events, but who was going to take the blame. Interjected here and there with the usual Lemly personal attacks: *The Bronze Star is several levels below from the highest award we can present our military,* or, *he was getting terrible grades later in high school so he probably would have ended up getting drafted and sent to Vietnam anyway. Or, he would have ended up like the homeless kids down at the University District.* Probably many of whom were also abused.

Lemly's closing arguments come to an end and I realize that I will never have to hear him utter another word in my lifetime. As I look at the jury, I see looks of disgust on their faces, one juror slightly shaking her head. I am thinking, *clearly they can see through Lemly's blatant efforts to shift the blame of negligence and failure to protect children to anyone but the Oblates.*

Michael Pfau's rebuttal, which ends the trial:

Occasionally, although rarely, Pfau would refer to his notes during the trial. For his rebuttal, I know that he had spent the weekend preparing. Lemly had gone first today, since he was granted more time to finish his closing that he started last Friday. Pfau had listened, rarely looking at him, scribbling a few notes, seeming to me like he was growing more irritated as Lemly rolled on.

Finally, as Judge Shaffer calls Mr. Pfau to present his rebuttal, he sets his pen down, closes his notebook on the table, stands and adjusts his trousers. There will be no notes on this day.

As with his opening arguments, Pfau presents his rebuttal standing in the forefront, facing the jury, appearing once again to be a confident (yet not arrogant) advocate explaining to the jury, in simple but comprehensive language, a summary of the trial and the reasons their verdict should be in favor of his client.

"Ladies and Gentlemen, this is my opportunity to respond to Mr. Lemly's statements, and statements that I thought he didn't emphasize, or statements that he omitted all together. I was struck by something he said at the end of his closing, and he said that Adamson's acts are the most reprehensible in this case. And I don't think anybody disagrees. But what he failed to mention were the other reprehensible acts. The failure to respond to the clear complaints of three children on four separate occasions is a reprehensible act.

"Failing not only to respond, but to immediately disbelieve those children, and to respond in the way Father Conrad responded is also a reprehensible act.

"To silence those children is a reprehensible act. To diminish their concerns, and diminish their complaints, that has enormous consequences, because Father Conrad had the opportunity to stop the abuse in 1959, in the fall of 1962 and a third time when Mr. O'Connor complained twice. That is what is at the heart of this case, his failure to act on the information he had.

"It is interesting in a case where a lawyer absolutely fails to mention facts that are so material and relevant to the case.

"And the inference is, when you don't mention it, it's because you have nothing to say, because the evidence is so strong that there can be no response. You put it in the middle of other testimony and hope the jury gives it less emphasis. Interesting. No mention of the contract in 1910, giving the Oblates total control of the parish. And did the Oblates have a responsibility to protect the children of St. Benedict Parish? Father Dillon testified *Yes, the Oblate seminary and the Oblate culture, it was their responsibility.*

"No mention at all by Mr. Lemly. No mention at all of Rob Kingsbury. No mention of Rob Kingsbury because there is no answer for Rob Kingsbury.

"Rob Kingsbury's testimony was crystal clear. *I told Father Conrad.* And Richard Fish's testimony was crystal clear. *I told the priest.* Remember the documents showing that the Oblates knew about Oblate B?

"*The police on the West Coast know what to do.* They knew what to do when informed about the sexual abuse of a child. So did Father Conrad.

"This would be a strong case if you had one student who told someone in a position of authority what happened, and they did absolutely nothing. And took the steps of trying to silence the victim.

"*Mr. Fish, Mr. Kingsbury, you are not to talk about Adamson. If you continue, you are going to hell.* And Mr. O'Connor, the eighth-grade class president. *This is the first time you've been in trouble.* And there is no mention of the Oblate files. Really, really important evidence in the wake of Father Carrignan's testimony.

"He was called to testify three, or five, different times. Because his testimony kept evolving. First, it was important to the defense, because that was how they were going to exonerate themselves. The distance between the Oblates and the Parish. But Father Carrignan went out of his way to explain what they would do if they heard about sexual abuse of a child. They would call the police, they would call the bishop, and they would take action. And amazingly, in the middle of the trial, under court order, they had to produce the documents which clearly showed how they dealt with sexual abuse in the 1960s. Coincidently, the years 1961-1965, the same time Father Conrad was dealing with it. They dealt with it in the worst possible way.

"They dealt with it by trying to cover it up. By trying to avoid scandal. No mention of the children who were also being abused by Oblates in California and Oregon, and Washington. It would be bad for the Oblates if the word got out about the scandal.

"It is incredible evidence about what the Oblates were doing at the highest level. And after looking through over 1100 pages of documents, it was revealed that Father Carrignan himself placed Oblate B, a known child molester in a school in 1974. Remember what Father Carrignan testified to under oath: *The Provincial at the time, Father McDonald, was all business. He got it done. He was by the book.* Through the documents, we revealed how Father McDonald was dealing with this. He was clueless. He was interested in avoiding scandal. He was praying that Oblate B would not stray again. And I asked Father Carrignan, under oath, and he said he didn't remember there being any problems in the 60s.

"Not once, in the 1100 pages of documents, is there ever any mention about the victims, not once are the children mentioned. So what do we see as a theme here? The Oblates are blaming everyone else because they want to minimize their exposure. And they blame Steve O'Connor in subtle and not so subtle ways, and I hope this wasn't lost on you. When you assume responsibility, when a religious organization assumes responsibility for the protection of children, the law in the state of Washington clearly states that you have a responsibility to protect those children.

"And you insinuate that we dishonor the Veterans who served in Vietnam by bringing up the almost two years Steve O'Connor spent in combat? Both experts, Doctor Conte, and for the defense Dr. McGovern agree, you cannot segregate the damages from Vietnam and the abuse. Are the subsequent damages of Vietnam a result of running away to not deal with the sexual abuse, Dr. McGovern? Yes, you cannot separate the events.

"When you allow a kid to get harmed to the level that Steve was harmed, then he will have a complex reaction to further traumas, whether it is combat in Vietnam or police work or whatever.

"What happened to Steve at St. Benedict's made him more susceptible to a bad outcome. It is probably one of the reasons he could never talk about the abuse. He was traumatized so rapidly, so thoroughly, and for so many years that he can't sort it out. I have never seen a case where the two opposing experts were in such agreement about the damage. Actually, it's refreshing.

"What comes up every time there is a major case such as this: *Oh boy, this shouldn't be a windfall.* Think about it. The entity that is negligent is suggesting that Steve O'Connor would receive *a windfall* if you awarded the damages that I suggested.

"It is interesting to think about a painting. If we were talking about someone who negligently ruined an expensive painting at a museum, it would be easy. "An appraiser would come in and say that through the negligence of, say, the person washing the painting, they ruined this painting. This Rembrandt's been ruined, and we agree that twenty million dollars is the damage. However, when we look at the canvas of a human life, it's suggested that those numbers are somehow not only unfair, but outrageous.

"Ladies and Gentlemen, if anything, I think those numbers suggested are conservative. And I talked to you about the four stages of the damages.

"*What would you give that seventeen-year-old boy?* And I suggested two to four million dollars.

"And I suggested those war traumas would be somewhere between two and four million dollars.

"Then I suggested, *what about the long years afterward where it is clear that Steve is still suffering?* And I said that if it was just that, the damages would be two million.

"Then there would be, *what are the damages after the 2008 reunion?* The defense says Steve should have seen a therapist. There is no evidence that Steve had a duty to mitigate his damages before 2008 because he had no idea what damage had occurred. It is that simple. He is a United States Marine. He is a police officer. He has dealt with these things in the past. He has a history of dealing with this in his own way, using his blockers.

"The experts agree. Dealing with this will be very difficult, very painful. But the damages go beyond what the experts agree on. Damages are the memories, which have not gone away. Damages are having to conceal what happened to you, to your wife and family and friends, for your whole life. It's the damage of having to look yourself in the mirror after you have been sexually abused in the worst way, and not liking what you see. I think nothing in this case demonstrates the damages more than when Steve told you about the St. Christopher medal.

"Ladies and Gentlemen, in all my years as a lawyer, I have never known a sadder, more heart-wrenching story. And the suggestion that he is not hurting now is amazing to hear from the defense. And it dovetails exactly with what Doctor Conte said was the saddest thing about Steve. And he said that Steve O'Connor does not realize the good he has done for others.

"And Mr. Lemly can get up and talk about his wonderful family, about his heroism in Vietnam, his resilience, that he is forged from a *different metal* than other abuse victims, and his courageous acts as a police officer. But if Steve O'Connor does not view himself as a worthy person, it means absolutely nothing.

"And I will leave you with the image of that videotape from the 2008 reunion interview. Watch the video tape, where he completely shuts down, then he expands on what he's always said to keep everyone at bay. *No, Adamson was a great guy.*

And at the very end of the tape, he cuts his wife off in midsentence, and says, *That's about it. It's been a wonderful life.* And I want to talk about that movie, the story....

"George Baily is saved by a guardian angel, who walks him through his life and shows him all the events, and that those events had meaning. He did good acts, he saved people. Likewise, at the end of the movie, the community comes together and validates who he is as a person. They validate the kind of life he led. And they validate how he has touched others.

"Steve O'Connor has led a heroic, but tragic, painful life. Ladies and Gentlemen, you are like that community. You can validate what he has suffered through. You can validate that it was not his fault. You can validate that it's not just something that happened in the past that should be just swept under the rug. That people made mistakes, and church members made mistakes.

"You can validate that Steve O'Connor had every right to come into this courtroom and tell what happened to him, and be compensated by those who were negligent for what he went through.

"Thank you, it has been a very long month, and I, like Mr. Lemly have complete confidence that your decision will be fair. Thank you."

CHAPTER 27

FACE IN THE MIRROR:
A TIME TO CAST AWAY STONES

Monday, July 2, 2012, 4:30 p.m.
King County Courtroom, Seattle

Judge Shaffer speaking to the attorneys and counsel:

"Be seated everybody. Okay. Well, folks, it's been a long trial, but a wonderful experience for this Court, because the quality of counsel has just been outstanding in this case. It was actually a pleasure to work with you all in jury instructions, and I cannot remember the last time I said that because you're all so bright and so attentive, and came up with such good arguments. And, frankly, I enjoyed getting the many, many briefs I got during the case because, again, they were so well written and well thought out, even when I didn't always rule in your favor. So I will—and most of all, I'm going to miss seeing everybody perform in court. It's really been a tremendously well-presented case. The facts of this case are heartbreaking, but they were also extremely interesting, and so it's also been very interesting for me, I think, and for the jurors to sit on this case, and to learn all the things that we have learned, so thank you, all of you, the work you put in. I want you to know that."

The jury is brought back in to receive their final instructions from the judge. She gives advice on how to proceed in nominating a foreman and the importance of all jurors being present when in deliberations. These twelve people now rise from their seats and begin to file out of the courtroom to begin consideration and discussion on all the testimony and evidence they have heard and seen these last four weeks—and come to a decision.

At this moment, I attempt to make eye contact with each and every one of them in a last desperate hope of getting a read on what they are thinking. I am not able to. In fact, there are no smiles, no frowns, and no hint at all of what they are thinking. As the jurors pass me, however, it seems as though more than a few of them express a look I'd seen as a police officer while at the scene of a serious vehicle accident: the curious, yet shocked gazes of those passing the carnage of twisted metal, twisted lives. We always referred to it as *morbid curiosity*. I reflect on this as I notice some of the jurors taking a quick peek at me, turning their heads if I catch their glance.

After thinking of how others were impacted by this trial, I reflect on its effect on me. And to quote a statement by one of the experts during the trial, "The damage is permanent." There was no fixing that. Was the whole endeavor I embarked on for almost three years ago worth it? I feel that the sacrifices, re-victimization, isolation and all the rest were necessary.

I taught myself a valuable life lesson. I would not have had to go through this if I had done the right thing in 1961, '62, '63, '64, '65, '66—and had the courage to protect that twelve-year-old boy, and all the following victims. Now, I know that I should have said more—told other people and not given up until someone, *anyone*, listened.

The trial is over for me. The results are a total vindication and disclosure. As for the carefree boy, dirt poor, yet rich in spirit, he will never again, cheerily hop onto his Roadmaster bicycle, fishing pole lashed across the handlebars, and venture out on an early Saturday morning to take his rightful place, at the edge of the most cherished fishing spot: the south end of the T-Dock on the east side of Green Lake. That twelve-year-old died the day he set foot in Dan Adamson's classroom. He died just as if he walked out in front of a bus. His soul was murdered, in a dreary old Catholic grade school named St. Benedict's, in a dreary old neighborhood called Wallingford.

Even though the trial is over for me, it certainly is not for my legal team. As we enter the elevator for the trip to the Columbia Tower, Suite 500, for our daily debriefing, the subject of jury deliberations comes up.

Jason Amala asks me, "What do you think, Steve?"

"Oh, I will squeak out a narrow win," I respond. "They will award one million to me, then place 90 percent blame on everybody but the Oblates, which means I will gross one hundred thousand, which I will owe to Michael Pfau, and I will be spending the next ten years doing dishes at Pfau, Cochran, Vertetis, Amala."

That is sure an icebreaker, as the whole elevator erupts into laughter. Jason then turns to Michael Pfau to get his response. I look at Pfau and think of a line in a Billy Joel song about *as the smile ran away from his face.* The elevator door opens and Pfau turns to look at no one in particular.

"High sevens," he states, then disappears as if he were a ghost to the confines of his office. No one would be knocking on that door for a while.

The closing arguments mark the first time since I met Michael Pfau that I have ever heard him utter a word concerning what we'd ask for in damages. As the "two million" became "four million," and the "four million" became "eight million" and the defense table gasped, it was lost on me. It really didn't matter at all. It never had.

I have found my time for purpose, and to quote Chief Bob Kane, "Your courage was tested, and not found wanting." I still had it, and that was good enough for me.

Let the jury bring back their verdict, let them voice their opinions, but whatever their decision, I know I can now look in the mirror and like what I see.

CHAPTER 28

BACKBLAST:
A TIME TO REFRAIN FROM EMBRACING

Thursday July 5th, 2012
King County Courthouse, Seattle

The law firm informs me that I'll be notified as soon as the jury reaches a verdict. I'll have an hour or so to be at the courthouse. I position myself close to downtown Seattle.

If there is no verdict announcement today, then I will have to wait through the upcoming weekend. I'm more concerned for my legal team than I am for me. I am pretty sure that these guys don't like to lose. Additionally, they invested three years of effort, with a great deal of cost, to bring this case to trial. Thomas Lemly will still get paid, win or lose. But my side, well, there's a lot to lose.

I know the consequences will be great for the defense if the verdict does not go their way. Big consequences. There is no doubt this is an important trial. It will be referred to in future litigation as a precedent-setting case. The Catholic Church, the Archdiocese of Seattle, the Dominican Order of Sisters, not to mention the defense lawyers, all have a big stake in this. The result will certainly be plastered all over the news and in the papers, no matter what the outcome.

By Thursday morning, I'm contemplating just what the hell am I going to do now that it is over. My feelings remain the same no matter what the verdict. I have a distinct urge to walk out of the courtroom, throw my black leather, bulging briefcase in the nearest garbage bin, and flag down the first cab that comes my way. The problem is, I will have no answer when the driver asks *Where to?* Do I say, *airport*, and then walk up to a counter and ask for a flight? I will be asked the same question, *Where to?* I have no idea, but I certainly have a sense of urgency. Maybe, for one of the very few times in my life, I will do whatever I feel like doing. Disappear. For a week, month, year, or forever. I do know this much: I have absolutely no desire to talk to humans again, not for a long, long, time.

The haunting thought of going *back* certainly crosses my mind. *Maybe I should just go back where I should have stayed.* During the time period of the trial, not in the courtroom, someone asked me, *Steve, what do you feel is the worse decision you made in your whole life?* That was an easy one. *I came back.* I should have just stayed in Vietnam in the first place. More often than not, I have felt that Vietnam was my reality, and that the rest of my life since has just been one more *Academy Award performance. Best Actor in a made up role.* Or maybe it goes further back than that, to a tap on the desk, in the sixth grade. The stubby fingers tapping, the stale smell of cigar smoke, and those wing walkers.

It is no surprise that by lunchtime I'm hoping to drive to Wallingford and spend the rest of the day walking around Green Lake. It is a beautiful summer day, like so many I experienced at that lake. Instead, Gail and I are in West Seattle hanging out with a friend, Ginny, when the call comes in at 1:30 p.m.

"Steve, you have fifteen minutes to get to the courtroom. The jury has reached a verdict."

CHAPTER 29

JUSTICE HAS ITS PRICE: A TIME TO HEAL

July 5th, 2012, 1:30 p.m.
Downtown Seattle

The three of us jump into Gail's minivan and make our way onto the West Seattle bridge, taking the 99 North exit, hoping there's no traffic. As I pass cars, weaving in and out, I'm giving instructions to Gail.

"I'll jump out a few blocks away from the courthouse and you park the car, then come to the courthouse as fast as you can."

It reminded me of police days, driving as if in hot pursuit, an adrenaline rush. I slam on the brakes as I spot a parking garage on the hill heading up Cherry Street, jump out of the car, leaving the door open, engine running, halfway in the street, halfway in the garage.

"Park the car, don't forget to pay and I'll see you there!"

My cell phone rings again, notifying me that the judge and the attorneys are already seated. My fast walk turns into a full sprint, and after getting through security check, I rush over to the elevators, repeatedly punching the up button.

Once on the eighth floor, I race down the hall and enter the courtroom, out of breath. Forget the state of my clothes, my casual sport shirt is now drenched in sweat. I take my seat at the witness table and compose myself. I am soon joined by Darrell Cochran.

The jury is not yet in the courtroom. And as I glance over to the defense table, there is no Tom Lemly, no Boris Gavaria, no Father Carrignan, only Candace Keenan. *How sad, they left the woman holding the bag.* Next, I turn around to scan the 'pews' in back of me. There are several rows of what I think are law students, some attorneys, and a current superior court judge who I recognize from previous sessions. I see Gail and Ginny enter the courtroom and take their seats about three rows back, but no Mr. Pfau. Jack Kennedy is there, along with Jason Amala and other members of Pfau's law firm. But as the bailiff announces *All Rise!*, there is still no sign of Michael Pfau. *This—the grand finale of five weeks of trial—and some of the main players are absent for the verdict.*

Compared to the previous four weeks, the events are unfolding at breakneck speed. As the judge directs the bailiff to retrieve the jury from the deliberation room, I have the urge to jump up and yell, *Wait—Wait, I'm not ready for this.* Controlling my anxiety as best as I can, I settle into my chair, hands placed on my thighs, feet flat on the floor, eyes dead ahead. But where is the Mighty Pfau?

Shortly, I hear the shuffle of twelve sets of shoes advancing by me. Then the jury members, one by one take their places in the jury box. The foreman of the jury is in the front row, seated nearest to the witness stand. Judge Shaffer states that the jury has reached a verdict.

I quickly realize that I completely forgot about the critical eight questions that the jury need to answer. It's been several days since I heard the questions when the jury received their instructions.[‡] I know there will be *yes* answers, and *no* answers, but a *yes* isn't necessarily good, and a *no* isn't necessarily bad. One needs to know what the question is—and I did not have that information.

Judge Shaffer asks the jury foreman, "What is your answer to question number one?"

He answers, *Yes—11 and No—1.*

Is that good, bad, or is it over? I knew that the wrong answer, whether yes or no, meant that it was over and we lost.

‡ See Appendix C for transcript of jury instructions, questions, and answers.

The judge says to the jury, "Then proceed to the second question."

Crap, this is a twisted version of Russian roulette.

0—No and 12—Yes

Is that good or bad? I am too petrified to glance at Cochran.

"What is your answer to question number three?"

The foreman responds, *Yes, Dominican Sisters of Holy Cross and Archdiocese of Seattle—these entities were negligent in this case.*

Yessss again? Is that good or bad?

"Then proceed to question number four."

Yes—11, No—1.

Dead silence except for my heartbeat, which I can hear revving up.

After what seems like an eternity, Judge Shaffer instructs the foreman, "Then proceed to question number five."

He answers, *Oblate Fathers Western Province, Inc., 80 percent, the Archdiocese of Seattle, 15 percent, Dominican Sisters of Holy Cross, 5 percent.*

Judge Shaffer asks, "What is the jury's answer to question number six?"

Eight million dollars.

Instantly, I feel a strong grip place a hold on my left arm. It is Cochran, who whispers, *Wait, Wait.* His grip not only catches my attention, but thankfully keeps me from keeling onto the floor, which I feel I am about to do. *Is that it? The wrong answer? Have I lost?*

At this time, he starts tapping on a blank yellow notebook that he places in front of him. I detect there is great importance he will reveal on this blank piece of paper, and my eyes remain fixed upon it.

My whole team seems to simultaneously jerk to attention in their chairs.

I have no idea what it means until I see Cochran sprawl the figure, *$6.4 million,* then circle it, at which time he grabs me by the shoulders and shakes me.

"What is the answer to question number seven?"

Another long pause from the jury foreman, followed by *Yes—11, No—1.*

Then they proceed to the last question.

"What is your answer to question number eight?"

No—12.

Judge Shaffer thanks the jury for their service and tells them they may leave the courtroom. She adds that if they so desire, they're free to speak to me, to the news media, to the attorneys, or anyone once they leave the courtroom. It is at this time that I turn to look at the pews in back of me. People are hugging, shaking each other, embracing. I don't see many dry eyes at this point. I then glance at my wife, Gail. From my vantage point, she appears to look as though she just lost her best friend. Head down, her hands folded together on her lap, in total silence. Maybe she's dismayed, feels sad for the church. I'm not sure what to make of her reaction; possibly she's in shock.

I hear people out in the hall—a large crowd is gathering outside. Cochran turns to me and says that they'll need me at the Columbia Tower as soon as I can get there. Later, I learn that pre-arranged news crews and other journalists are waiting to interview me.

I can only muster the strength to plop back down in my seat as everyone exits the courtroom. My strong, muscular legs fail me— do not respond. I cannot move. The courtroom is empty and silent except for one other person. I look straight ahead and catch the outline of a figure at the entrance to the judge's chambers. It is Judge Catherine Shaffer, and our eyes lock. I see her now, away from the bench, standing there, so small and distant, yet so large a figure. I can only respond with a feeble lifting of my hands, and to shrug my shoulders as if to say, *now what?*

She removes her hands from the confines of her robe, and slowly, softly claps them together three times, turns, and disappears into her chamber.

I am now left to myself, but not for long. As the voices in the hallway grow louder and louder, the urge comes back. *Is there a backdoor, how do I get away?*

But before I address that issue, I must come to grips with myself here and now, in this empty courtroom. I have no confusion, however with one reality, as I murmur to myself— *that's as far as I can hit the ball.* What do I do to follow this up?

The silence is, in the next moment, interrupted with a whisper inside of my ear: *Tell the story, tell the world what really happened to the children.*

Tell all about the crimes, cover-ups, all of it. From this moment on, my vow forever is to be the voice of the victims, the voice of the survivors.

I stand, proud, take one last look at the courtroom, and then turn to face what would be next.

Out in the hallway, I talk with several of the jurors and individuals. One person from the crowd introduces herself as a Seattle Police Officer. Shaking my hand she says "You're the bravest cop I've ever met." Another person, a juror, hugs me and says, "We just want you to be OK, to live a life in peace."

Shortly after, I am whisked away by my 'handlers', up the four blocks to the Columbia Tower. News crews from all the local television stations have the cameras on me, as I am interviewed by multiple reporters. Whatever thoughts I have of escape are nothing more than thoughts. I am surrounded. The lead story on all stations at the five o'clock news is the verdict. Apparently, a film crew was set up at St. Benedict's that afternoon, and as the image of the front stairs leading up to the school is shown, a camera pans over to the fence that borders the playground. Surveying the scene, a reporter begins her narrative: *Behind the fence, beyond the basketball court, Stephen O'Connor recalls a childhood lost after fifty years of secrets and sadness....*

The next morning brings the clarification from Cochran that Michael Pfau had left for a previously scheduled commitment in Europe and that's why he was not there the day of the verdict. Additionally, I am notified that I need to stick around because I would be interviewed on the afternoon radio shows.

No thank you, Mr. Cochran, you fill in for me. I am not doing it.
Maybe now is the time? Yes, now. Find me a taxi.

It's not to be. I am not really going to alter my personality and do something *I want to do* for a change. I'm used to making sure others are taken care of, sacrificing what I want to do—making sure the family is provided for— monetarily, fixing up cars, or driving people places, remodeling houses or entertaining the kids and grandkids on a weekend, even when I crave some peace and quiet, solitude. Maybe a trip to Glacier Park...or back to Vietnam.

But no, my family notifies me that my eldest daughter, Stephanie, has arrived in town, with her three young daughters in tow, and that everyone has decided I should spend the next day at the zoo with the grandchildren. Perfect. I can go look and see if the leopard is still pacing back and forth, aimlessly, hopelessly searching for an escape route. *Oh boy, can I relate to that.*

EPILOGUE

A TIME FOR PEACE

December 21, 2012

A s I sit perched in front of my living room window at my white colonial-style house in Spokane, I look out at the peaceful setting before me. The front lawn is covered in a recent blanket of snow. The frosted trees and the sweeping valley below lies still and frozen. As darkness sets in, the Christmas lights strung across the brick entry begin to glow under the translucent layer of snow and ice. Soon, my quiet scene will be interrupted by the arrival of four grown children, spouses in tow, and the clamoring of no fewer than seven grandchildren. All descending from various corners of the northwest for a "classic" O'Connor Christmas.

It is a rare occurrence, as is with most large families, getting everyone in one place, at one time is, in itself a Christmas miracle. I have only recently found out that the gathering is going to be without absentees, and the thought crosses my mind, *I wonder if they are choosing to come to see if I am "all right," or just out of morbid curiosity.*

Either way, time is short and I have until tomorrow afternoon to get myself together. Outward appearance is not the issue. I just hope they don't search beyond that. Some of the last three years might get spilled on them accidently. Please just don't ask, *How are you doing, Dad?*

My sarcastic answer would be brief, and perfectly rehearsed: "Ha. Look kid, never feel sorry for a multimillionaire."

I have played this part—my whole adult life— and this season will be no different. Perfectly behaved, jovial, polite, and attentive.

The trial ended on July 5th of this year and as 2012 comes to a close, I have much to be thankful for, most of which is about to arrive in the form of a multitude of family. But for the first time in my life, there is more. A crushing burden has been lifted from me. The twelve-year-old finally had his story told. His voice was released at last, not in a small way, because of the efforts of Michael Pfau and his team. I had found the courage to fight yet one more war. But this war had a purpose, and it needed to be fought.

As with Vietnam, I knew there would be permanent damage. I know that it will be with me for my remaining days, and will invade my peace, unwanted as is the pain in my leg when the cold winter comes, or the changing of the seasons, which bring an inability for me to adjust to the frigid temperatures. Probably just a psychological reminder of the sweats, shakes, and chills of a long-ago fever in a long-ago place. Like Vietnam, *back like malaria* the trial will come to me, invade my thoughts and interrupt my sleep. Maybe I will be able to deal with it, maybe it's a good thing. I need to be reminded that my child self was finally given a voice. I need to be reminded of the evil that took place at St. Benedict's for so long. I need to remember the victims and survivors whose lives were permanently damaged in a place that was purported to be a safe environment. I must vow to never give up the cause.

As I reminisce on the events of the last three years, some blur to dullness, others are vivid and sharp. Aside from the case, with all its twists and turns, there was another aspect that really had nothing to do with the events themselves, or maybe it did. Many times I reflected on its significance to me: my fledgling days at Seattle Prep, where I had visions of graduating at the top of my class. Possibly a future student body president. Maybe a scholarship somewhere to a prestigious Jesuit University. It might have been, but was probably nothing more than a dream. However, I always remember something Pfau would say about some of his clients who were drug addicts, alcoholics, criminals, thieves, or in other ways outcasts from society: "I wonder what they would have been if they had not been molested as a child."

Nevertheless, I think about my experiences in the last three years with Pfau's law firm. Even though I may never have graduated from an Ivy League school or reached anywhere near their level, I, a high school dropout, got to walk with giants. The walls of their offices are filled with diplomas from Boston College, Michigan Law School, Seattle University, and the University of Washington. On the other hand, they know little of what they would soon learn about Vietnam, police work, or the sordid crimes committed at St. Benedict's. I had gotten my *Master's in Death, and Dying* from Rice Paddy University, before I was old enough to complete high school. *I wish they weren't exposed to what they had to listen to. I wish I hadn't had to tell it at all, but in the end, there really wasn't a choice. Not in my mind anyway. The 100th anniversary set it all in place. They were not going to get away with covering it up anymore. There was really no choice.*

I am old now, having survived a lot longer than many Marines who served with me in Vietnam. I am thankful for that, and most of all, thankful that I met Michael Pfau, who brought the twelve-year-old child to life again. Hopefully, I will continue to watch, with humor, my grandchildren growing older, and my children grappling with the same sadness and gladness that comes with parenting.

And I will always take great pleasure, whenever I am able, to witness the sunsets over the Pacific Ocean on the Central Oregon Coast. An unbroken river makes its descent through the coastal mountain range, ending its journey to the Pacific just north of a beach house perched high above the ocean. And on a rare occasion, one can observe the sun rising above the river estuary, the sun sinking into the ocean, and the rising of a full moon over the coastal mountain range, all in one day.

Randomly, occasionally fleeting, but at other times dogged, tenacious, and debilitating, *it arrives* as I knew it would—intrusive thoughts and remembrances from long ago, the past that is never dead. Vietnam, St. Benedict's—those wars. And I hear the words of a juror after the trial, "We just want you to be OK."-

Sometimes late at night
when I am bathed in the firelight
the moon comes calling a ghostly white
and I recall, I recall!
     —Bob Seger

313

NW FRIDAY

Jury awards $6.4M to victim in Catholic-school sex case

BY ALEXA VAUGHN
Seattle Times staff reporter

The thought of the deepest, most violent jungle in the Vietnam War seemed peaceful to Steve O'Connor compared with what he said he experienced as a student at St. Benedict School, a Catholic school in Seattle's Wallingford neighborhood.

If he'd died, he said, he would no longer have to replay memories of being raped and abused weekly

from 1961 to 1964 by lay teacher Daniel Adamson. He wouldn't have to think about how his father and the school's priests ignored his requests for help either, he said.

That's why O'Connor, now 65, says he dropped out of high school at age 17, why he enlisted as a Marine and served through two gruesome tours in Vietnam. He then did his best to block out the horrific memories of abuse and death as he

moved on to become a police officer, marry and have four children, but it wasn't easy.

After hearing his story in a four-week trial, a King County Superior Court jury Thursday awarded O'Connor $6.4 million in his lawsuit against the order of priests, his lawyers say. The jury found that the Missionary Oblates of Mary Immaculate had refused to help when a teenage O'Connor reported the

abuse.

O'Connor's is one of the largest awards to a victim of a Catholic-school sex-abuse case in state history, according to his lawyers.

The Oblates order, based in Rome, has been investigated for covering up or ignoring child sex abuse several times before, and has insurance that helps cover the cost of lawsuits concerning it, according

See > **SEX ABUSE, B2**

INSURANCE CLAIM FOR DEAD CAT SCRATCHES BACK

TACOMA MAN ACCUSED OF FRAUD, ATTEMPTED THEFT

No feline, charges say

BY CHRISTINE CLARRIDGE
Seattle Times staff reporter

A 29-year-old Tacoma man who filed a $20,000 insurance claim for the death of a cat he claimed to have loved "like a son" has been charged with insurance fraud and attempted theft.

According to the charges filed last week in Pierce County, Yevgeniy Samsonov's beloved cat never existed and photos he submitted to bolster his claim had been pulled from the Internet.

"We've handled some pretty

Seattle Times headline July 6, 2012.

Author speaking with Marty Baron, editor of the *Washington Post*. As the former editor of the *Boston Globe*, Baron is portrayed in the movie, *Spotlight* because of the investigation he led focused on the Boston Catholic Church.

ARCHDIOCESE OF SEATTLE
OFFICE OF THE ARCHBISHOP
PH. 206-382-4886
FAX: 206-382-3495

710 9TH AVE
SEATTLE, WA 98104-2017
www.seattlearchdiocese.org

March 31, 2016

To the Parishioners and School Parents of St. Benedict Parish

My dear brothers and sisters in Christ,

Easter greetings in the Lord!

I am writing to provide you with some information to supplement the recent communication from Deacon Roy Harrington and Mr. Brian Anderson regarding Dan Adamson, a teacher and principal of St. Benedict Parish School from 1958-1974. Adamson died in 1975. I believe it is important to understand the extent of harm done by him.

The Archdiocese of Seattle has been involved in five lawsuits and two pre-litigation claims regarding Adamson. We settled six of these cases, and the seventh was filed more recently, so we have not yet entered into settlement discussions. We are also aware of one additional allegation.

We know that it is very likely that there are additional victims of the terrible and evil actions that Adamson perpetrated against innocent and vulnerable children. I personally am deeply saddened by the egregious acts suffered by some of your parishioners during those years, and I express my deep regret and apology to you all. I urge anyone who was harmed by Adamson to contact Denise Aubuchon, our pastoral outreach coordinator, at 800-446-7762, or an advocate of choice.

Please join me in praying for all victim survivors of child sexual abuse. May the Lord heal all hurts.

Sincerely in Christ,

+Peter Sartain

Most Rev. J. Peter Sartain
Archbishop of Seattle

Letter from the Seattle Archbishop to parishioners of St. Benedict parish, 2016.

March 18, 2016

TO: Mr. Stephen O'Connor

Dear Steve,

Thank you for meeting with me earlier about your concerns regarding the announcement made at St. Benedict's about Dan Adamson. I very much appreciated our conversation and gained some important insight by listening to your perspective. Thank you for your candor and courage in pursuing the truth. On a personal level, I also enjoyed our conversation very much.

I am enclosing for you a copy of my letter we have asked the parish and school leadership to share with parishioners and school families the week after Easter. Like you, I was not happy with the initial announcement and felt that more information should be shared with parishioners. I thought you would be interested in seeing my letter. We are also discussing the kind of language used in public statements of the Archdiocese regarding child abuse, and I thank you for heightening my awareness of how important that language is. And lastly, I want to repeat my offer to meet again if that would ever be of help in any way.

With every best wish and prayer for you and your family, I am

Sincerely in Christ,

+Abp. Sartain

Most Rev. J. Peter Sartain
Archbishop of Seattle

Encl.

Letter from the Seattle Archbishop to author, 2016.

THE VARSITY at PCVA.

Jack Kennedy of PCVA meeting with the author and Michael Pfau.

The author with Michael Pfau, 2017.

Christmas with family, 2012.

APPENDIX A

LEGAL DEFINITIONS

Borrowed Servant Doctrine

n. An employee whose services are, with the employee's consent, lent to another employer who temporarily assumes control over the employee's work. Under the doctrine of *respondeat superior,* the borrowing employer is vicariously liable for the borrowed employee's acts. But the borrowing employer may also be entitled to assert immunity under workers'-compensation laws. Also termed borrowed servant; loaned employee; loaned servant; employee *pro hac vice*; special employee.

Circumstantial Evidence

n. 1. Evidence based on inference and not on personal knowledge or observation. — Also termed *indirect evidence; oblique evidence.* Cf. *direct evidence* (1). 2. All evidence that is not given by eyewitness testimony.

Direct Evidence

n. Evidence that is based on personal knowledge or observation and that, if true, proves a fact without inference or presumption. — Also termed *positive evidence.* Cf. *circumstantial evidence.*

Legal Standing

n. A party's right to make a legal claim or seek judicial enforcement of a duty or right. To have standing in federal court, a plaintiff must show (1) that the challenged conduct has caused the plaintiff actual injury, and (2) that the interest sought to be protected is within the zone of interests meant to be regulated by the statutory or constitutional guarantee in question. — Also termed *standing to sue.*

Proximate Cause

n. 1. A cause that is legally sufficient to result in liability; an act or omission that is considered in law to result in a consequence, so that liability can be imposed on the actor. 2. A cause that directly produces an event and without which the event would not have occurred. — Also termed (in both senses) *direct cause; direct and proximate cause; efficient proximate cause; efficient cause; efficient adequate cause; initial cause; first cause; legal cause; procuring cause; producing cause; primary cause; jural cause.* Cf. (in sense 2) remote cause.

Statute of Limitations

n. 1. A law that bars claims after a specified period; specif., a statute establishing a time limit for suing in a civil case, based on the date when the claim accrued (as when the injury occurred or was discovered). The purpose of such a statute is to require diligent prosecution of known claims, thereby providing finality and predictability in legal affairs and ensuring that claims will be resolved while evidence is reasonably available and fresh. — Also termed *nonclaim statute; limitations period.* 2. A statute establishing a time limit for prosecuting a crime, based on the date when the offense occurred.

Statute of Limitations Trigger

For many years, Washington State required those who sought to hold an alleged abuser accountable had to file their claim within three years of their 18th birthday. Washington is one of the many states that has incorporated a "delayed discovery" rule into its SOL. Delayed discovery is designed to take into account the nature of sexual abuse and how memories of the event may have been blocked, repressed, or otherwise forgotten. It therefore permitted prosecution of an abuser within three years of the date that the memories are discovered. *Legalmatch.com Law Library*

Superseding Cause

n. An intervening act or force that the law considers sufficient to override the cause for which the original tortfeasor was responsible, thereby exonerating that tortfeasor from liability. — Also termed *sole cause.*

Summary Judgment

n. A judgment granted on a claim or defense about which there is no genuine issue of material fact and on which the movant is entitled to prevail as a matter of law. The court considers the contents of the pleadings, the motions, and additional evidence adduced by the parties to determine whether there is a genuine issue of material fact rather than one of law. This procedural device allows the speedy disposition of a controversy without the need for trial. — Also termed *summary disposition; judgment on the pleadings.*

All definitions from *Black's Law Dictionary* (10th ed. 2014) unless otherwise noted.

APPENDIX B

LIST OF WITNESSES

6-6-12. Robb Kingsbury—for the Plaintiff

6-6-12. Richard Fish—for the Plaintiff

6-11-12. Mary Santi—for the Plaintiff

6-11-12. Fr. Ciaran Dillon—for the Defendant

6-12-12. Mary Santi—for the Plaintiff

6-12-12. Fr. Gerald Brunet—for the Defendant (videotape)

6-12-12. Gail O'Connor—for the Plaintiff

6-13-12. Gail O'Connor—for the Plaintiff

6-13-12. Robert Kane—for the Plaintiff (deposition)

6-13-12. Stephen O'Connor—Plaintiff

6-14-12. Stephen O'Connor—Plaintiff

6-18-12. Stephen O'Connor—Plaintiff

6-18-12. Fr. Ronald Carrignan—for the Defendant

6-19-12. Dr. Jon Conte—for the Plaintiff

6-20-12. Dr. Jon Conte—for the Plaintiff

6-20-12. Fr. Ronald Carrignan—for the Defendant

6-25-12. Fr. Ronald Carrignan—for the Defendant

6-25-12. Sr. Joan Unger—for the Defendant

6-25-12. Dr. Kevin McGovern—for the Defendant

6-26-12. Dr. Kevin McGovern—for the Defendant

6-26-12. Christine Taylor—for the Defendant

6-27-12. Jerome O'Connor—for the Defendant (deposition)

6-27-12. James O'Connor—for the Defendant

6-27-12. Fr. Ronald Carrignan—for the Defendant

6-28-12. Fr. Ronald Carrignan—for the Defendant

APPENDIX C

JURY INSTRUCTIONS, QUESTIONS & ANSWERS

Official transcript: the jury brings the following verdict, read by the Court in the presence of the Plaintiff and respective counsel:

1) Do you find that defendant was negligent in this case?

Answer: 11 (Yes) 1 (No).

2) Was such negligence the proximate cause of injury or damage to the Plaintiff?

12 (Yes) 0 (No).

3) Do you find that any of the following entities were negligent in this case?

Dominican sisters of Holy Cross 12 (Yes) 0 (No). Archdiocese of Seattle 12 (Yes) 0 (No).

4) Do you find that such negligence is a proximate cause of injury or damages to Plaintiff?

Dominican Sisters of Holy Cross 11 (Yes) 1 (No).
Archdiocese of Seattle 11 (Yes) 1 (No).

5) Assume that 100 percent represents the total combined negligence that was a proximate cause of plaintiff's injuries or damages. What percentage of this total negligence is attributable to defendant and what percentage is attributable to each non-party whose fault was found by you, if any?

Oblate Fathers Western Province, 80 percent
Archdiocese of Seattle, 15 percent
Dominican Sisters of Holy Cross, 5 percent

6) After segregating and not including damages, if any, caused solely by Daniel Adamson's intentional acts, what do you find to be the measure of plaintiff's non-economic damages proximately caused by the defendant's and /or other entities' or persons' negligence?

$8,000,000.00

7) Did Plaintiff commence this action within the statute of limitations period?

11(Yes) 1(No).

8) Were Father Conrad and Father Dillon both borrowed or loaned employees or agents of the Seattle Archdiocese?

Yes (0) No (12).

Stephen J. O'Connor is the youngest of six children raised in a very traditional pre-Vatican II Catholic household. He spent his childhood in the Wallingford district of Seattle, Washington in the early 1960s.

Steve served in the United States Marine Corps from 1966 to 1973. He was an infantryman in Vietnam for almost two years, from April 1967 through March 1969. He received multiple awards for bravery, including two Purple Hearts and the Vietnamese Cross of Gallantry.

After many years in the electronics industry, Steve began a career in law enforcement. He served with the Stanwood Washington Police Department and the Snohomish County Sheriff's Department. During his police career, he was also a certified D.A.R.E. officer, graduating over 600 students through the Stanwood School District program. He also was assigned as an undercover narcotics detective with the Snohomish County Narcotics Task Force. He received multiple awards and commendations during his career, including the highest law enforcement award for bravery, the Medal of Valor.

Steve is married to his childhood friend, Gail, whom he met in the second grade. They have been married for over forty-eight years, and continue to be blessed with a close relationship with their four children and seven grandchildren. Gail worked for over forty years in the medical profession, mostly in pediatric care. She retired in 2013 from Sacred Heart Children's Hospital in Spokane, Washington. Steve and Gail divide their time between Spokane and the Central Oregon Coast.

Steve continues to be a forceful voice and a fervent, outspoken advocate for victims of child sexual abuse at the hands of the Catholic Church.

CPSIA information can be obtained
at www.ICGtesting.com
Printed in the USA
BVHW030815050819
555096BV00011B/370/P